Postcard History Series

Along Broadway

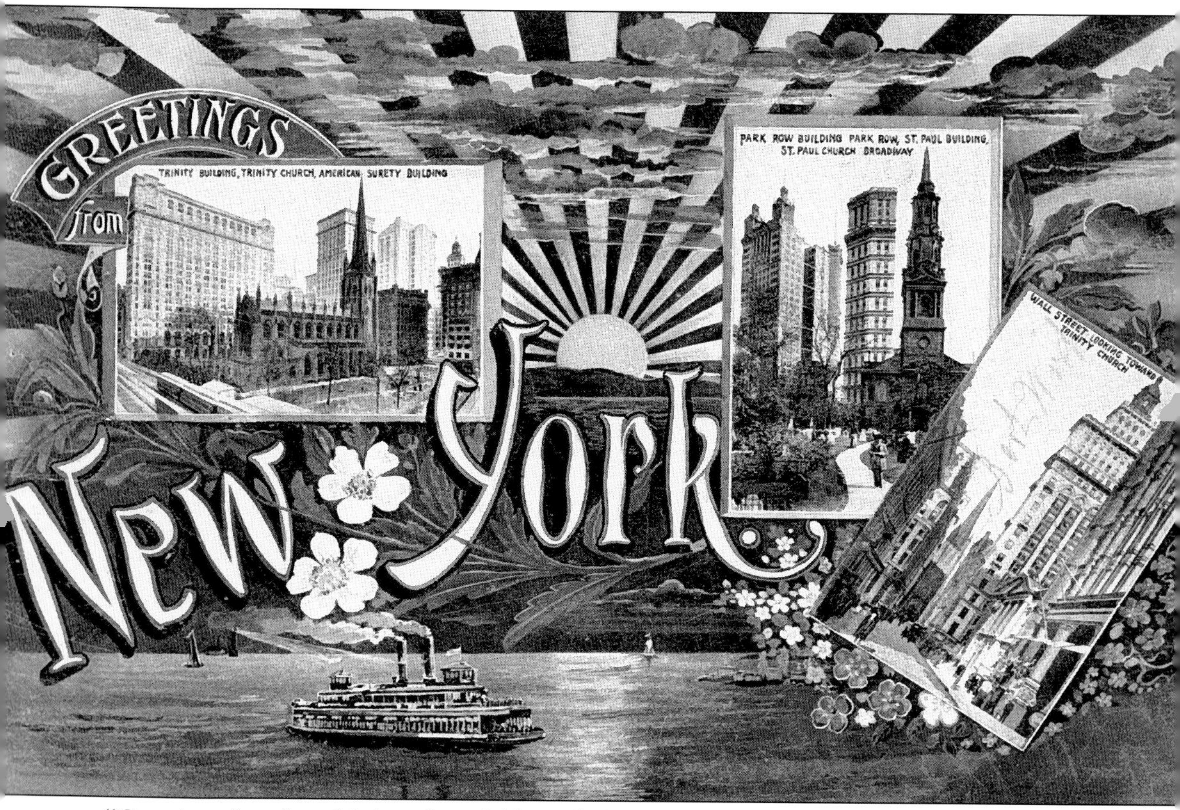

"Greetings from" multiviews invariably include Broadway.

On the front cover: Please see page 71. (Author's collection.)

On the back cover: Please see page 34. (Author's collection.)

POSTCARD HISTORY SERIES

Along Broadway

Randall Gabrielan

ARCADIA PUBLISHING

ISBN 978-0-7385-5031-2

Published by Arcadia Publishing
Charleston, South Carolina

Printed in the United States of America

Library of Congress Control Number: 2007922155

For all general information contact Arcadia Publishing at:
Telephone 843-853-2070
Fax 843-853-0044
E-mail sales@arcadiapublishing.com
For customer service and orders:
Toll-Free 1-888-313-2665

Visit us on the Internet at www.arcadiapublishing.com

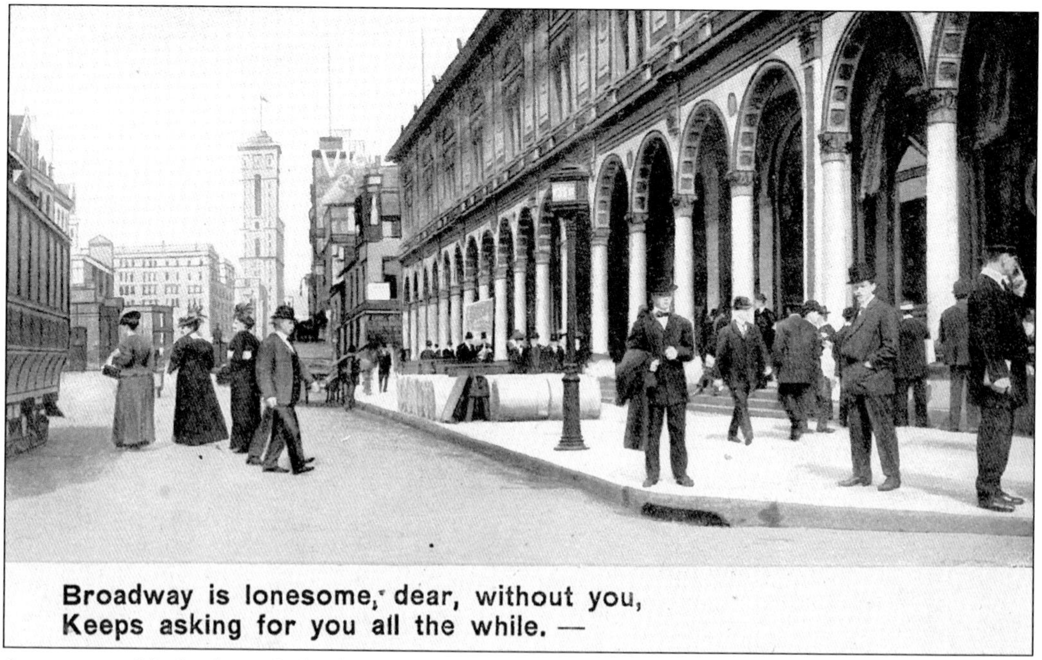

A century-old city hyperbole claims, "Broadway is lonesome, dear, without you, keeps asking for you all the while."

Contents

ACKNOWLEDGMENTS

Joan Kay, one of New York's foremost postcard figures, lent generously for some of the better images. Robin Kaller of Kaller Historical Documents gave liberal access to an extraordinary collection of stereographs. Robert Schoeffling located a copy of *Both Sides of Broadway*, published during the postcard craze, 1910, and accessed for a number of postcard-type images. Robert Pellegrini lent the proverbial last, but not least, image. John McGrath also proffered assistance. My heartfelt thanks to all.

INTRODUCTION

"There is only one Broadway," exclaimed an exuberant 1905 buyer of an appealing parcel. While others may replicate the name, the "only" Broadway in New York is the one-word metaphor for an industry, the big time, the main road, a New York state of mind, and even New York itself. This Broadway, the world's best-known street, needs no other identification. Established in 17th-century Dutch New York, Broadway grew with the city, not only as a thoroughfare but as a conveyance of an expanding city, carrying progress with the tide of time, section by section, with each part reinventing itself after the older Broadway and New York moved on. Broadway had a rival for a brief spell around the 17th century when maritime trades were a lifeline to European civilization, but Pearl Street, a counterpart closer to the East River that was then the main dockage area, became just another business street. It was Broadway that carried the growing city. Broadway's expansion took it to the environs of Columbus Circle as the city was preparing to unify itself in the 1890s, but anticipating the next century's growth, outlying paths known as the Boulevard and the Bloomingdale Road were rebuilt, widened, and made part of Broadway. The likely course of this main stem was foreseen even prior to European settlement. The "new" Broadway of northern Manhattan followed the paths of the Native Americans, not necessarily by design, but because modern engineers found that the Native Americans had chosen the likeliest courses for easy passage.

The concept of Broadway, or even Manhattan moving uptown, embraces the moving character of an area as buildings and their tenants change over time, seen in business, residential, lodging, and entertainment patterns. Broadway is about buildings, people and moving them about, and how their ability to move impacts the size, type, and location of buildings. The changing character may be seen in residential patterns. While in compact early New York, virtually all activity, including returning home, was confined in a small area, when business needed expansion room, residences were taken over and people moved, often establishing new neighborhoods. Once the island was built out and certain industries relocated or ceased, the process at times reversed itself, but this volume is confined to the limitations of 200 images and does not explore, say, the adaptive use of redundant offices as residences. Lodging patterns not only present a vivid example of a city on the move but can be traced herein chapter by chapter. The regular shifting of hotel districts is one of the clearest in New York real estate patterns.

A few words about postcard publishing will help heighten an appreciation for the illustrations. Most collectable cards were issued between 1905 and 1915, the period of a collecting craze. The first mass-produced popular imagery, their antecedent is represented by several choice examples, one being the stereograph. Beginning in the 1850s and continuing into the early-20th century (although by 1900 interest in them was fading), stereographs are two similar images mounted side by side on cards, intended to be seen through viewers that would add the appearance of three-dimension depth to the image. They were an enormously popular parlor entertainment in the Victorian period and are collected today, although generally without the fervor of postcard collecting.

Early postcards printed in Germany were often graphic masterpieces. Tariffs steered market share to inferior American printers, a significant timeline within that period was March 1, 1907, when postal regulations permitted a message on a postcard's address side. Prior postcard publishers left small blank spaces on the picture side, or front, for messages. Use of the back for writing was accompanied by a line of division separating the message from the address halves, so cards once having an uninterrupted space for an address, or undivided back, were succeeded by cards with a line down the middle, or a divided-back card. Most cards in this book are from the 1905 to 1915 era. The fading of the craze and the dominance by American printers devolved into the next category, the white-border era, so named because images were surrounded with a four-sided white space, ostensibly to save ink. Many are awful. The era, arising around 1915 and mercifully ending around 1930, is the nadir of postcard production. Photographs printed on postcard stock, popular nationwide in the 1905–1915 era, continued to be produced in bulk quantities in New York, mitigating the white border and its successor period, one distinguished by omission here, the linen era, cards so-called because the rough texture of the paper seemed not unlike linen. They absorbed well new inks of the time and were a product that could produce brightness and warmth that can make an otherwise dismal printing process possess a characteristic charm. Linens, beginning around 1930, continued into the 1950s, overlapping with the chrome period. Appearing like photochromes, early examples were often produced from the Kodachrome film introduced at the chrome era's beginning, around 1940, and continue to date. Cards continue to be published in New York but in fewer numbers as the medium is falling from use as few actually write. Slogans on postcards are at times inaccurate, which may account for differences between the illustrations and the text.

One

Broadway's Bowling Green Beginnings

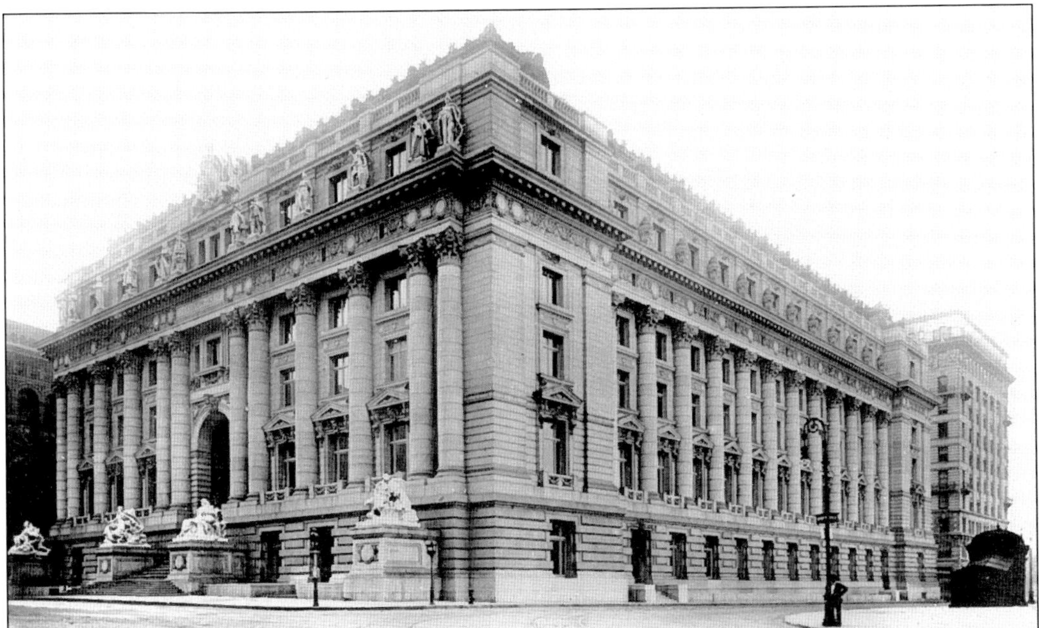

Cass Gilbert's great Beaux-Arts United States customhouse reflects the significance of customs duties as the major source of federal revenue prior to 1913. Constructed 1899–1907, the building's grandeur, emphasized by rich sculptural decoration, conveys its stature as a "Temple of Commerce." The larger *Continents*, so prominent at eye level, may prompt one to overlook the 12 figures above the cornice, executed by various sculptors, representing history's successful nation and city-state traders. Abandoned in 1972 by customs, the richly decorated interior is Smithsonian's National Museum of the American Indian, since October 1994.

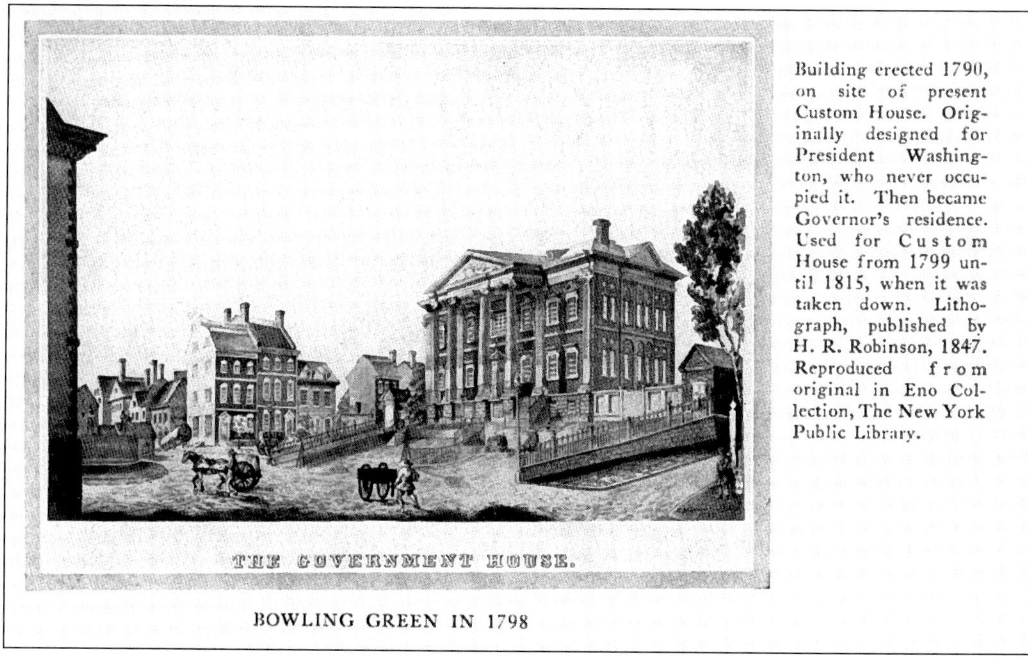

Historic print postcards are typically of mediocre graphic quality, rarely convey the artistic vitality of original imagery, and are disdained by collectors. The front of this card provides historic background. Amos Eno was a major New York real estate figure.

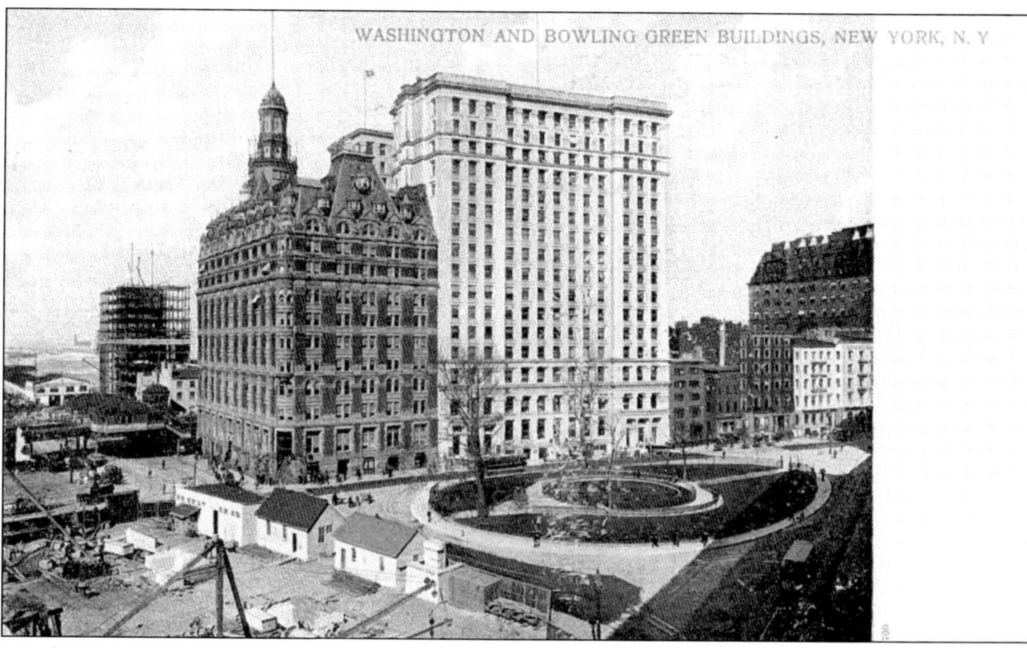

Much happened at Broadway's foot around 1902. The customhouse was under construction as the skeleton of the Whitehall Building neared completion. Abraham DePeyster had been on his pedestal for six years, while 1 and 11 Broadway were new. The 1890 Columbia Building at right sported its original three-story roof capital.

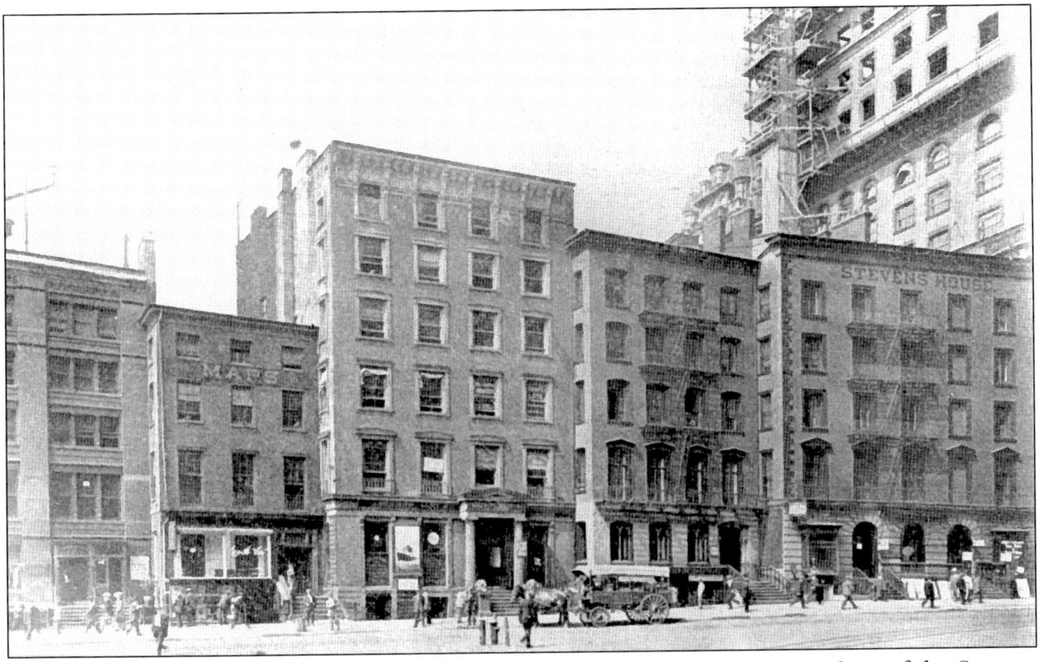

Joseph and Lorenzo Delmonico's 1846 restaurant and hotel were an antecedent of the Stevens House, reorganized as such in 1856 and later lending its name to two office buildings. This strip was replaced by the Cunard Building in 1921.

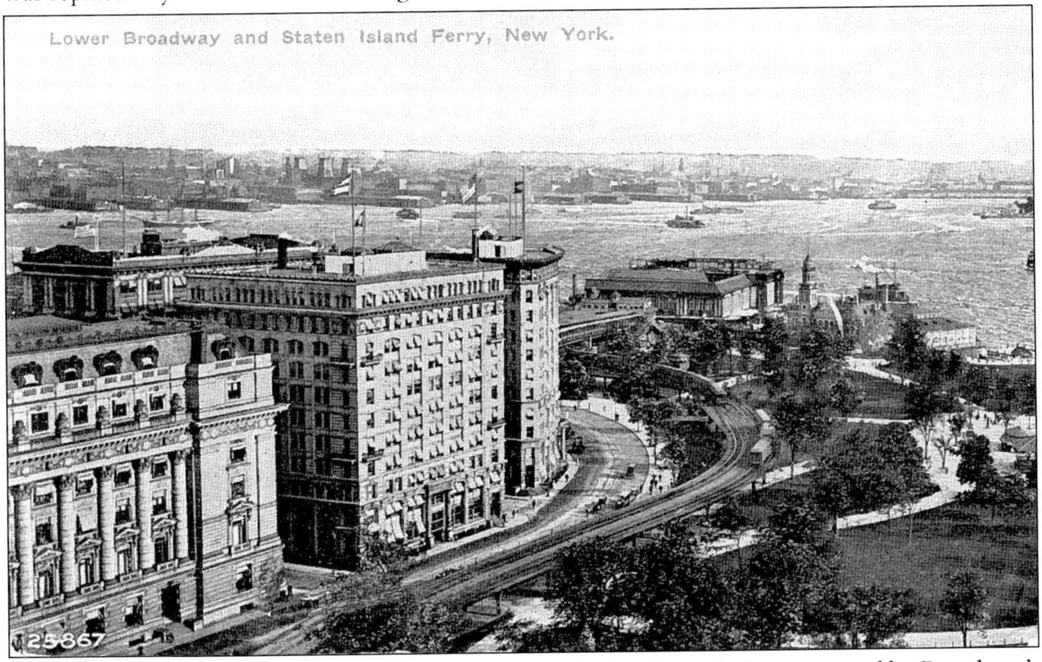

The sensibility of the "Lower Broadway" designation in the slogan is demonstrated by Broadway's continuation at State Street, as pictured, and Whitehall Street to the east, two thoroughfares that are practical extensions of Broadway, linked by the customhouse at its foot, and partially at left. The two buildings beyond it are the no-longer-extant Battery Park Building, center, and the Cheeseborough Building, right. Part of the Maritime Building is at the top left.

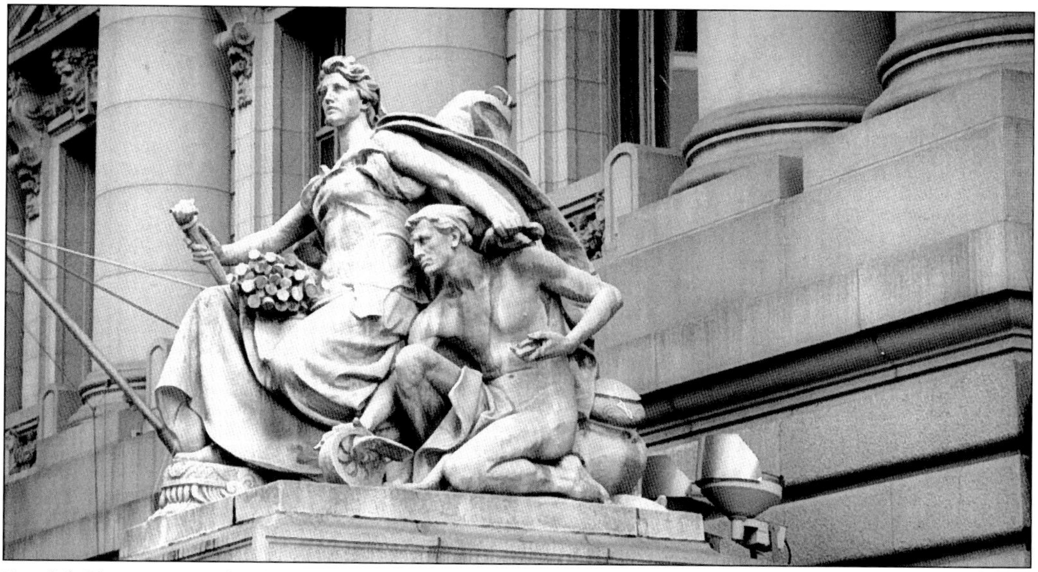

Daniel Chester French's four-year undertaking to design, create, and install the four figure groups *The Continents* represents his most significant architectural commission. The four, following design changes during their creation, were executed in Tennessee marble by New York's noted carvers, the Piccirilli brothers. Seated *America* holds a torch, the sheaf of corn in her lap representing the American idea of plenty. The kneeling *Labor* holds a wheel of progress. A Native American peering over *America*'s right shoulder is obscured when viewed looking southeast, thus reminding that one joy of seeing sculpture is the multiple imagery by changing perspective.

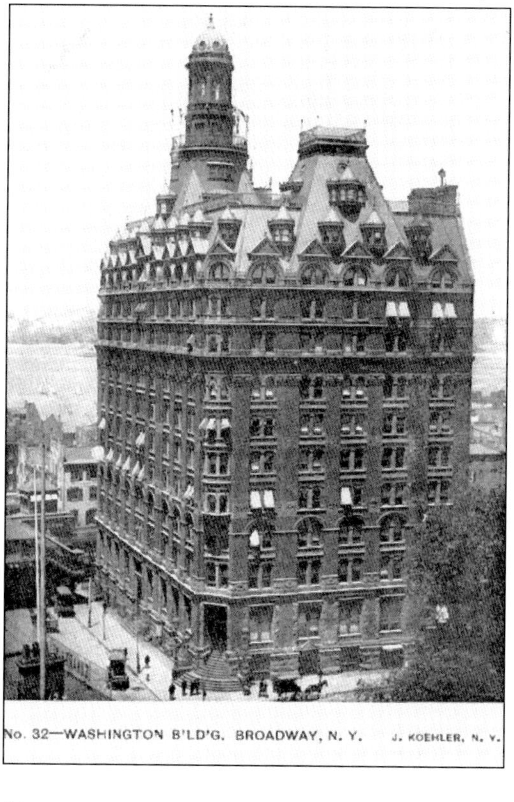

The Washington Building, built by the Washington Building Company from 1882 to 1885 at 1 Broadway, the former site of the Washington Hotel, was designed by competition winner Edward H. Kendall. The two-story mansard and the tower, added in 1887, enhanced visual impact from the harbor. The card is from around 1902, but the image is earlier as the edges of the view west are absent the adjacent 1895–1898 Bowling Green Building and the 1902–1903 Whitehall Building (17 Battery Place) beyond the elevated station. See page 17 for a reincarnation.

George Edwin Bissell (1839–1920) came late to sculpting, beginning in his family's stone business, then traveling to Europe in 1875 to study ancient Roman art and bronze developments practiced in Paris. He developed a portrait style reflecting the emerging Beaux-Arts and the naturalness of Roman portraiture. Abraham DePeyster was a prominent Colonial public and business figure and one of the wealthiest. This statue, commissioned by a great-great-great-grandson, is the most prominent of several done for the family. Modeled from Michelangelo's *Moses* in Rome, this figure was installed 1896 in Bowling Green Park.

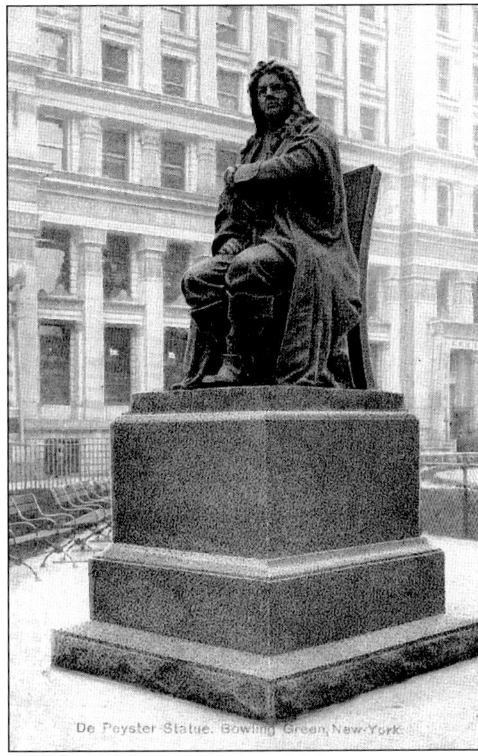

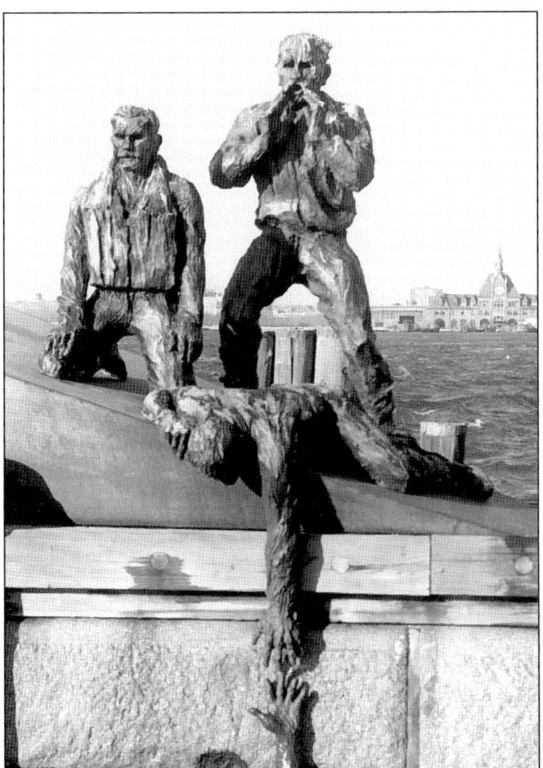

Broadway, the site of most early monuments, became hazardous from growing congestion. Most were moved to city parks, where new statues are typically mounted in homes better suited for permanent installation. Battery Park is a notable example. One newer monument that uses the water's edge for enhanced emotional impact is Marisol's *American Merchant Marine Memorial.* Dedicated on October 8, 1991, it honors a force whose sacrifices were too often overlooked. The former Central Railroad of New Jersey terminal in Jersey City's Liberty State Park is in the background.

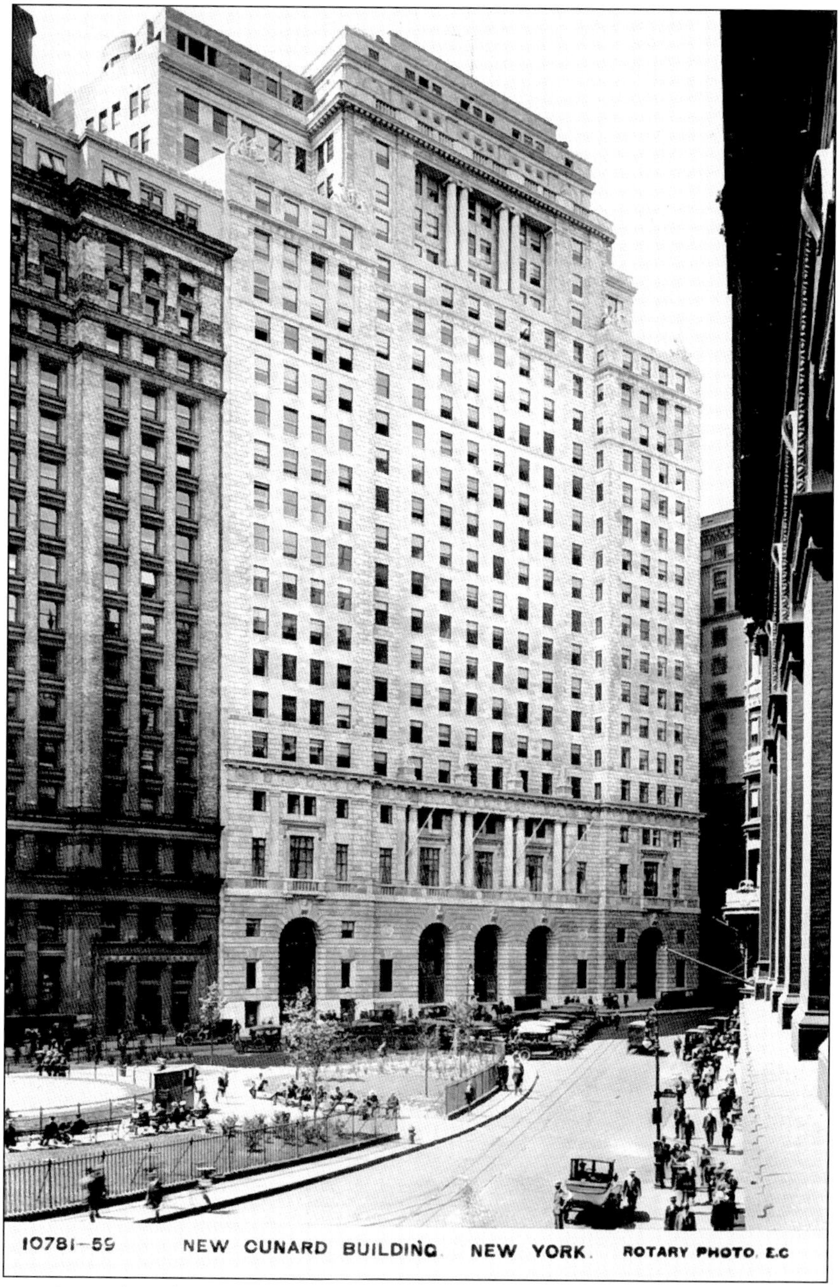

The 22-story Cunard Building, designed by Benjamin Wistar Morris with Carrere and Hastings, completed in 1921, was the booking office for its oceanic transportation. Cunard's departure in 1968 left a challenge for adaptive use of the building's signature architectural highlight, its lobby. The 183-foot-long space with a 68-foot-high dome decorated with maritime murals by Ezra Winter has a grandeur rarely encountered in an office. The installation is marred by the occupancy of the Bowling Green Post Office, a tenant since 1977. The building, a designated New York City landmark since 1995, fills the block to Greenwich Street and complied with the 1916 zoning law without conspicuous setbacks. A glimpse of the Bowling Green Building is at left.

The nine-story structure at right, designed by Ebenezer L. Roberts and completed in 1886, was the origin of the Standard Oil office. It expanded to the north with a nine-story building, which was enlarged and built up in 1896, as pictured at left, to a design by Kimball and Thompson. They were also the architects of Manhattan Life in the background, pictured around 1905.

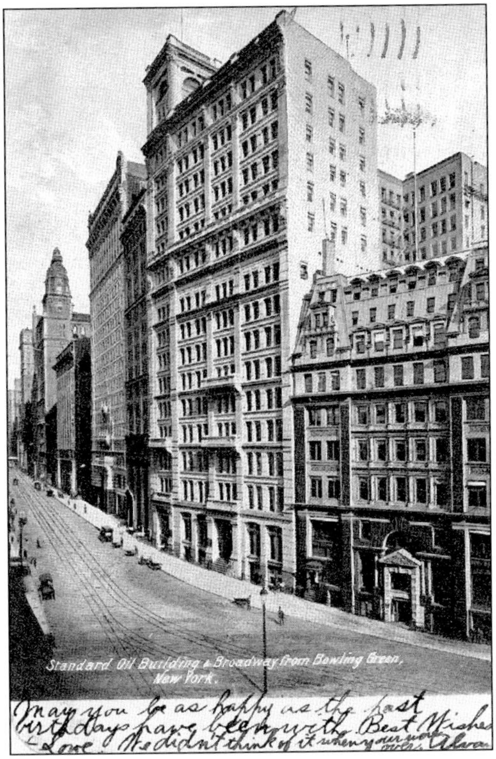

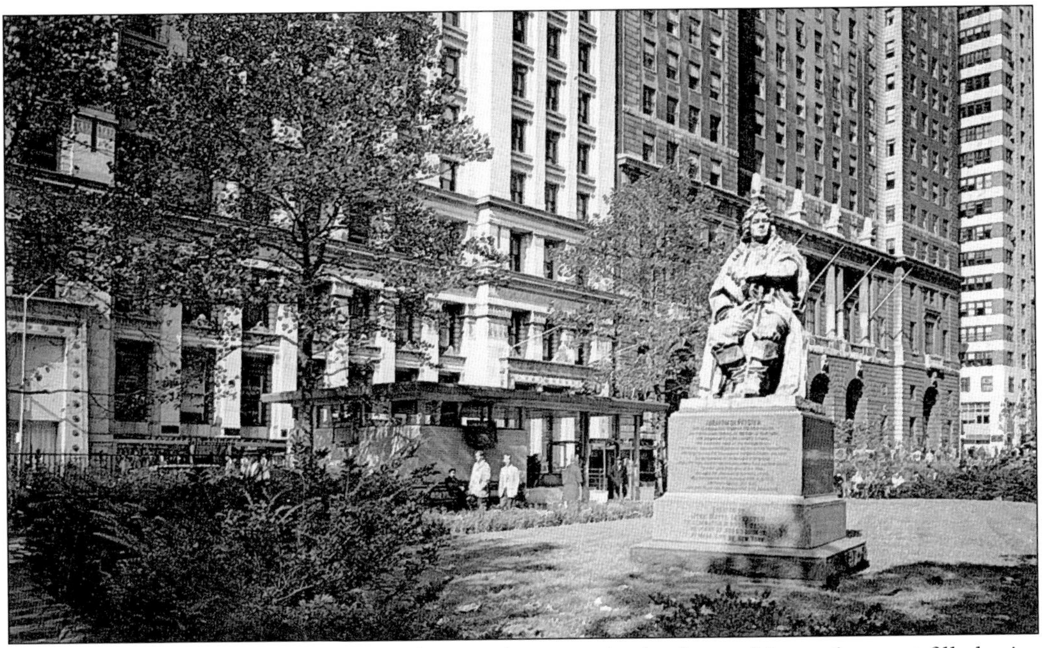

Abraham DePeyster is pictured in his former placement in the front of the park, a spot filled prior to the Revolution by a statue of George III, destroyed in an act of rebellious fervor. DePeyster was moved to Hanover Square in 1972, where he rested on a new pink granite pedestal until taken away on October 30, 2004, his second home given to the British Memorial Garden. In 2007, DePeyster is in storage, awaiting reinstallation.

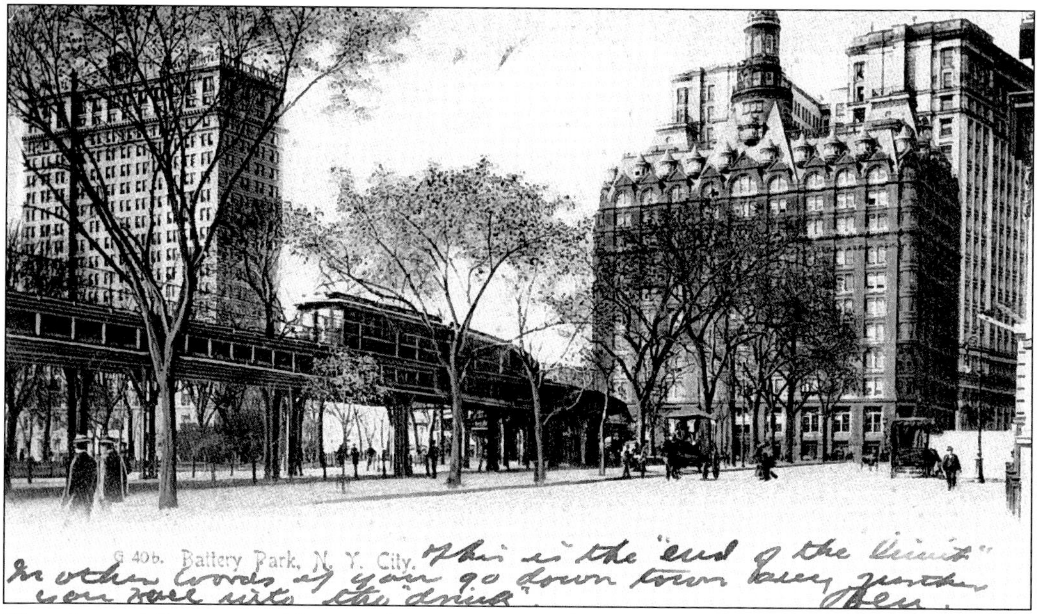

The elevated line wound its way into Battery Park and the ferry terminal emerging from between the Whitehall and Washington Buildings. Land south of Bowling Green is fill, accounting for Broadway's not beginning at the actual tip of present-day Manhattan. The card is a *c.* 1905 Rotograph.

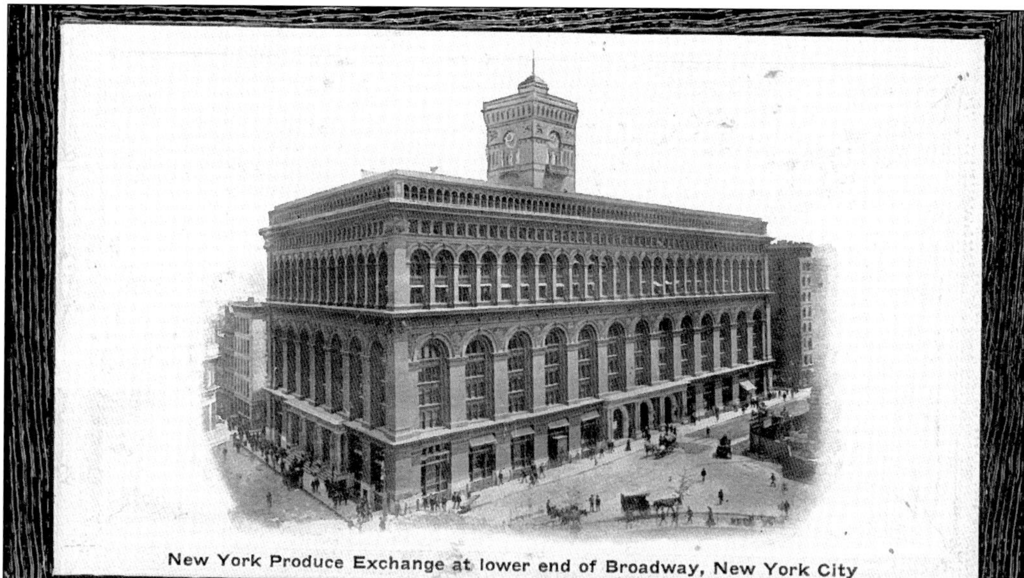

The New York Produce Exchange, chartered in 1862, built in 1884 this headquarters—trading floor at 2 Broadway, the southeast corner of Beaver Street. The elevated perspective depicts well its arched windows, doubling in number at each level. Designed by George B. Post and Company, the east elevation's 11-story, 200-foot-tall clock tower was a favored vantage for photographers. This masterpiece was demolished in 1957, replaced by the glass and metal office now on the site. The edge provides interest around 1905, an arc of Bowling Green, a customhouse construction fence, and Whitehall Street as a natural extension of Broadway.

Bowling Green, actually leased as a bowling green in 1733, known earlier as the Parade, an open space in front of the foot of Fort Amsterdam, is the city's oldest park. This *c.* 1915 image depicts at right the Produce Exchange Bank, and the Columbia Building, between the two taller structures at left. Also pictured on the bottom of page 10, that building's three-story roof had been rebuilt and fire escapes added, reminding one that 1890 fire code may not have been enduring. Looking straight down a 15-story open staircase is frightening, not for height but the fire potential.

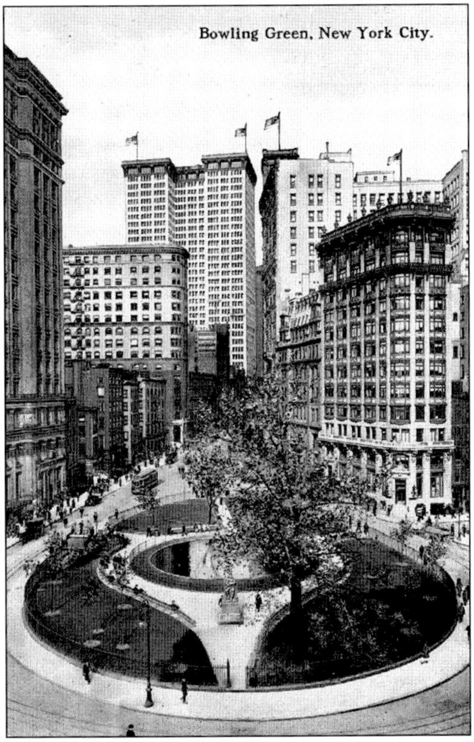

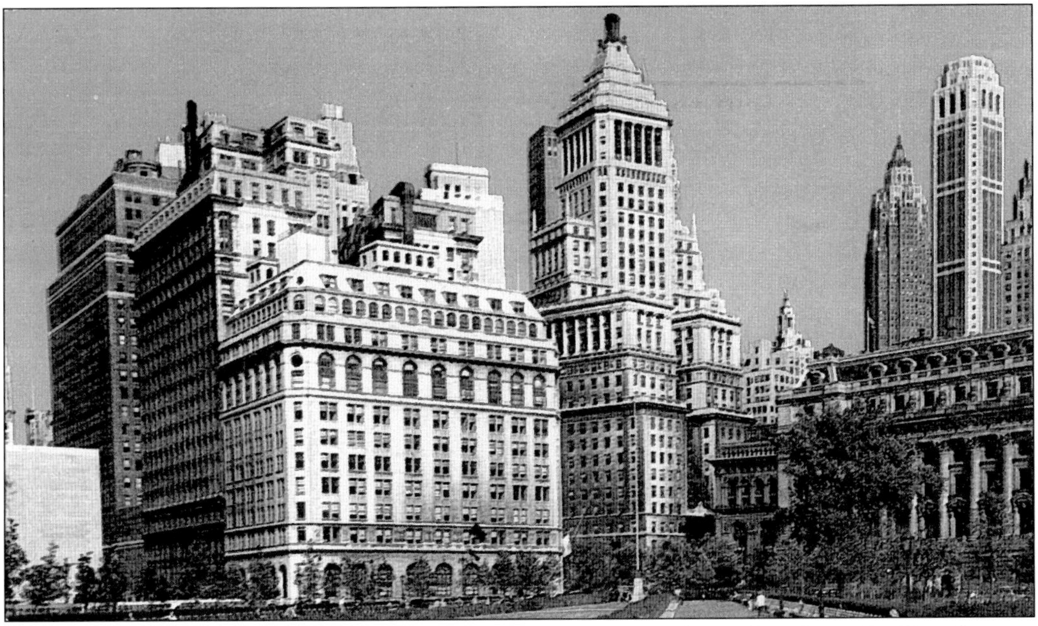

The International Mercantile Marine, a merger of shipping firms, hired W. B. Chambers to rebuild the Washington Building in a neoclassical style. The 1919–1921 project, at center, has its maritime origins depicted, via facade ornaments. Adjacent is the Greenwich Street elevation of the Bowling Green Building, while the customhouse is at right. On the edges of Broadway, above it, are the Cities Service Building at 70 Pine Street, left, and the City Bank Farmers Trust at 22 William Street.

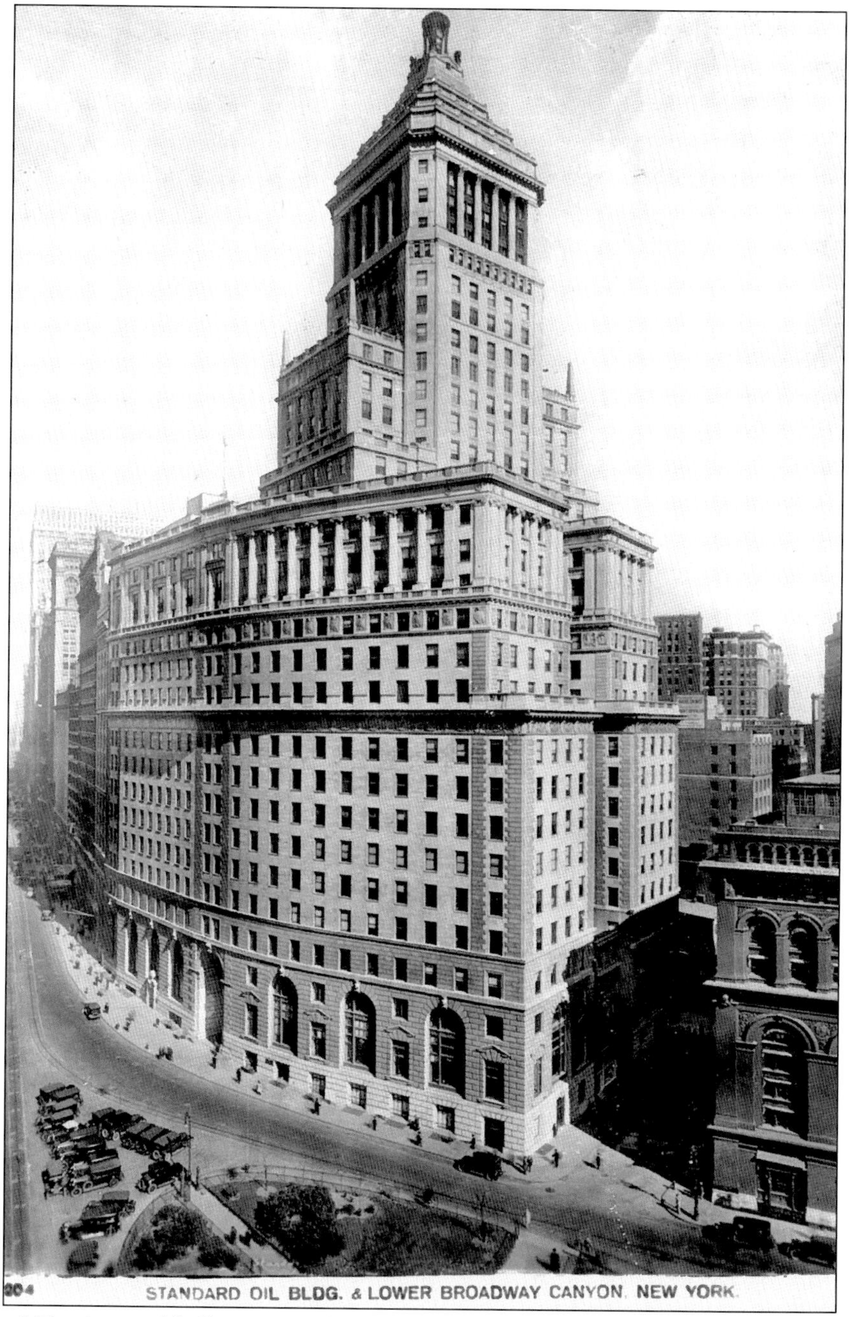

Carrere and Hastings, with Shreve, Lamb and Blake, designed Standard Oil's new headquarters at 26 Broadway, erected 1922–1926. A plaque at the entrance succinctly describes their intent: "The curved base and skewed towers are part of a complex Renaissance-inspired design that reflects the alignment of Broadway and the irregular pentagonal plot. The prominent tower is crowned by a bronze brazier surrounded by flaming torches. These symbols of the corporate power of the oil industry growth were meant to be visible to travelers entering New York harbor." Visible on the edges of the *c.* 1930 photographic card—it predates 1 Wall Street—are the northern arc of Bowling Green and the Produce Exchange on the south side of Beaver Street.

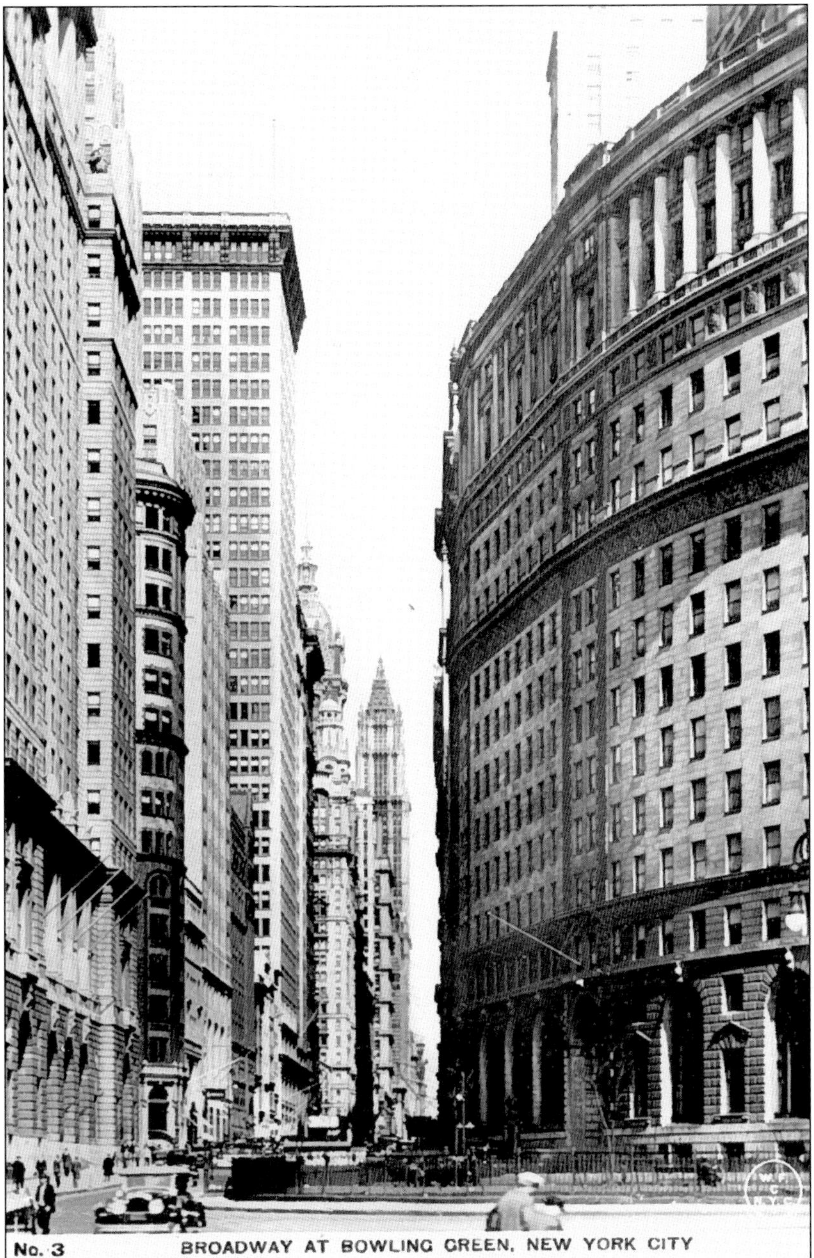

No. 3 BROADWAY AT BOWLING GREEN, NEW YORK CITY

This photographic card suggests the pedestrian's challenge of capturing the cityscape. The artful composition of Standard Oil, at right and opposite, needs height and/or distance to be perceived properly. Looking up from two blocks away will permit seeing the top of Adams Express (left, middle), but the view at grade is generally less than seen on page 22. Two-dimensional viewing also has challenges, as the Woolworth Building in the background could be at the end of a row rather than considerably separated, obvious on page 34. The Cunard Building (page 14) is flattened at left. The image dates from around 1928, or after the 1926 Standard Oil and prior to the destruction of the rounded-corner 1890 Columbia Building, replaced by the present 29 Broadway, 1929–1931.

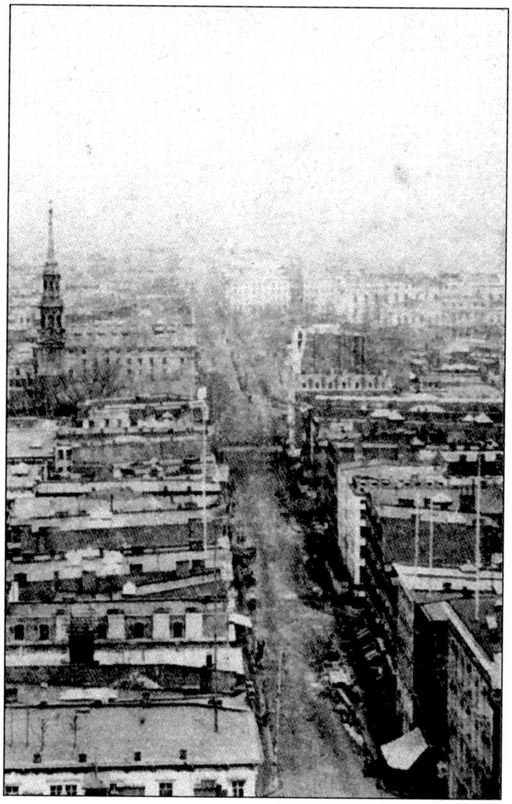

The *New York Times* on February 14, 1882, mildly ridiculed "the mania for high places," noting, "For many years the tall spire of Trinity Church was the favorite climbing round," "towered above all the other heights and gave rural visitors a chance to scan the symmetrical outlines of ten thousand picturesque chimneys." It claimed, "It is no small undertaking to climb the steep winding stone stairs up past the bell-ringing room . . . and then still up without any rest to the dizzy height where the stairs end . . . seeing all of lower New York at his feet." It added, "it makes the flesh creep to go up and look down." The American Illustrated Stereographs of New York seen below gave the viewer, perhaps around the 1860s, a comparable experience without leaving home. The view west toward the Hudson was a rather prosaic, even wash on a line. The view north (Anthony's Stereoscopic Views No. 6603, also 1860s, at left) has one identifiable landmark, St. Paul's steeple. What would be considered the city's first skyscraper, the Equitable Building, would be completed in 1870 near the right lower edge. By the 1905 postcard mania, nearly all these buildings had been replaced. (Courtesy of Robin Kaller.)

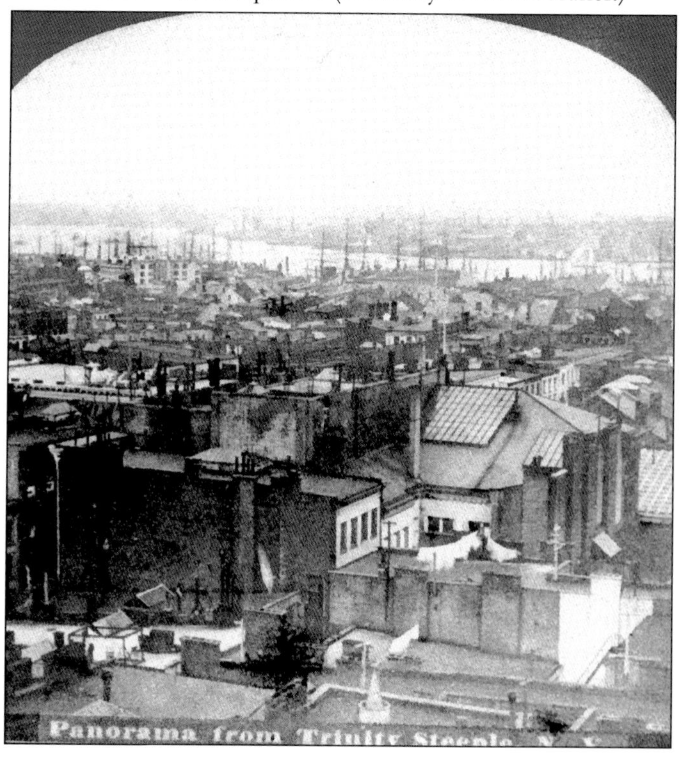

Two

Around Wall Street

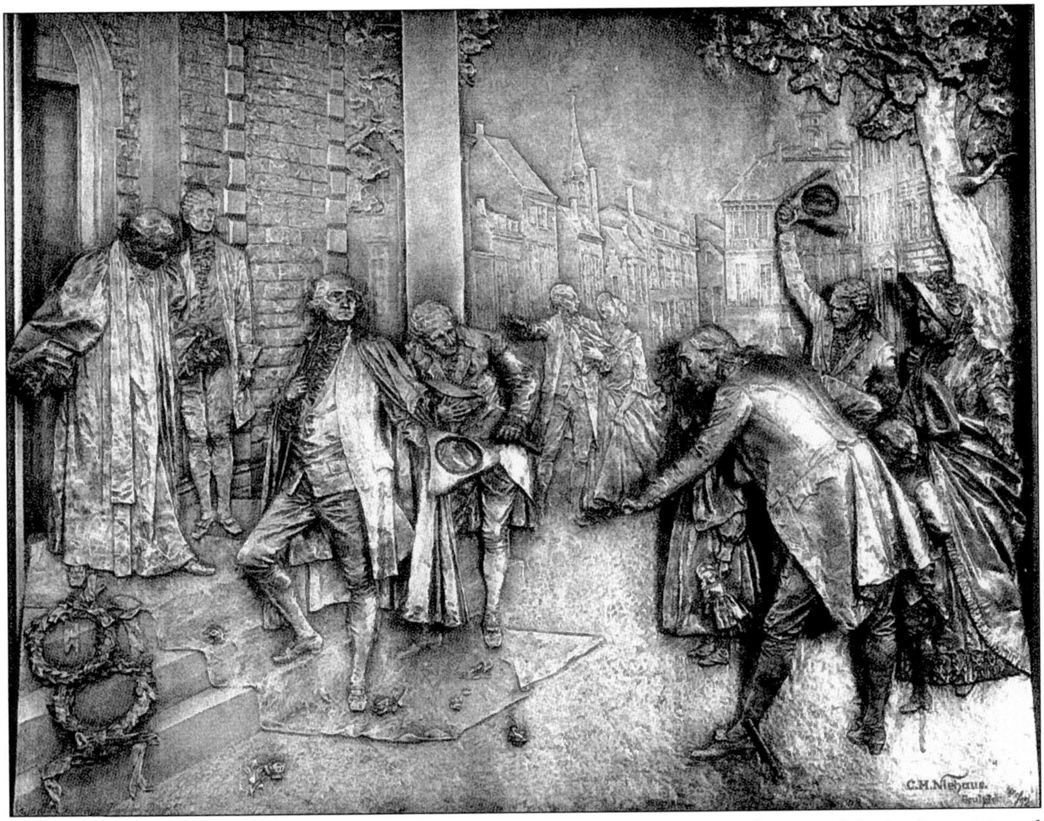

Trinity Church's artistic bronze doors were designed by leading sculptors of their time. Noted portrait sculptor Charles Henry Niehaus (1855–1935) executed the 12.5-foot-high South Doors, which depict significant figures in the history of Manhattan and Trinity and were installed in 1893. Each panel is 2 feet 8 inches wide by 23 inches high. This contemporary card depicts *President Washington at St. Paul's Chapel after his inauguration April 30, 1789.* The Thanksgiving service was held there as Trinity was being rebuilt after its 1776 fire.

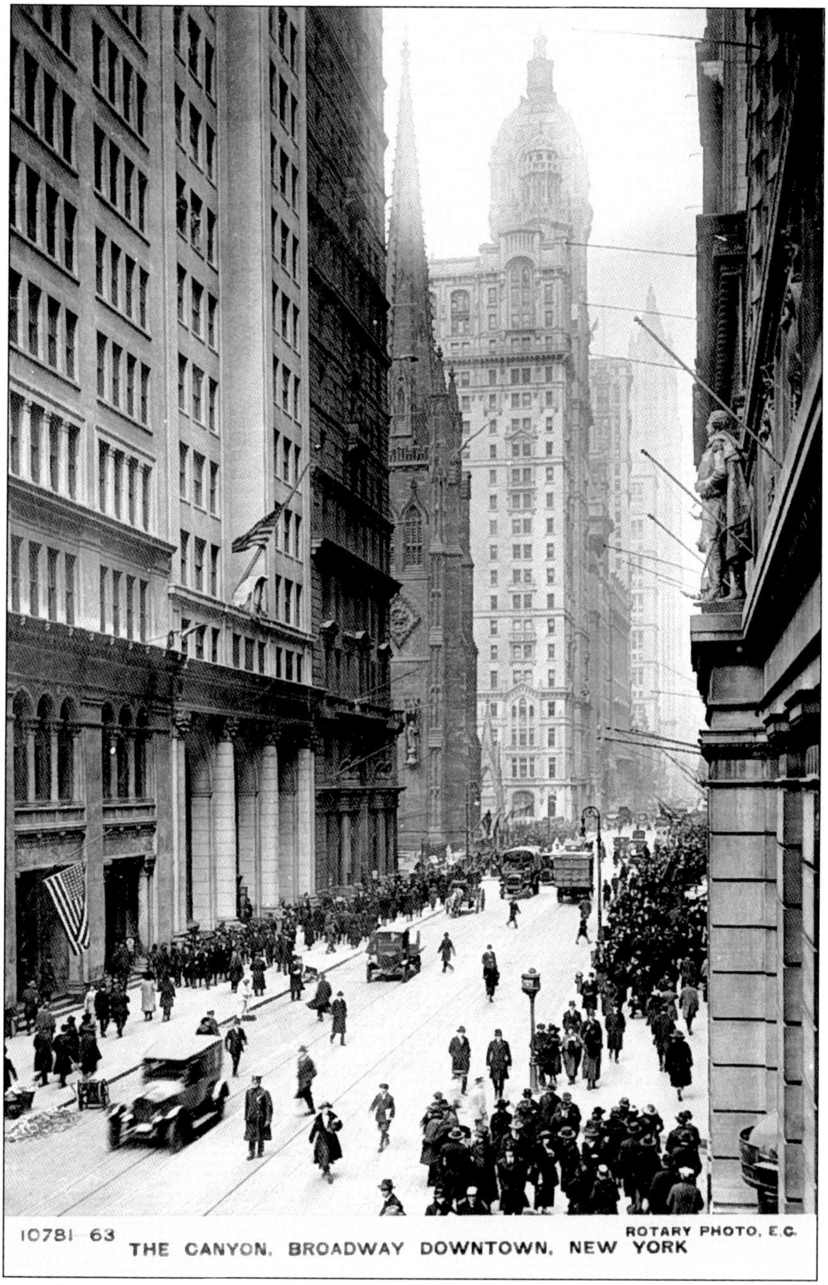

The canyon of Broadway alludes to the continuous lines of tall buildings constructed with compatible masonry material, best portrayed by the three offices at left. Closest to the edge at No. 61 is the 1914 33-story, 424-foot Adams Express Building. Adams, a leader in the 19th-century rapid and secure delivery business, merged into the Railway Express Agency, familiar into the third quarter of the 20th century. Adjacent are No. 65, the 1917 23-story, 297-foot American Express Building, and the Empire Building. Clearly visible beyond Trinity Church on the west side are buildings described in these pages, including the Trinity Building, the Singer Building, and the Woolworth Building. Part of the canyon's eastern wall is on the opposite and preceding pages; at right is one of the four sculptures at 52 Broadway.

Exchange Court was built 1896–1898 at the 52 Broadway corner with Exchange Place, designed by Clinton and Russell. Four statues by J. Massey Rhind, standing figures of George Clinton, Peter Stuyvesant, Henry Hudson, and Gen. James Wolfe, stamped the structure's character. Removed for unknown reasons at an unspecified date prior to 1950, the statues wound up in a junkyard. Wolfe was "repatriated" to Calgary, Alberta, while the three others were installed in a park in Kingston, New York, where they remain. In 1979–1980, loss of integrity followed loss of statuary when the building was stripped to its 12-story skeleton, six floors were added, and the entirety was clad in metal and glass.

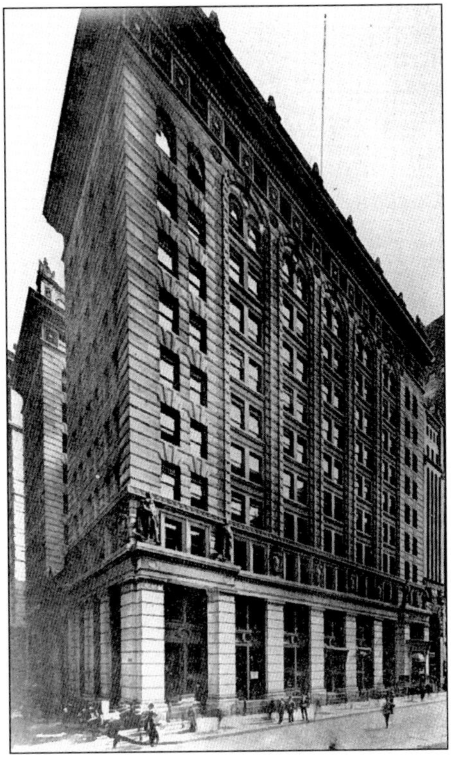

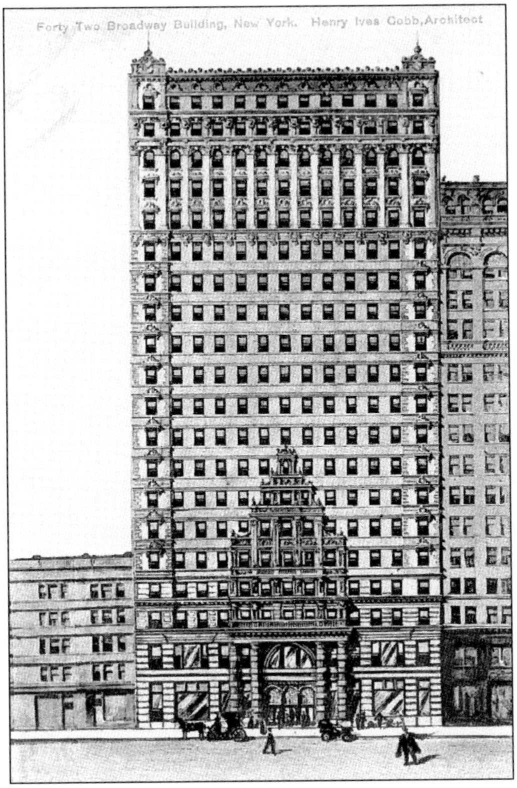

Henry Ives Cobb designed the 22-story, 243-foot-tall 42 Broadway, completed in 1903. The shaded area over the entrance suggests the type of step-gabled building erected by the Dutch in the latter 17th century. Although still clearly discernible in darker stone, the appealing outline can be easily overlooked.

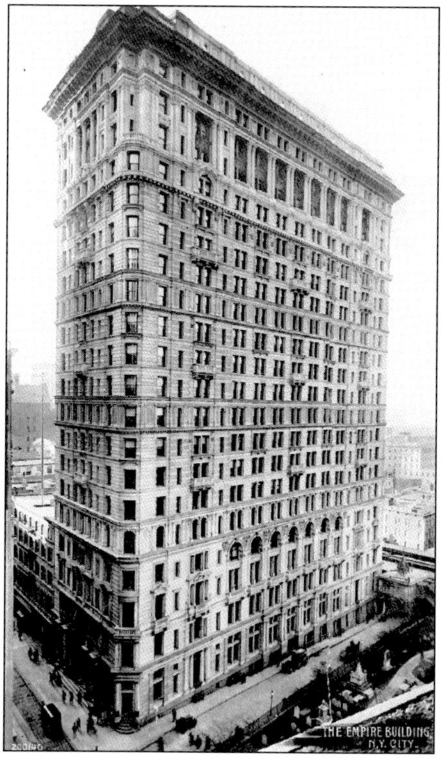

The 20-story, 293-foot Empire Building was completed in 1898 at No. 71, the southwest corner of Rector Street, opposite Trinity Churchyard. Kimball and Thompson's neoclassical design contrasts with Francis H. Kimball's Gothic offices north of Trinity. Empire would have been confusing after a similarly named, famed skyscraper opened in 1931 and was renamed for a subsequent owner, United States Steel. This 1910 card looking southeast depicts the elevated station on Trinity Place and the pyramid of Alexander Hamilton's monument.

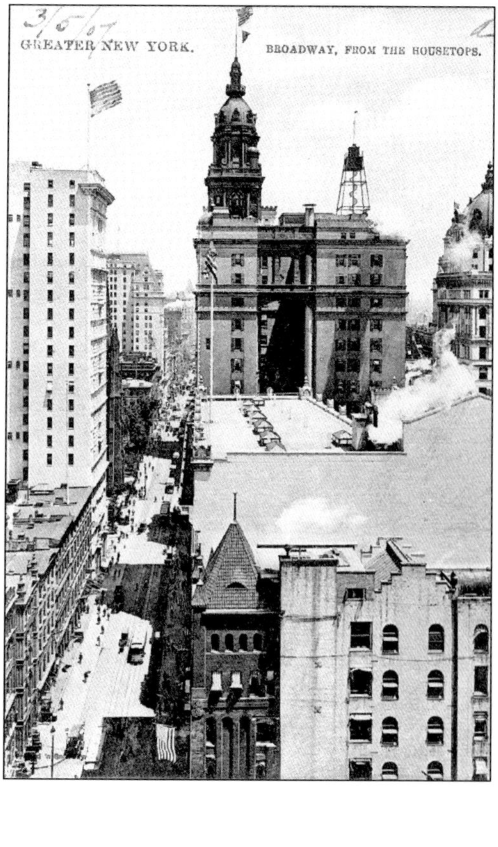

The view from No. 42, bottom of preceding page, shows that buildings with finely finished masonry facades often possess prosaic sides. The tower at center is Manhattan Life's, while a partial view of the dome on the 1897 Commercial Cable Building is at right. The flag flies on the Empire Building, while City Investing is behind it. Several skylights depict the roof of 52 Broadway. The low-lying buildings at left around 1905 were replaced by buildings pictured on page 22 within 10 years.

Manhattan Life, at Nos. 64–70, stood in the center of the east side block between Exchange Place (foreground) and Wall Street. Completed in 1893 to Kimball and Thompson's design, the building was taken down for Irving Trust. The 1893 Consolidated Stock Exchange is in the foreground. Completed in 1888, the exchange, which had grown by merger, left for Broad Street in 1907. The image is dated 1895, the card seven years later.

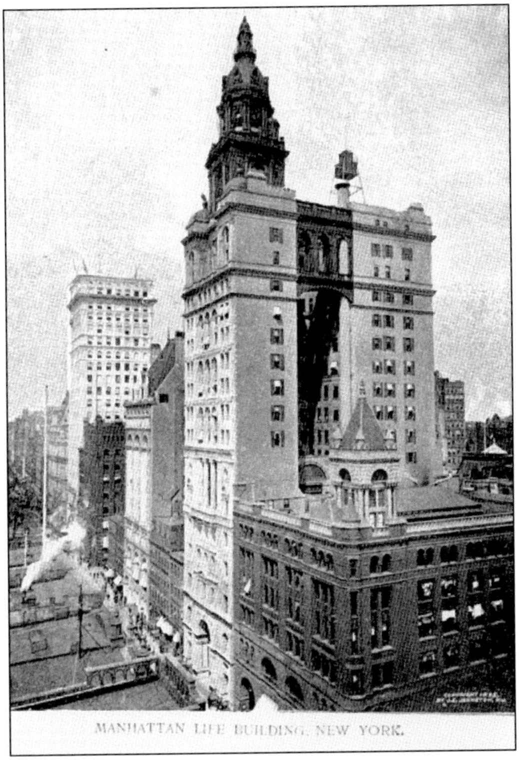

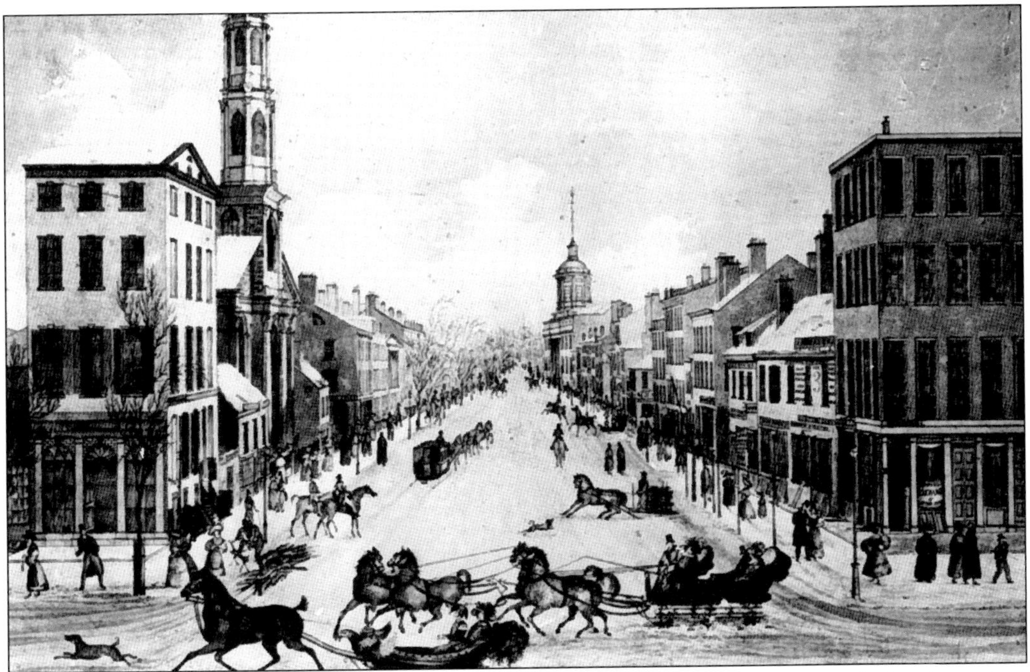

A bank had long been on the northeast corner with Wall Street. The steeple at left belonged to the Presbyterian church, there from 1811 to 1845 when lost in the July 19 conflagration. Indeed, much of the surrounding landscape east of Broadway to Water Street was destroyed by the fire and subsequent explosion that began in a factory on New Street.

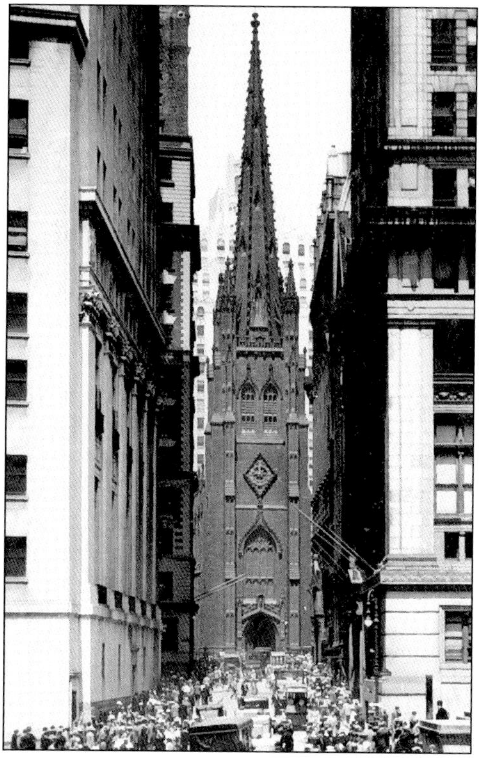

Trinity Church seen from Wall Street is the quintessential Financial District image. Surrounding buildings provide dating aids on older images, but they are unchanged since this 1930s view. The spot marks the separation of Broad Street at the left, where the New York Stock Exchange stands, and Nassau Street at right, where the edge of Bankers Trust at 14 Wall Street is visible. The structures on the west side of Trinity Place are behind the church.

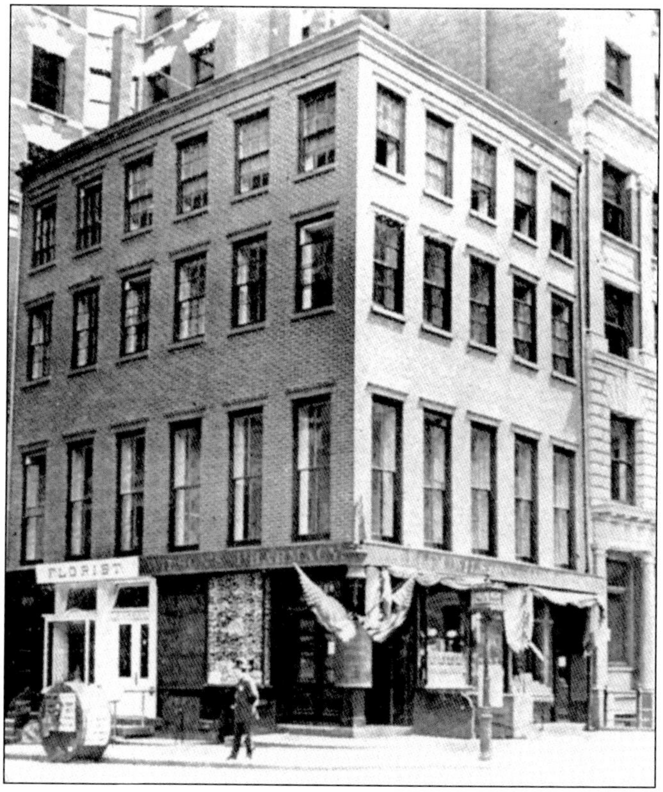

This "shabby old building," as characterized by the *Times* of March 3, 1896, soon gained renown as the county's most valuable piece of real estate. Benjamin D. Sillman long retained the southeast corner of Wall Street, even in the face of advancing construction, perhaps from sentiment. The 29-by-39-foot property yielded an astonishing $700,000, or $4 per square foot, when sold by his estate in 1905 to the Mercantile Trust Company of St. Louis. A buyer representative exclaimed, "There is only one Broadway, only one Wall Street and only one Number 1 Wall Street." They built the tiny tower of 18 stories visible on page 29.

The southeast corner of Wall Street demanded higher utilization once a larger lot could be assembled. Broadway's art deco masterpiece soars over Trinity's steeple, the five-story 1 Wall designed by Voorhees Gmelin and Walker, completed 1931 and known historically for builder Irving Trust. This building towers over the prosaic 2 Wall Street, completed in 1933 to Walker and Gillette's design for the First National Bank, and the southern expansion of American Surety.

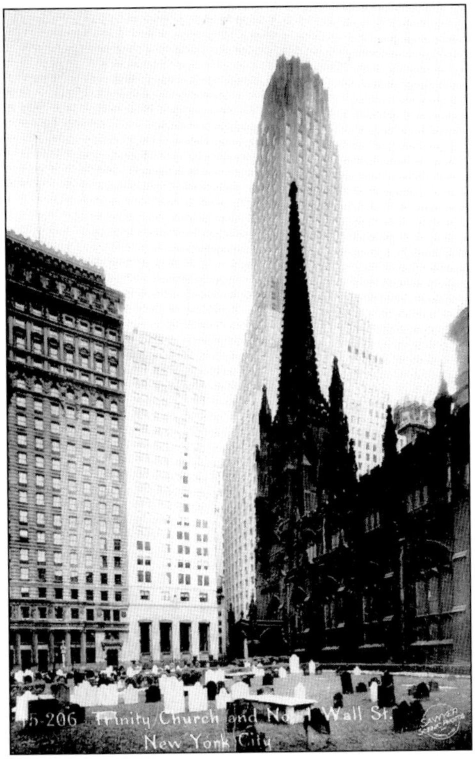

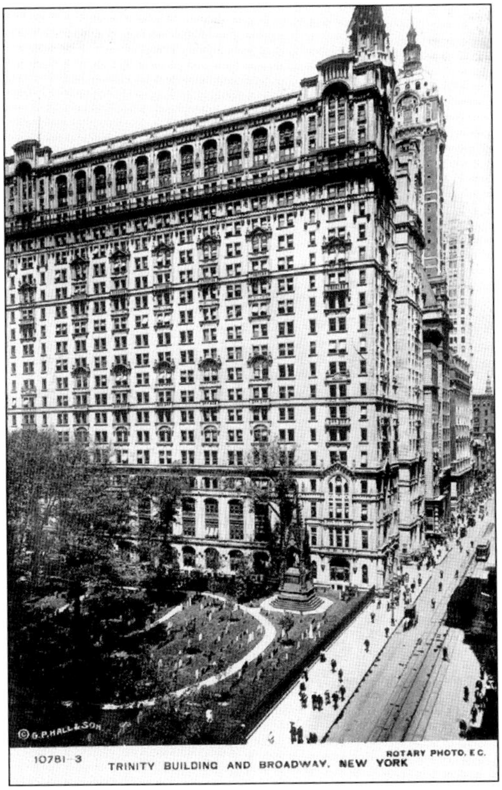

The United States Realty and Construction Company, organized in 1901, bought the old Trinity Building and another office north of Trinity Churchyard, hoping to relocate Thames Street 28 feet northward. Initially unsuccessful, it built in 1905 a three-bay, 21-story, limestone-clad office at No. 111, designed by Francis H. Kimball. Overlooking the yard, it was unfinished on its north as expansion was anticipated. The Soldiers Monument in the foreground honors unknown soldiers and sailors of the Revolution.

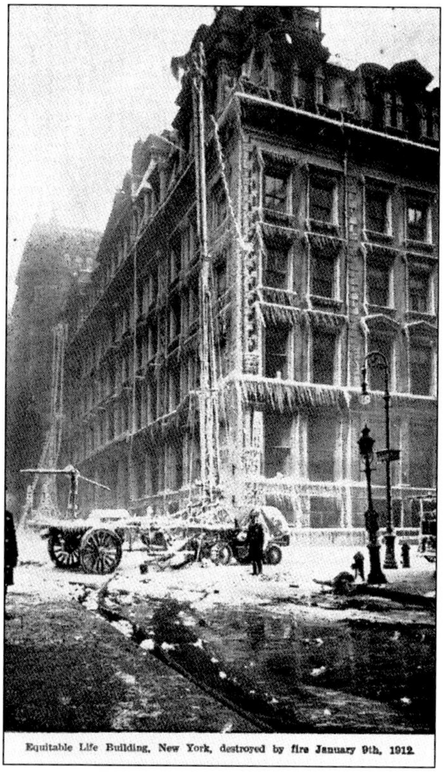

The 1870 Equitable Building at 120 Broadway, designed by Arthur Gilman and Edward H. Kendall, is considered New York's first skyscraper, its attainable height elevated by inclusion of the first office passenger elevator. Spanning the Pine-Cedar block, the appealing, technologically advanced building became a powerful symbol of the Equitable Life Assurance Society. Alas, the place was destroyed by fire on January 11, 1912, a blaze pictured on numerous photographic cards, the news pictures of the day. This dismal printed example reflects an enduring interest in the image. The block's symbolism took a darker character.

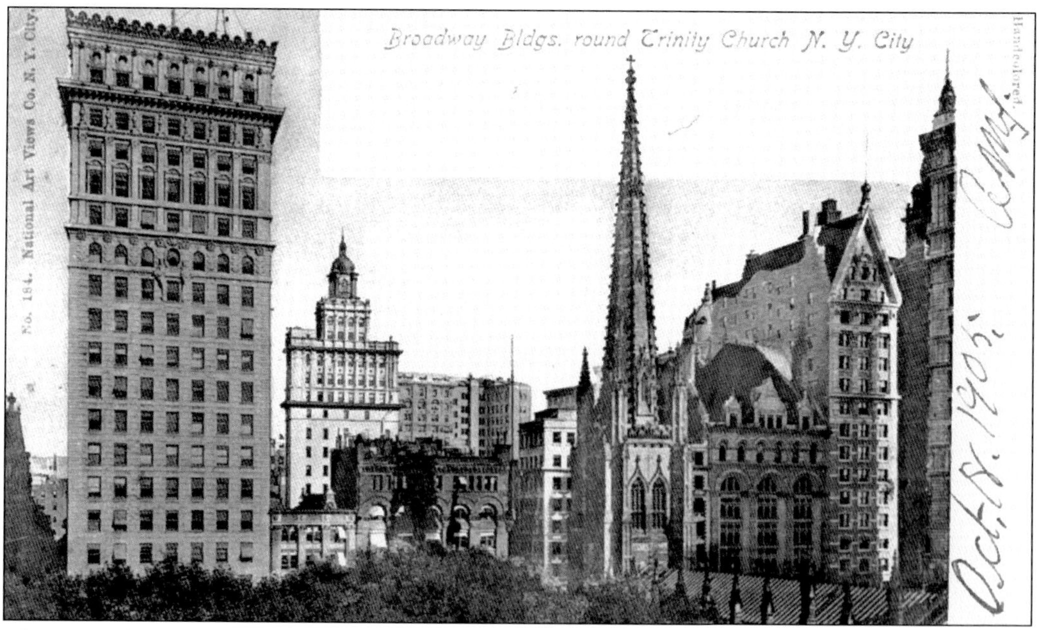

The east side of Broadway is pictured from the American Surety Building at left to No. 74, the gable-roofed, slender tower with the finial. Demolition of the Schemerhorn Building adjacent to the former would provide space for its southern expansion. The United Bank Building adjacent to it would be replaced by that pictured on the top of 27. In the background stands the Gillender Building, a 25-foot-wide office at Nassau and Wall Streets with a brief life span of 1897–1912.

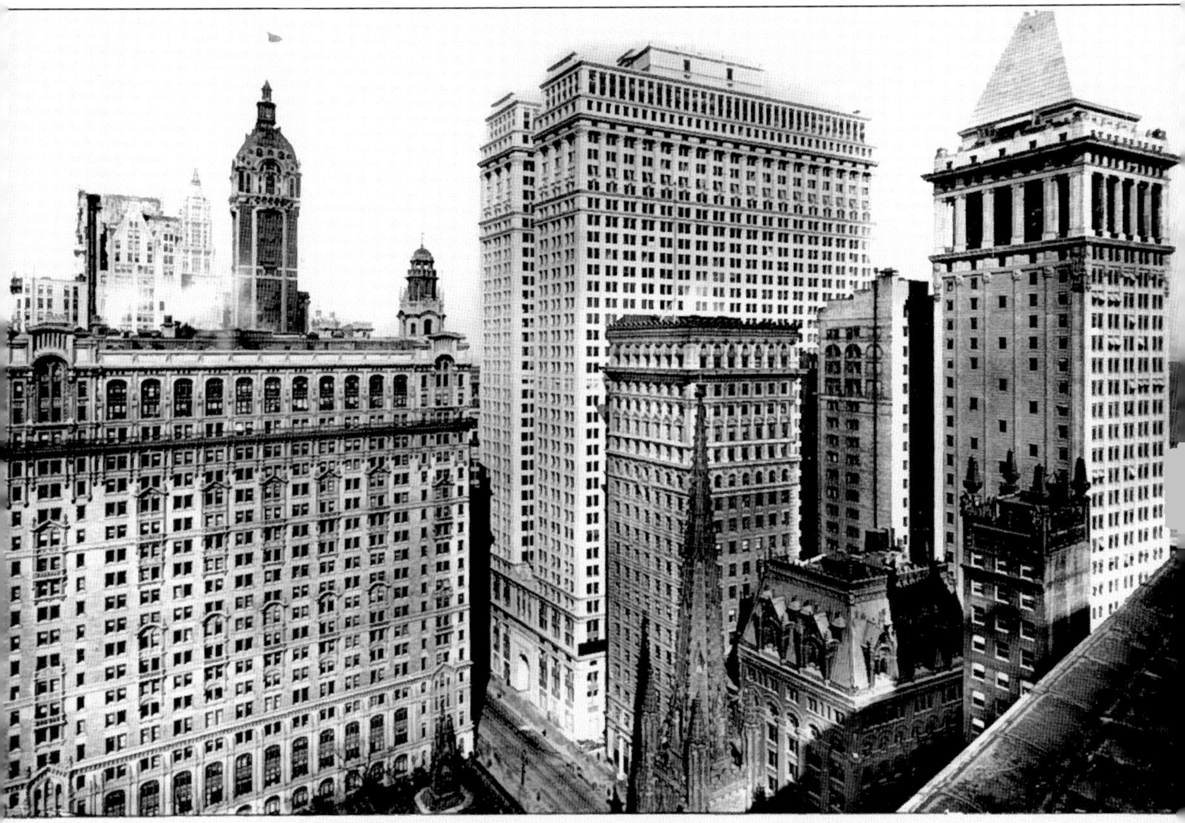

EQUITABLE BUILDING & SURROUNDING SKYSCRAPERS, NEW YORK. (c) Irving Underhill

Easily overlooked on this two-block view from Wall Street to Cedar Street is the diminutive 18-story tower that was 1 Wall Street from 1906 to 1930, at lower right, its finials outlined against Bankers Trust. It was facetiously known as "the chimney building," or the bandbox. Bankers Trust at 14 Wall Street, completed on the site of the Gillender Building, is the background tower on the preceding page. The American Surety Building at 100 Broadway, designed by Bruce Price, dominated the block when completed in 1896. It was dwarfed by the 1916 Equitable Building at No. 120, a structure instantly disdained for its bulk and effect on darkening its surroundings. This building is often wrongly attributed as the motivation for the 1916 zoning law, which had been years in the planning. History has treated the Equitable Building kindly; it was designated a national historic landmark in 1986. The Trinity Building from page 27 is at left, while Singer and City Investing loom overhead.

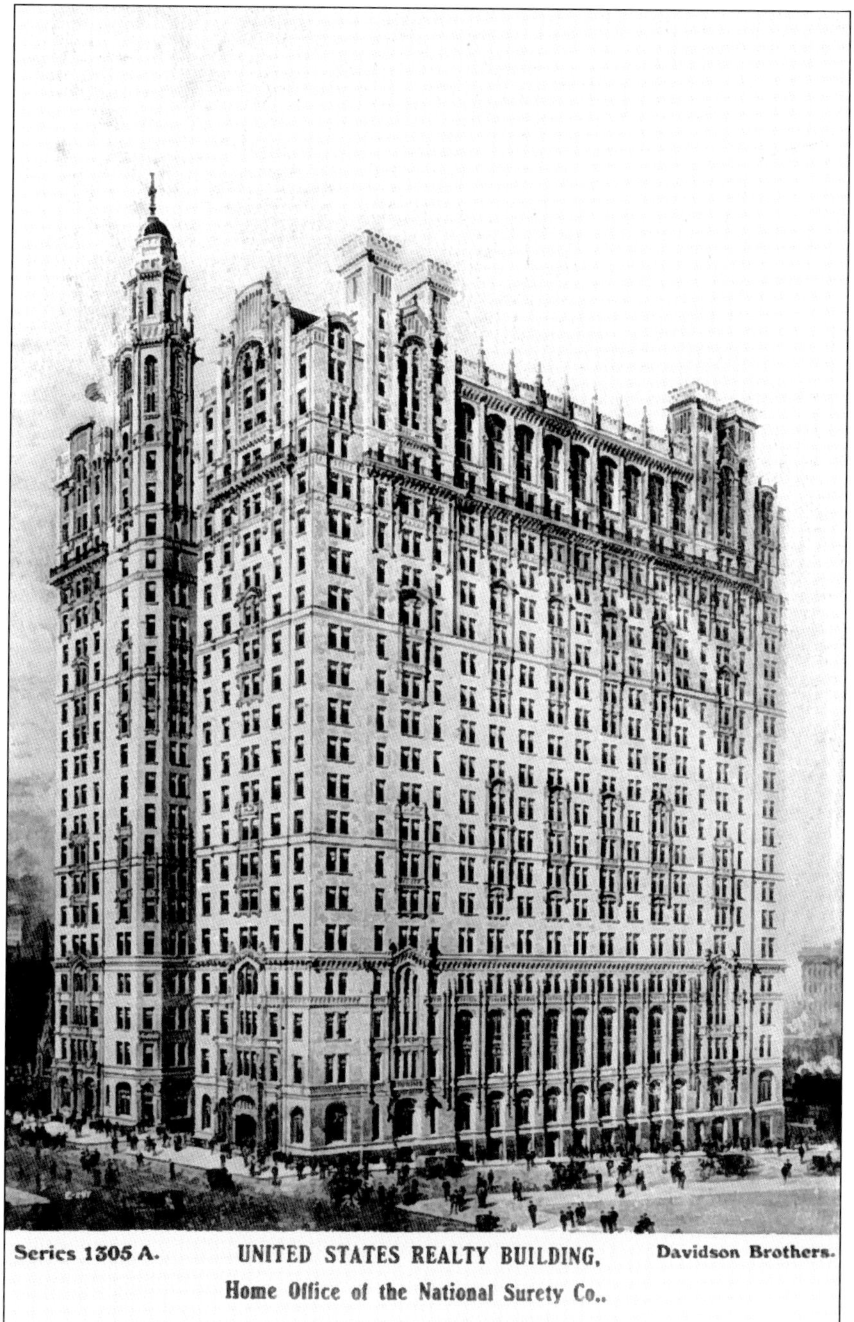

United States Realty expanded the Trinity Building with the section under the tower and hired Francis H. Kimball for its companion at right, the United States Realty Building at No. 115. The latter employs the Trinity's design elements, although in a symmetrical layout. However, the approximate 23-story, 308-foot buildings are sufficiently alike for casual reference as "twins." Dark, narrow Thames Street separates the two, while basement windows above grade at right reflect the drop in elevation at Trinity Place. The *c.* 1907 card appears as a real photograph, but it is a highly detailed rendering.

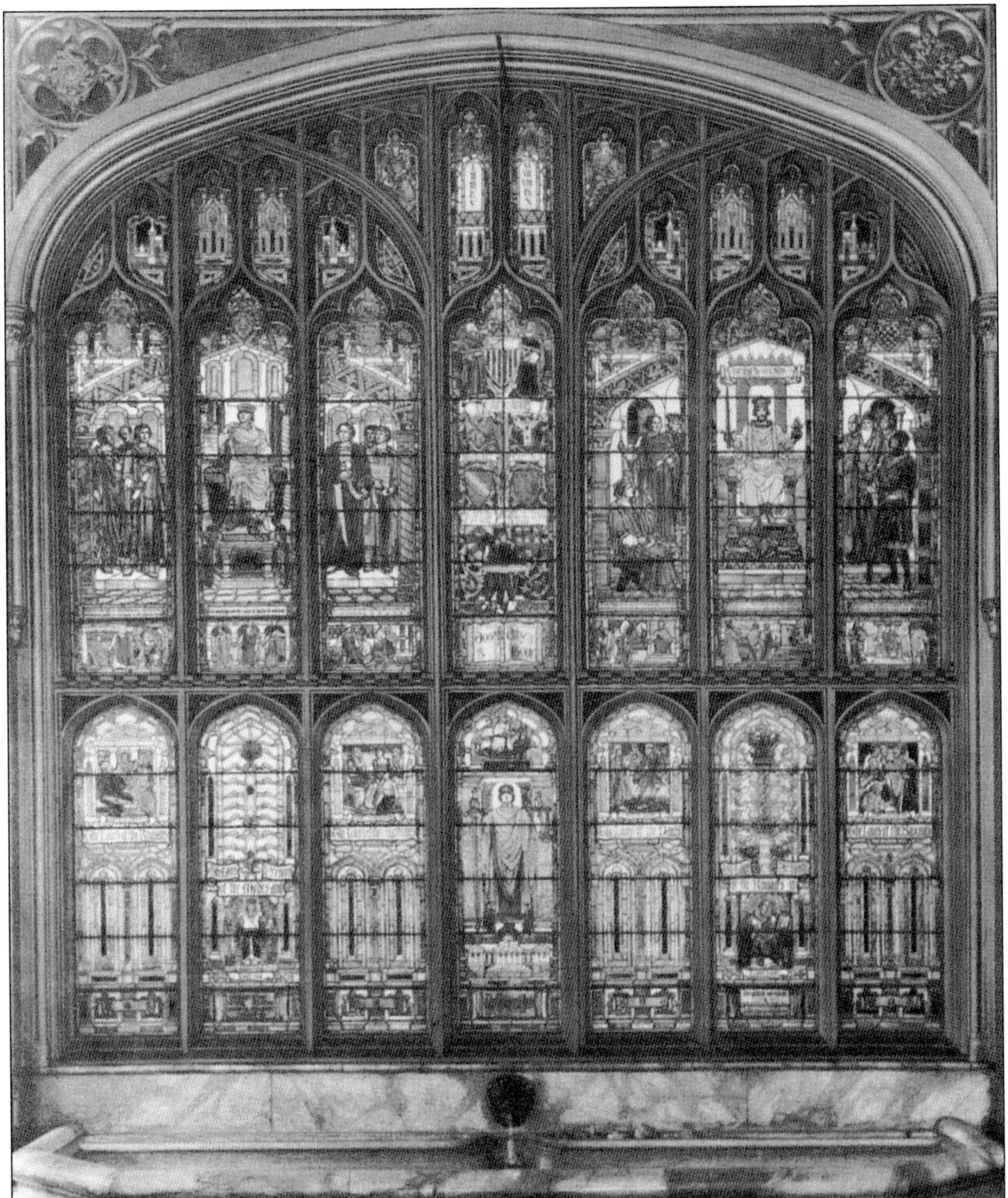

The Lawyers' Club, founded 1887 as a "day club," evolved into a luncheon club. First housed in the Equitable Building, it rebuilt at United States Realty after the fire, occupying the top two floors. Its 17-by-20-foot stained-glass window depicting the history of law provided a spectacular focal point. Henry Davison, a lawyer turned interior designer, laid out its quarters and planned the window, designed by artist J. Gordon Guthrie, whose ecclesiastical work is in a number of city houses of worship. Three sections divide the window. Key symbols are the Ten Commandments at top center, Roman and English law, and their antecedents, left and right. The window's story reflects the legal roots that evolved into law, symbolized by justice and her temple, bottom center. The window's future, an issue at the club's 1979 disbanding, remains in place, inside an office. The club reproduced the window in color as both a menu cover and a 1950s postcard.

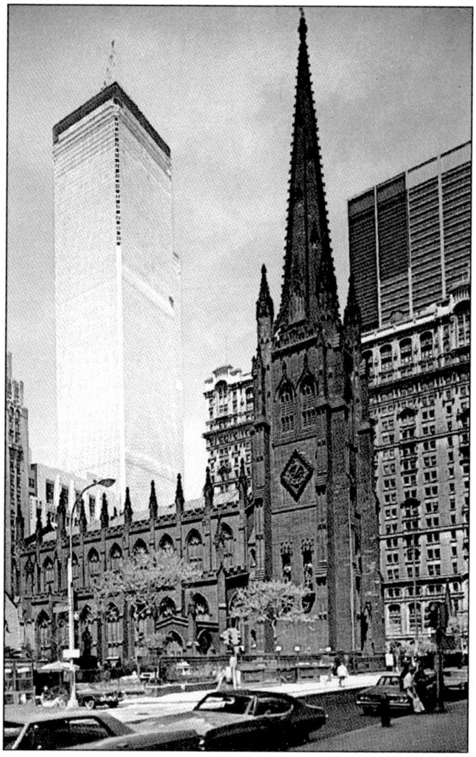

The backgrounds of often-published Trinity Church can be as revealing as their subject. The south tower of the World Trade Center is nearing completion around 1969, while the 743-foot, 54-story United States Steel Building, better known as 1 Liberty Plaza, is at right over the Trinity Building, occupying the former sites of Singer and City Investing. The top of the American Stock Exchange on Trinity Place is visible over the lamppost. Imagine parking now on Broadway and Wall Street.

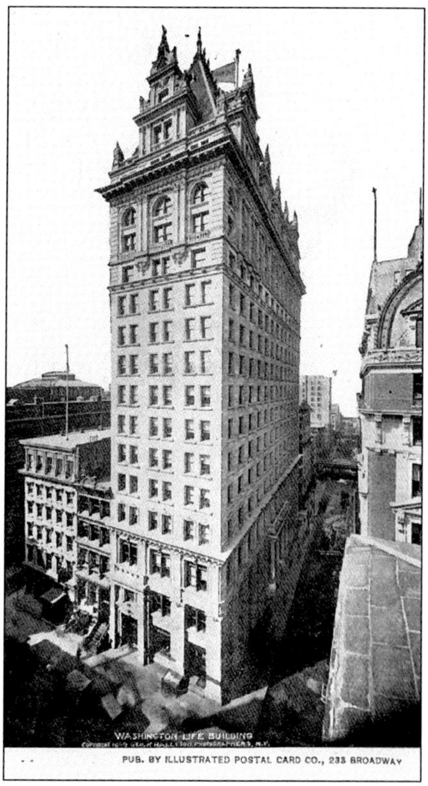

The Washington Life Building on the southwest corner of Liberty Street extended west to the former one-block-long Temple Street. The site is now part of Liberty Plaza, which runs west to Church Street and was set aside to permit construction of adjacent 1 Liberty Plaza. The 19-story, 278-foot building, completed in 1898, was designed by Cyrus L. W. Eidlitz.

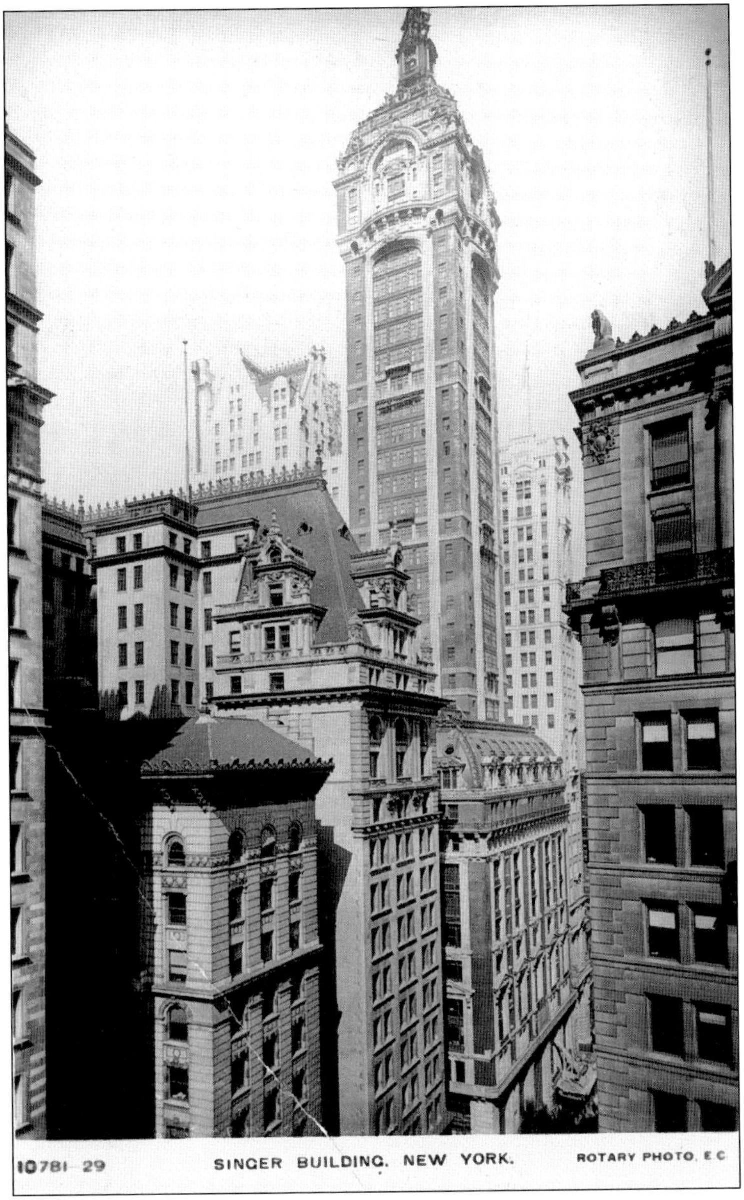

The title of "world's tallest" was changing frequently when the Singer Building was completed in 1908. Three of its predecessors are pictured on page 49 and elsewhere. The 47-story, 612-foot Beaux-Arts tower, designed by Ernest Flagg, was added to an existing 11-story base and built as a corporate symbol to reflect the power of sewing machine maker Singer Manufacturing Company. Singer soon lost the tallest title to Metropolitan Life but remained distinctive due to its shape and prominent location, even after Woolworth soared to downtown's highest in 1913. Indeed, the artful towers were as bookends, linking the few blocks of financial and civic centers. Singer had a well-visited observation deck, closed after becoming a popular pinnacle for those seeking to end it all. Pictured in front of City Investing (next page) and Washington Life (preceding page), Singer now holds a dubious distinction, the tallest building ever demolished. Demolition began in August 1967 for replacement by 1 Liberty Plaza, on the edge of page 32 top, its site also including City Investing.

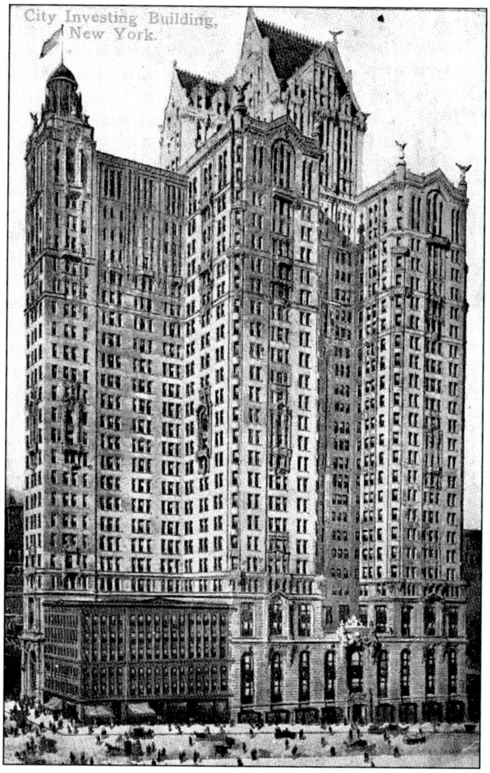

The City Investing Building was nearly always pictured on its north elevation as the narrow 37-foot Broadway facade would have been unrecognizable. Designed by Francis H. Kimball and completed in 1908 (with Singer), the building spread west to Church Street; two north wings provided light within its enormous bulk. Thirteen acres of floor space made City Investing the largest office in area. Its 34 stories and 480 feet were in the shadow of Singer, conveniently omitted, as this *c.* 1910 image is a rendering. The older Wessels Building remained on the Cortlandt Street corner.

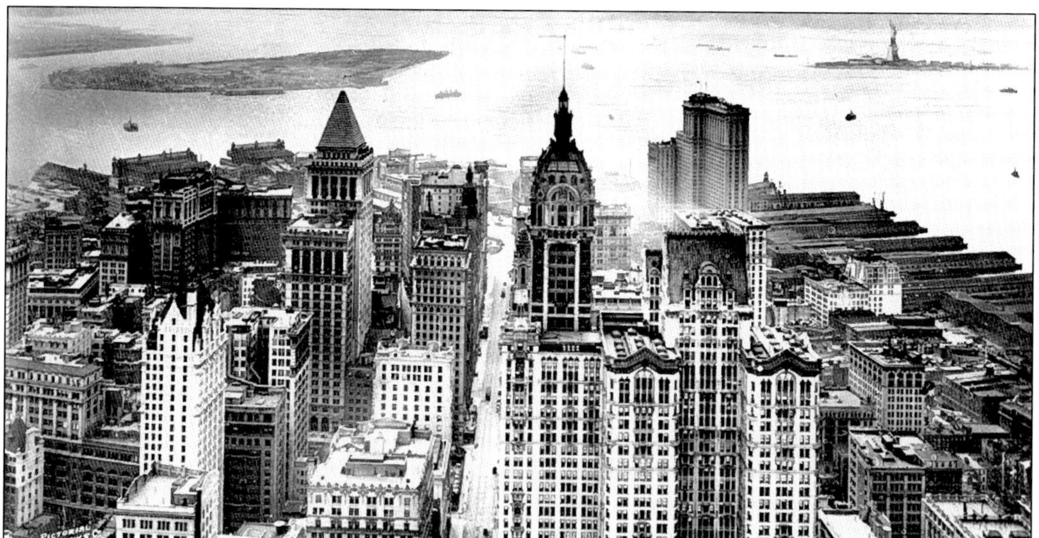

Broadway south from the Woolworth's seems to empty into New York Harbor, although it begins there. City Investing's bulk is prominent in the foreground, but Singer always towers above. American Surety is opposite Singer, while the pyramid belongs to Bankers Trust. Unseen elsewhere are Liberty Tower, left foreground, at the northwest corner of Liberty and Nassau Streets (Henry Ives Cobb, 1910) and the Whitehall Building at 17 Battery Place, right background. Its 1911 32-story northern extension obscures the 1903 origin of a second important maritime building, prompting the industry's move from the fading structures once lining lower Broadway.

The Mutual Life Insurance Company Building at 140 Broadway, the southeast corner of Liberty Street, designed by John Kellum and pictured in *Both Sides of Broadway*, was initially the four-story base completed in 1865. Inspired by the 1870 Equitable Building and pursuing the era's Second Empire craze, the mansard was added in 1871. It was destroyed for the 1913 Guaranty Trust Building, which in turn was demolished in 1964 for the building below.

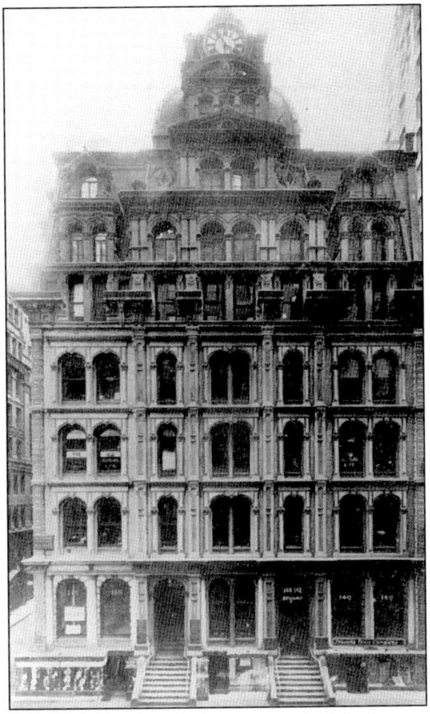

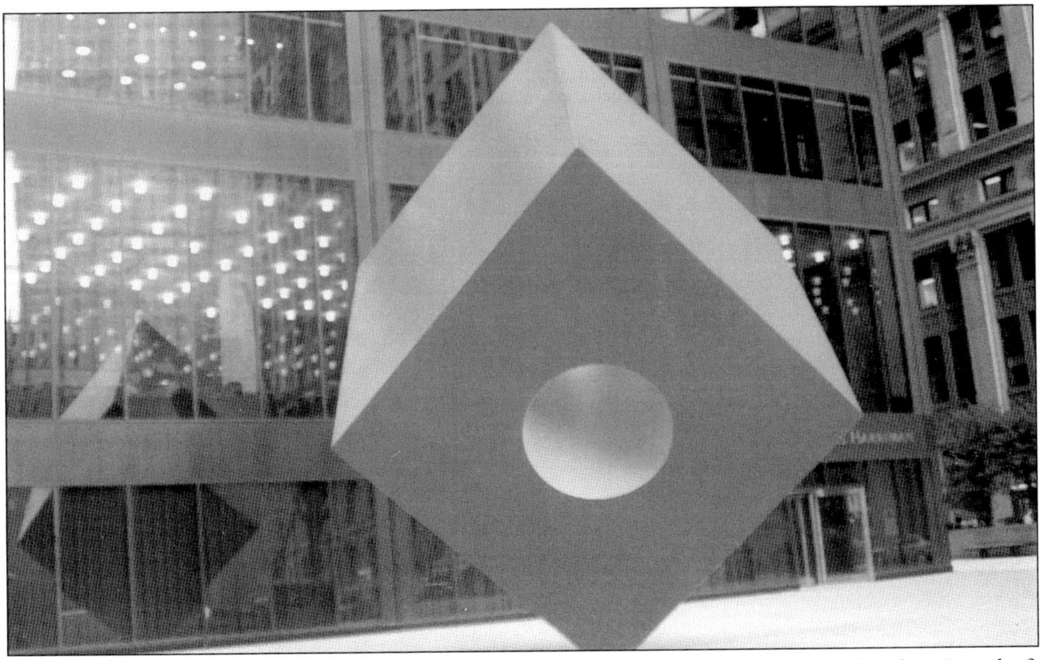

The 1967 52-story Marine Midland Building at 140 Broadway, designed by Gordon Bunshaft of Skidmore, Owings and Merrill and one of the finest skyscrapers built under the 1961 zoning law, stands amid a plaza over a full square block. The facade can be seen approaching from the east, but Isamu Noguchi's *Red Cube* hits all passersby. The shape was the architect's second choice for a decorative sculpture. The artist planned the cylindrical hole mounted at a tilt, creating one of the city's most compelling pieces of street art.

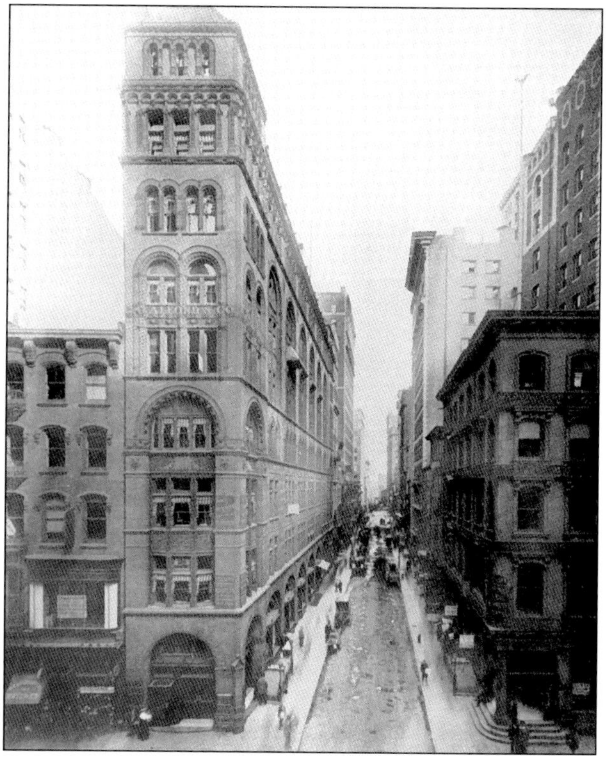

Francis H. Kimball's Romanesque Revival 1889 Corbin Building is one of downtown's most appealing buildings, albeit one often overlooked. Built of redbrick and terra-cotta trim over a brownstone base, the Broadway facade is 20 feet, but the eight-story building extends 161 feet east on John Street. Once threatened with destruction, the Corbin Building, added to the National Register of Historic Places in 2003, will survive construction of the Fulton Street Transit Center. The basement and ground floors will be incorporated into the station, while upper stories will be otherwise used. The illustration's perspective, from *Both Sides of Broadway*, makes narrow John Street appear even more so.

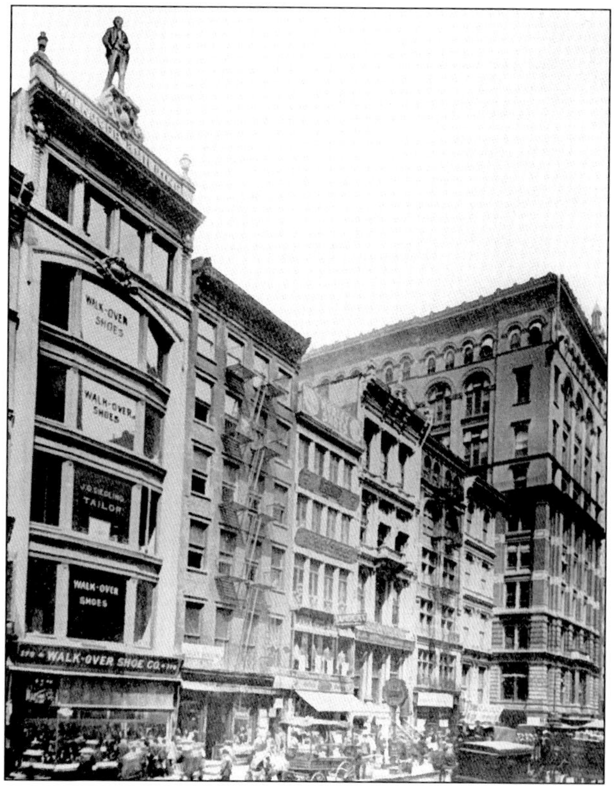

The shabby west side between Cortlandt and Dey Streets looks as if development jumped by. However, peering past the contemporary storefronts and signage reveals a fine mid-19th-century row. The Walkover Building statue catches the eye in this *Both Sides of Broadway* illustration. The man, right hand in pocket, left on stomach, is symbolic of the George B. Keith Company, former Brockton, Massachusetts, maker of the Walkover brand shoe. He also graces its stock certificates. Preservation of architectural statuary in New York has a spotty history. Neither the provenance nor disappearance of this figure is known, nor if it was sculpture or promotional kitsch.

Three

St. Paul's to City Hall

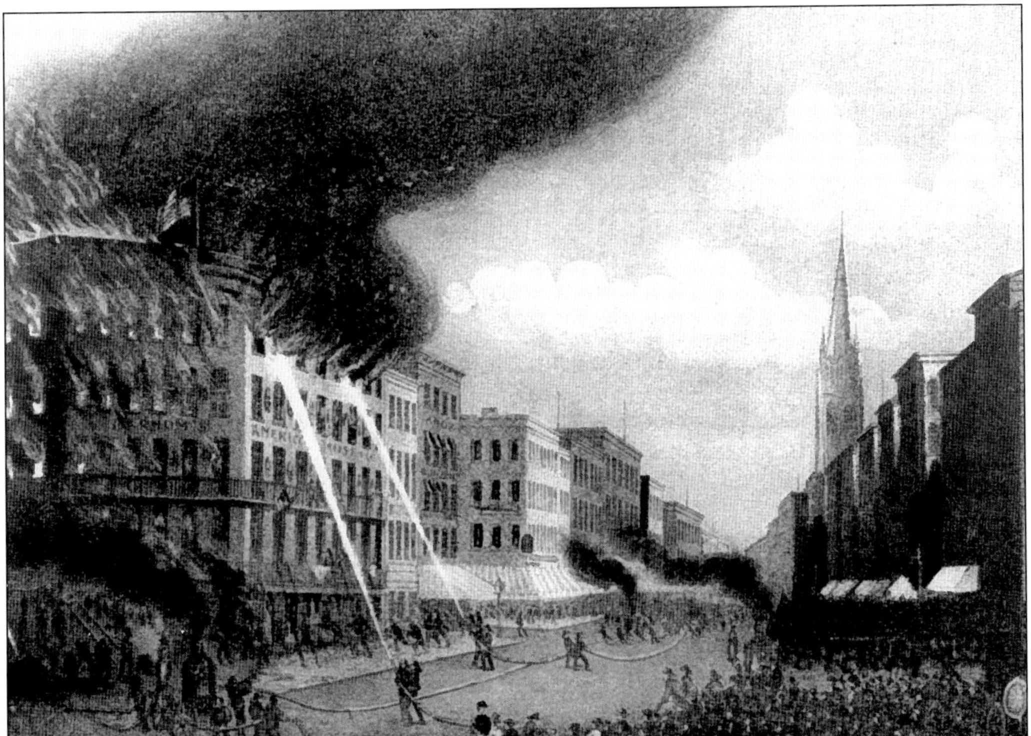

"Disastrous Fire" headlined the *Times* the day after Barnum's American Museum burned to the ground on July 13, 1865. The blaze, which began in a defective boiler and destroyed nine other buildings, was long regarded as one of the city's most spectacular fires. The news was filled with tales of escape and death, the latter limited to the animal members of Barnum's curiosities. A dead whale lay in the street for days. P. T. Barnum, a spectacular showman, was a substandard fire insurance risk. All his places prior to 1874 were destroyed by fire. This old print has been often reproduced.

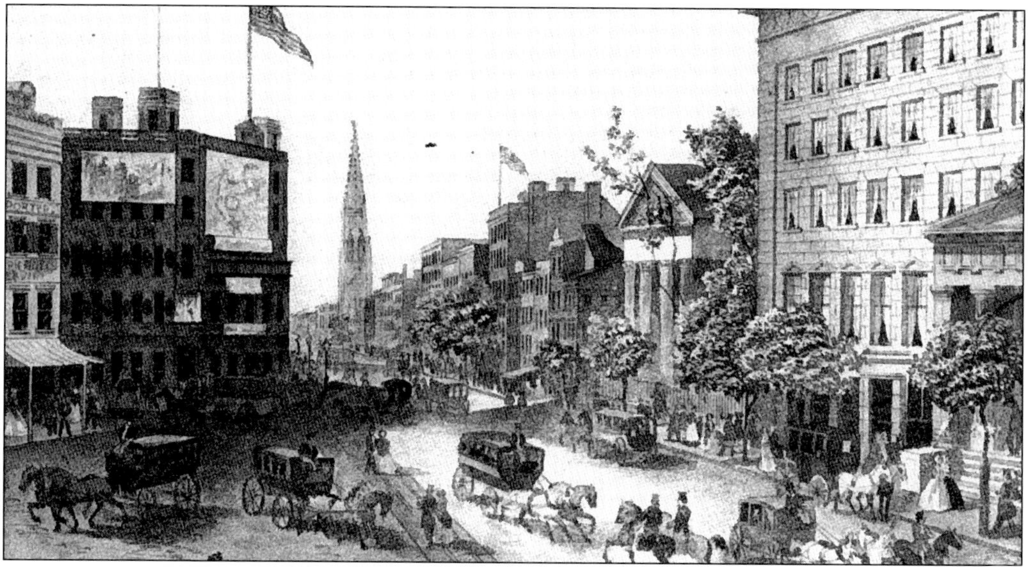

P. T. Barnum attained showman's fame in 1835 when he exhibited an old lady reputed as George Washington's nurse. He bought Scudder's Museum's collection in 1841 and opened the first of a series of museums, collections of oddities rather than artifacts. His American Museum is pictured with the flag on the southeast corner of Ann Street opposite the columns of St. Paul's. Trinity Church is in the background, the Astor House is at right in a street lined with modest-height buildings, typical and necessary prior to the prevalence of elevators. A well-known print was crudely reproduced on a postcard around 1920.

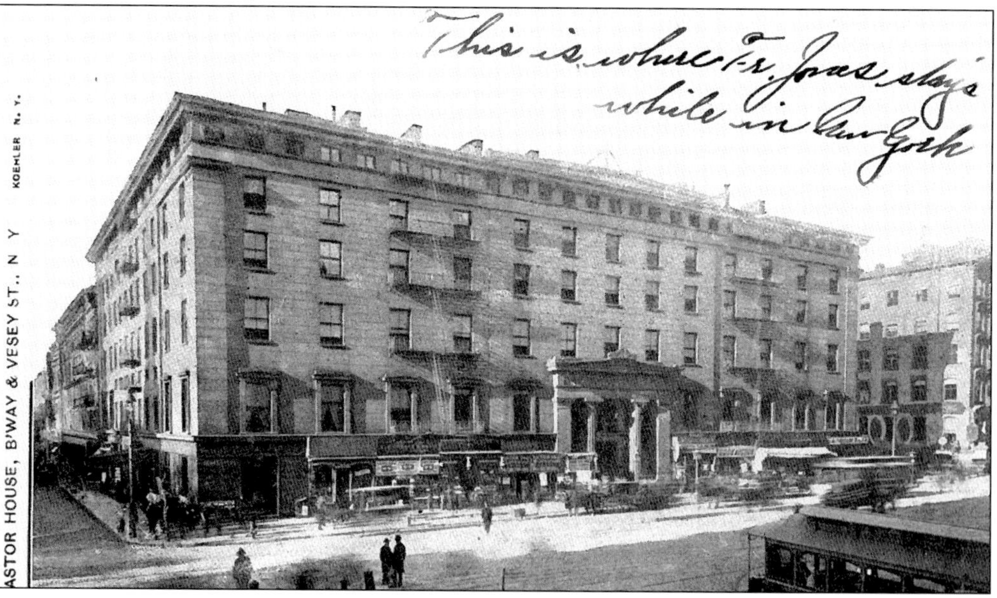

John Jacob Astor's namesake Astor House was the city's premier hostelry for decades. Construction began in 1834 in a fashionable residential block, prompting a change in character of the surroundings with the northward move of public facilities. Isaiah Rogers designed the Greek Revival building, which opened in 1836. Change in neighborhood later gave the Astor a commercial following. Demolition occurred in two parts, beginning with the southern section in 1913. The block pictured on page 49 illustrates replacement structures.

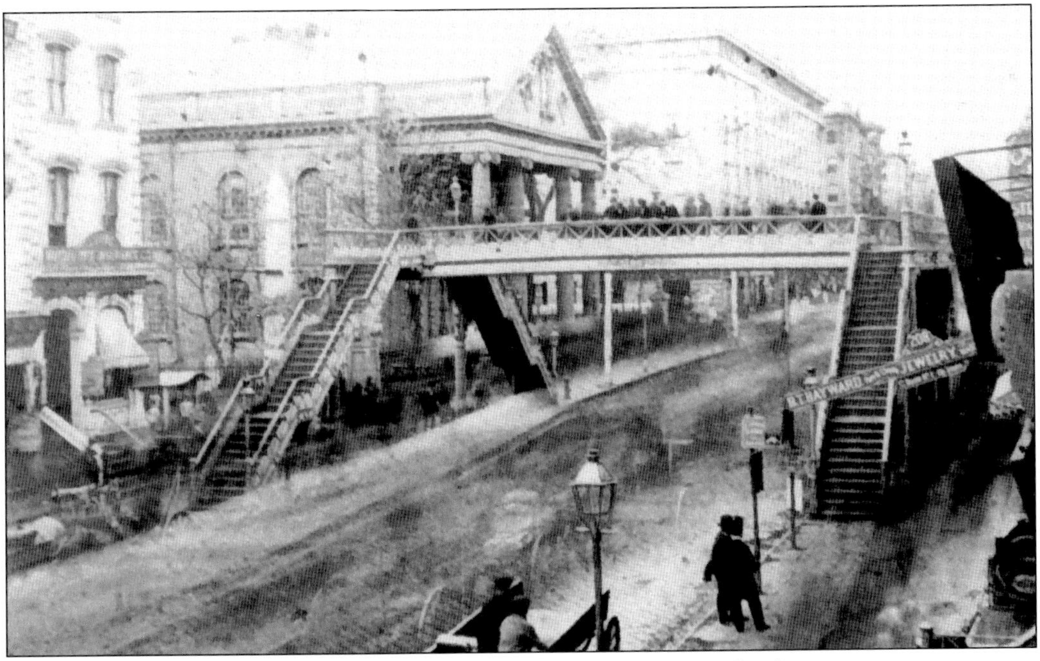

By the 1860s, Broadway's woeful congestion at Fulton Street was due in part to convergence a block north with the Eastern Post Road, its beginnings now Park Row. Water and other effluent contributed to the perilous crossing by foot. The Broadway Bridge, promoted by alderman Charles E. Loew and named for him, provided a remedy when opened for traffic on April 15, 1867. Enthusiastic initial response prompted the *Times* on May 2, "This bridge is so successful we ought to have more of them." Knox the Hatter disagreed. Claiming the bridge interfered with his business, he sued and won. The bridge was closed in December 1868 and dismantled. (Courtesy of Robin Kaller.)

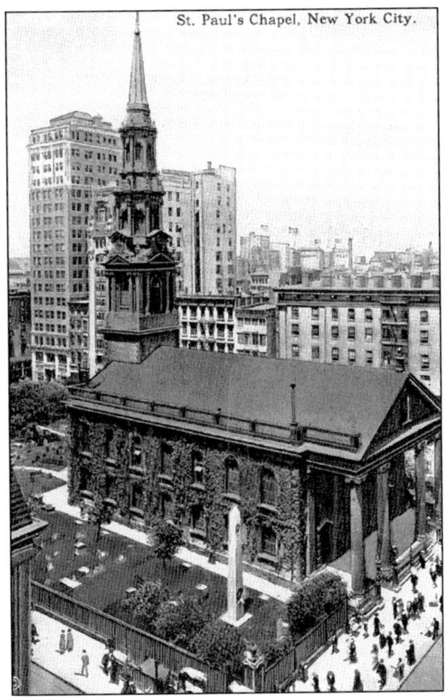

St. Paul's, a chapel of Trinity Church, built 1764–1766, is Manhattan's oldest house of worship. Modeled after James Gibb's St. Martin-in-the-Fields, London, the design is attributed to Thomas McBean. Built of local stone, Manhattan mica-schist, St. Paul's fills the west side block between Fulton (bottom) and Vesey Streets. The Thomas Addis Emmett monument is prominently viewed from above. The 30-foot-high marble obelisk, designed by artist Charles C. Ingham and executed by sculptor John Preece, was carved from a single block of stone.

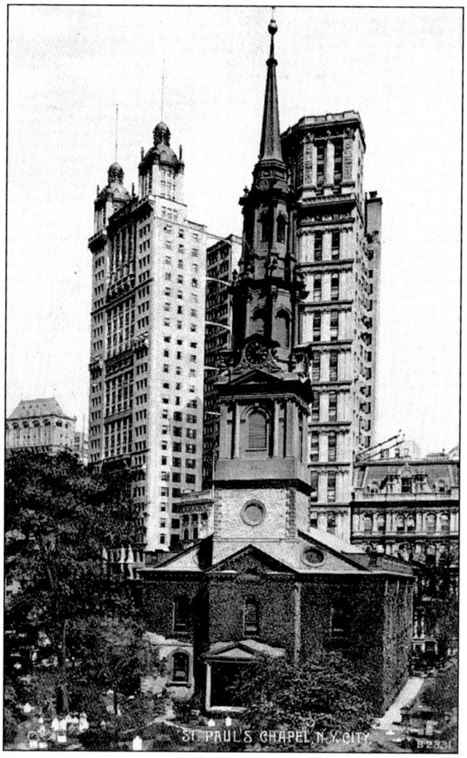

The frequently illustrated St. Paul's can provide a good perspective of its surroundings, including this *c.* 1910 photographic card depicting the 1904 Donn Barber–remodeled National Park Bank Building at right. At left the arcaded loggia of Robert H. Robertson's 1895 150 Nassau Street rises from the trees, while the south elevation of the Park Row Building shows a break for one of its two light courts.

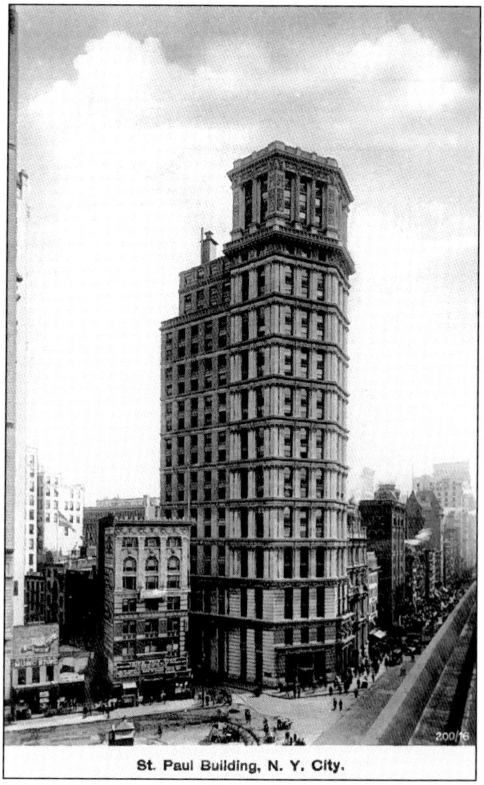

After completion in 1899, the 307-foot, 25-story St. Paul Building briefly held the distinction as the world's tallest. The George B. Post–designed tower replaced the Tribune Building, built on the Ann Street corner of the fire pictured on page 37. The photographer's view south—he apparently did not want to lean over the Astor's roof—includes the Fulton Street block to be the site of the Fulton Street Transit Center. The handsome southeast corner office was long ago replaced by a prosaic taxpayer. The St. Paul Building fell in 1954 for the present glass tower at No. 200.

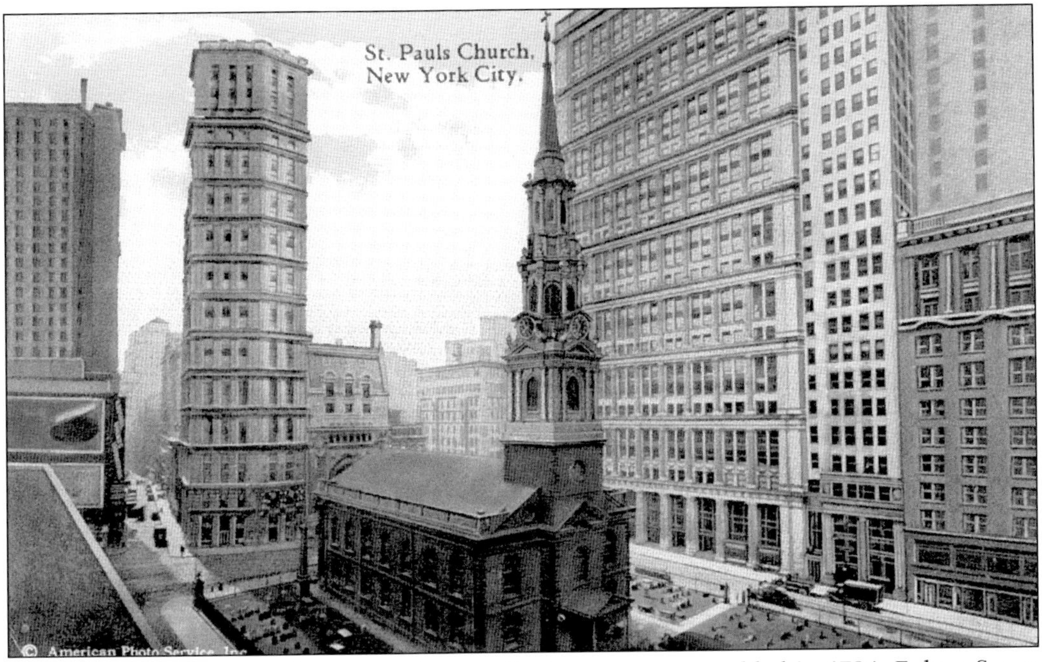

St. Paul's tower, designed by James Crommelin Lawrence, was added in 1794. Fulton Street at right was the only downtown river-to-river street until its western stem was taken by the World Trade Center. The former AT&T headquarters is on the southwest corner, designed by William Welles Bosworth and built in 1913 and 1916 in two sections now seamlessly joined. Ann Street's dingy three blocks, left, are best remembered in Charles Ives's song, lyrics from Maurice Morris's 1921 poem: "Quaint name Ann Street/ Width of same ten feet/ Narrow yes Ann Street/ Rather short Ann Street."

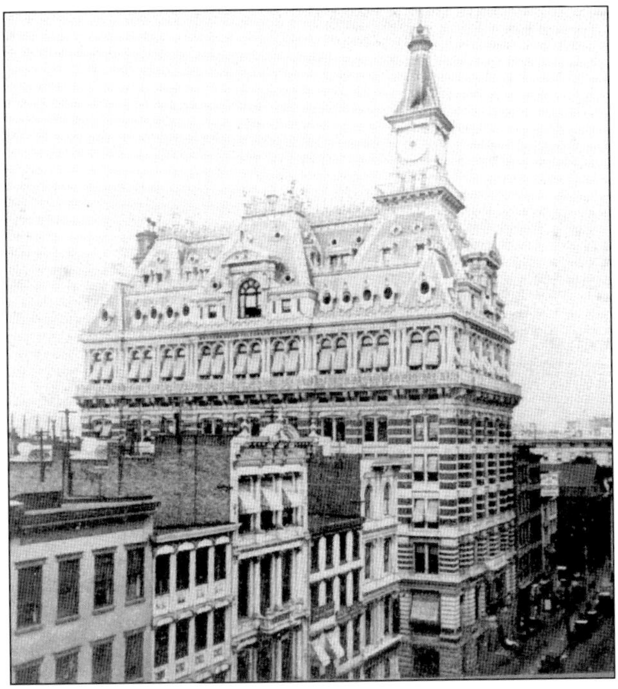

The Western Union Building on the southwest corner of Fulton Street, completed in 1875 to a design by George B. Post, provided a solid symbol of its owner's might. The distinct three sections of this Second Empire–style building embraced the classicist aesthetic of base, shaft, and crown, and it is topped with a richly decorated mansard surmounted by a tower that enclosed a time ball. Visible at top, the ball, which was dropped at noon to mark midday, appealed to both passersby and mariners. It was like New Year's Eve every day! (Courtesy of Robin Kaller.)

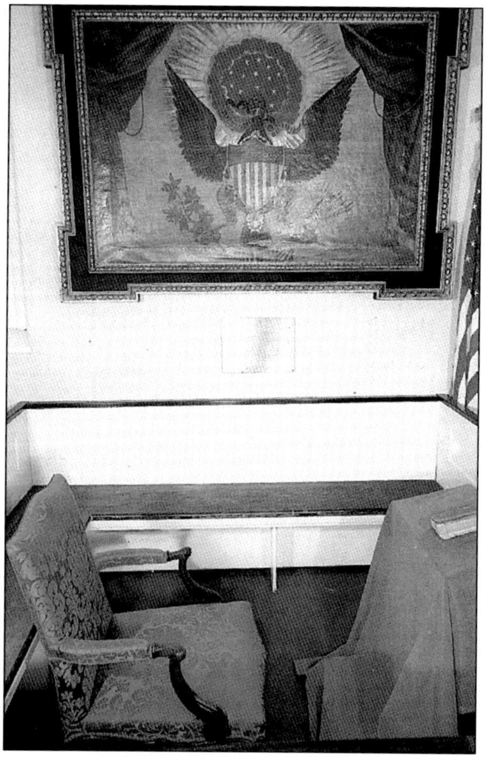

George Washington was St. Paul's principal historical association; the first president worshipped here for the nearly two years New York was the nation's capital. He is honored by the Washington Pew, set off along the north wall as a shrine. Above is the first oil painting of the great seal of the United States, adopted in 1782 before the states were truly united by the 1787 ratification of the Constitution.

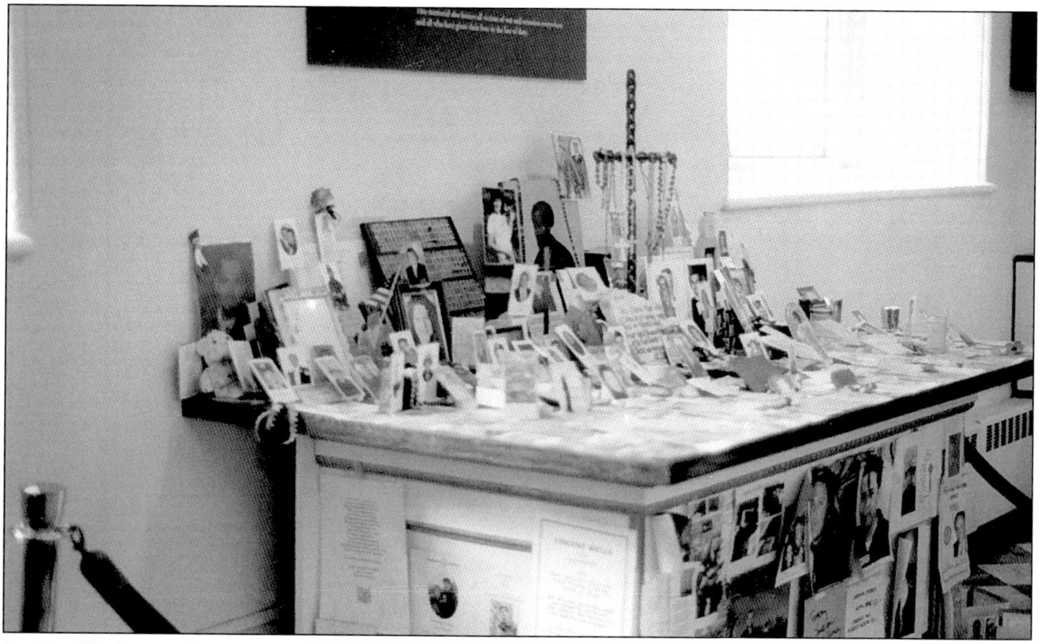

St. Paul's, located across the street from the World Trade Center, and miraculously spared by the collapse of the twin towers, immediately became a place of refuge and rest for recovery workers at ground zero. The notes and pictures seeking information about the missing, initially scattered at random in the surrounding area, were collected and organized in their own shrine on the chapel's south wall.

The card focuses on the huge new Hudson Terminal at the end of the McAdoo Tunnels, widely known as the Hudson Tubes, now the PATH, an acronym for successor Port Authority Trans-Hudson, which faced Church Street. It also provides a glimpse of the forgotten rear of the St. Paul Church Yard. The foreground pictures the Trinity Vestry Office in the center and the St. Paul School Office at right, while a few graves provide contemporary perspective of a totally changed landscape. The two offices were demolished around 1930 for a Church Street widening project. The 19-story, 275-foot-high Hudson Terminal's floor rentable space made it the world's largest by that standard. The buildings, which helped propel downtown as a major office center, opened in 1908 and were demolished in the 1960s for the World Trade Center.

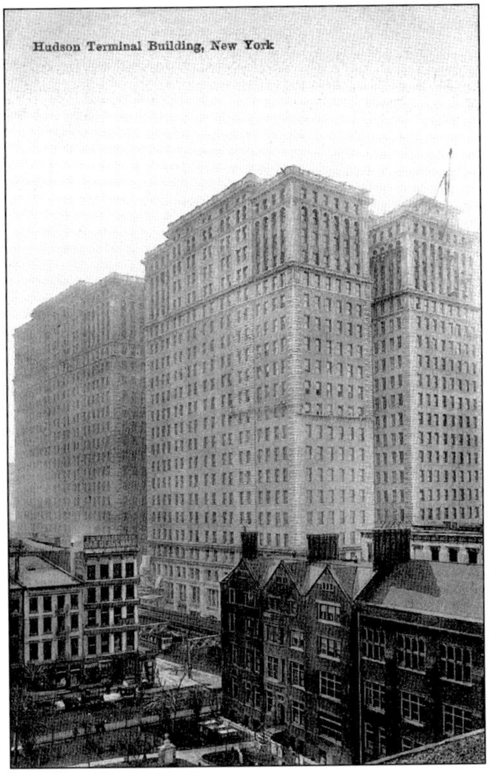

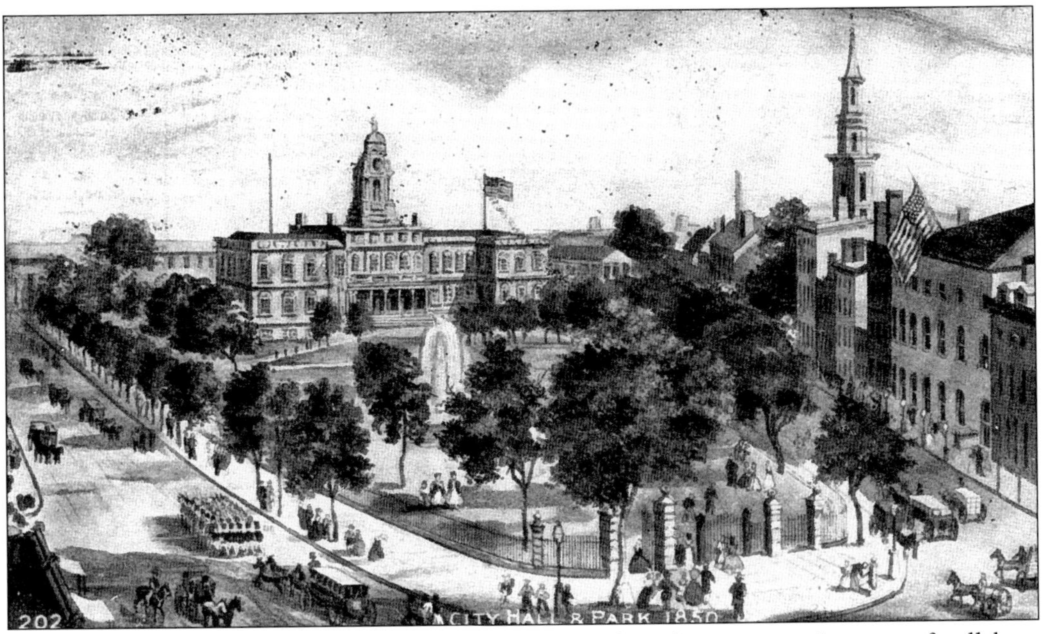

City Hall Park, pictured in an 1850 print, was from its earliest days an attractive array of well-kept lawns and groves of trees. Liberty poles were erected in the Revolution, but the area also included the Corporation Yard for the maintenance of fire and related equipment. Temporary charitable buildings were located behind New York City Hall. The Park Theater is showing the flag at right, while the steeple belongs to the Brick Presbyterian Church on Beekman Street.

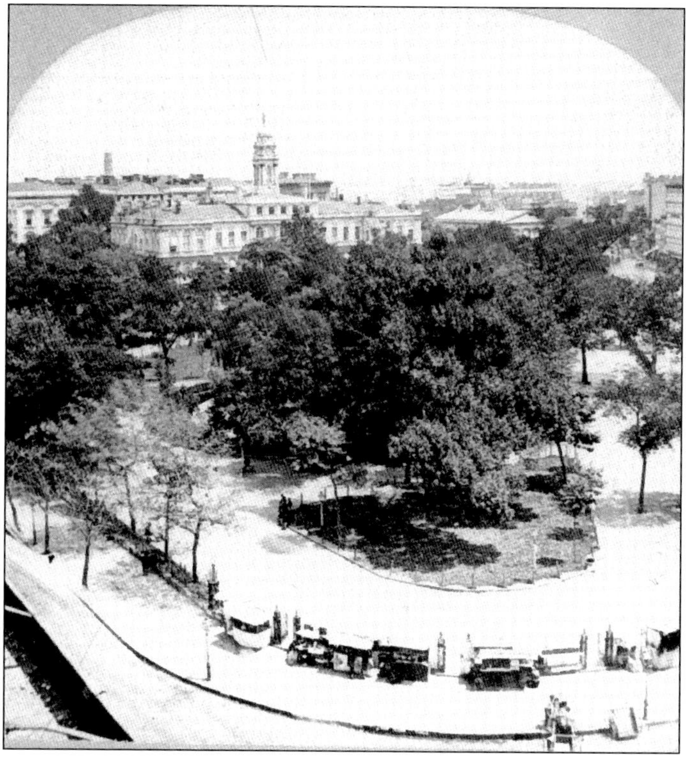

By the 1860s, wide walks surrounded the park's perimeter, apparently built around growing trees, which in the 19th century included elm, willow, poplar, and catalpa. At that time, the city considered expanding the park to the east across Park Row. Slicing off a major piece of parkland today would be unthinkable. The gesture was not popular in the late 1860s either, but it happened. This stereograph omits its publisher. (Courtesy of Robin Kaller.)

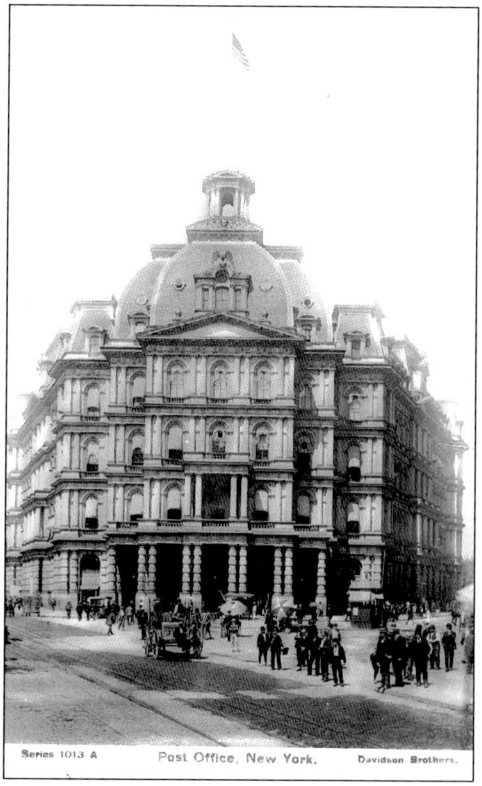

The federal government bought the tip of the park for $500,000 and sponsored a design competition where the five top finishers collaborated on plans modified by Alfred B. Mullet, who received credit for the finished design. Work proceeded slowly after the August 1869 groundbreaking as funds trickled and the project expanded. The post office was finally occupied in August 1875. The Second Empire design was artful, but the public disdained the poorly sited building and was glad to see it go. In retrospect, some preservationists reflect that the building had its merits.

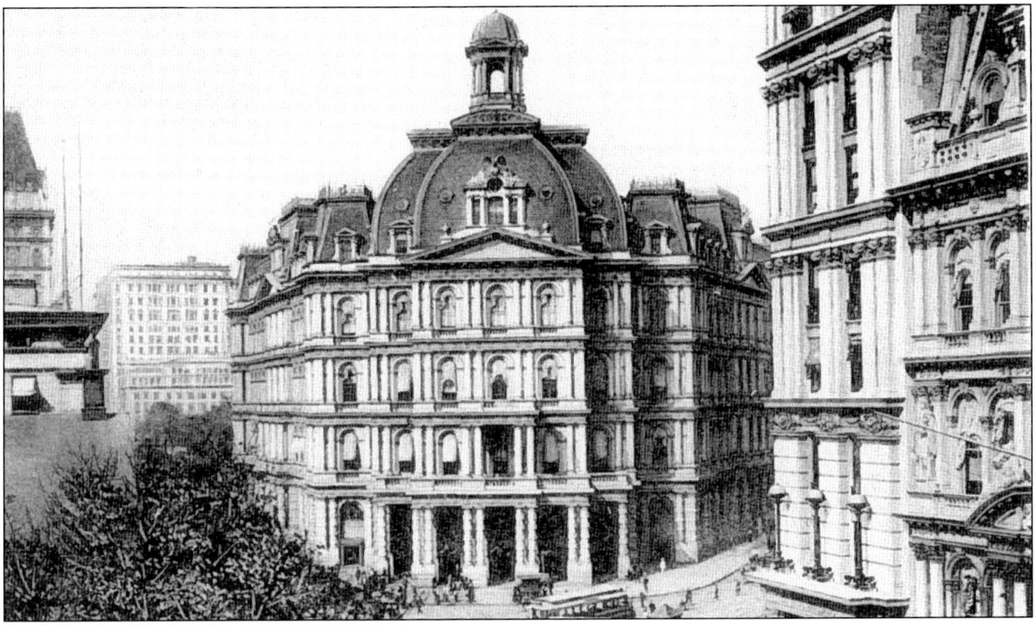

The street context around 1905 suggests the unpopularity of the post office, which was demolished in 1938. The view north obliterates New York City Hall and darkens the entrance to Park Row. It also provides a glimpse of the Karl Bitter statues *The Races of Man* above the entrance to the St. Paul Building. When that building was demolished, they were eagerly sought by several would-be rescuers. The figures traveled to Indianapolis, where they were installed in a grotto in Holliday Park, a place popularly called "the ruins."

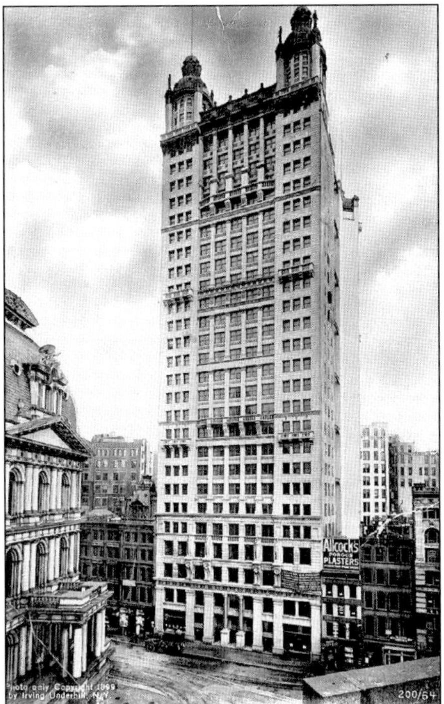

Park Row Building, New York.

The Ivins Syndicate had Robert H. Robertson design its 32-story, 386-foot-high office, which, when completed in 1899 at 15 Park Row, was the world's tallest, a designation held until 1908. The early name of Syndicate Building was replaced by the enduring Park Row Building. The little visual stimulation of the facade, which rises straight up, includes the two towers and four idealized female figures sculpted by J. Massey Rhind. They can be spotted standing on the massive third-floor brackets. Photographer Irving Underhill added his 1899 date, but the card dates 10 years later. The balcony and decoration of the post office look appealing as seen in a manner that the usual straight-on images of this building miss.

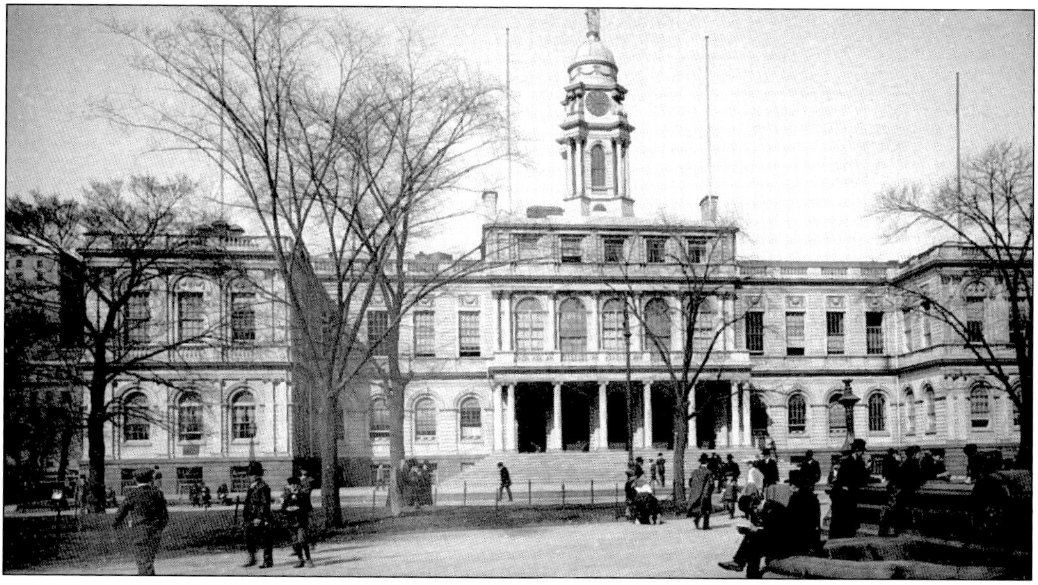

When New York City Hall was built from 1802 to 1811, its location just south of Chambers Street was so far at the northern reach of the city, the north elevation was left bare of marble cladding. The reasoning was simply, "Who would notice?" The design was a collaboration between Joseph Francois Mangin, generally credited with the exterior, and John McComb Jr., who is believed to have designed the interior. A lengthy preservation project from 1954 to 1956 replaced the original Massachusetts white marble cladding and brownstone base with Alabama limestone over a Missouri granite base.

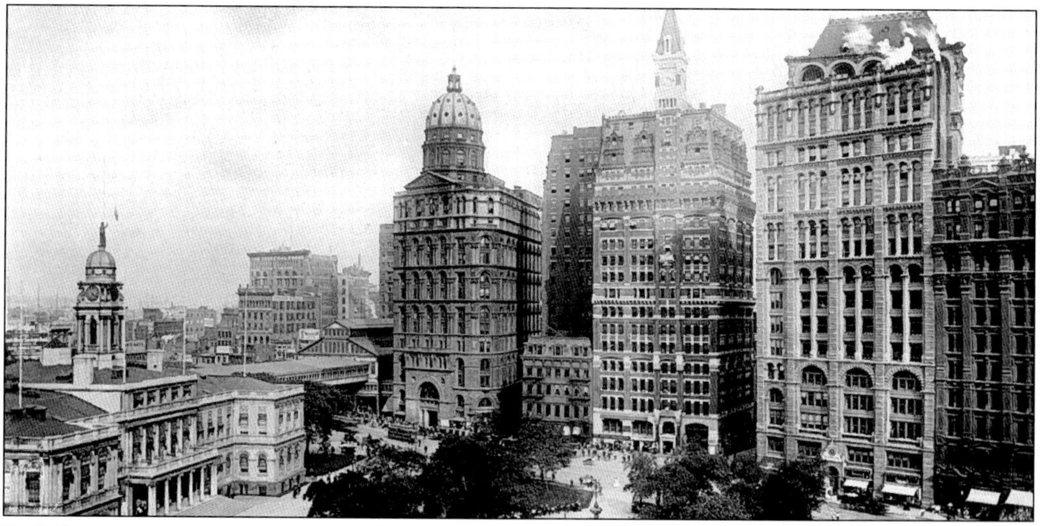

Park Row was newspaper row in the latter 19th century, its juncture with Nassau and Spruce Streets known as Printing House Square. The gold dome belonged to the 16-story World Building, designed by George B. Post, which was completed in 1890 and demolished in 1955–1956. The entrance to the former trolley on the Brooklyn Bridge is below. Richard Morris Hunt's design for the Tribune Building, completed in 1875, was an initial 9 stories but was later expanded to 19; it fell in 1966 for the construction of Pace University. Post's 1889 13-story Times Building was also expanded in 1905 after the newspaper departed for 42nd Street and now survives as residences. Most of the rich, terra-cotta-decorated Potter Building is pictured at right.

The core of the early civic center is pictured around the 1920s, including the Municipal Building, 580 feet high and 450 feet wide, completed in 1914 to William Mitchell Kendall's design. Directly behind New York City Hall is the courthouse, begun in 1861, designed by John Kellus and Leopold Eidlitz, and designated the New York County Courthouse but universally known as the Tweed Courthouse for the crooked politician who oversaw and stole from the project, making it a universal symbol of official corruption and greed. The mansard belongs to the Beaux-Arts 1899–1911 Hall of Records at 31 Chambers Street, while the Emigrant Industrial Savings Bank is at rear. Entrances to the now-closed New York City Hall station remind one that the original subway turned around in a loop under the park.

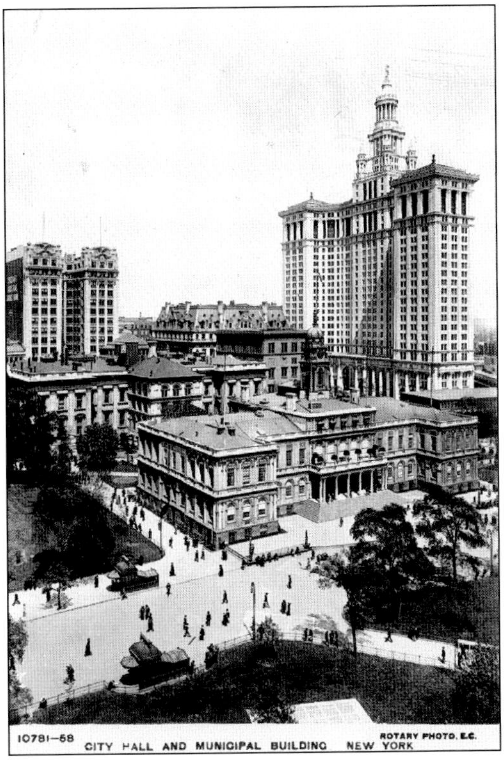

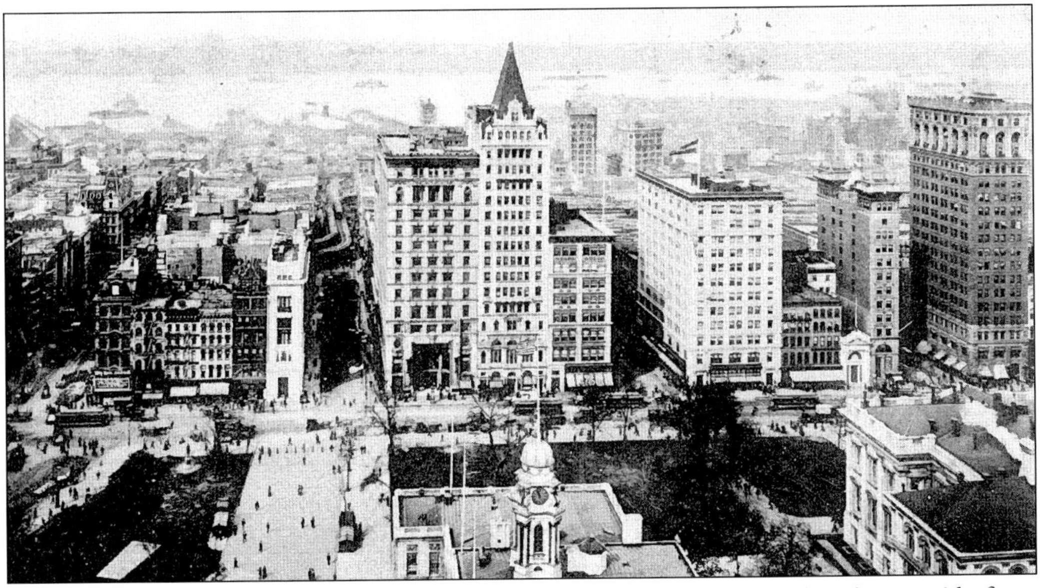

The *c.* 1908 avian perspective from New York City Hall depicts Broadway's west side from Park Row to Chambers Street (right). Peer west on Murray Street where the elevated railroad curves in the distance. Both corners had been recently built, the slender 1908 Importers and Traders National Bank on the south and the 1894 Postal Telegraph Building north. Adjacent is Home Life and the 1900 Rogers Peet Building right of it. The Tweed Courthouse is at bottom right and the 1899 Broadway Chambers Building over it. The sharp eye can spot the original location of Nathan Hale's statue.

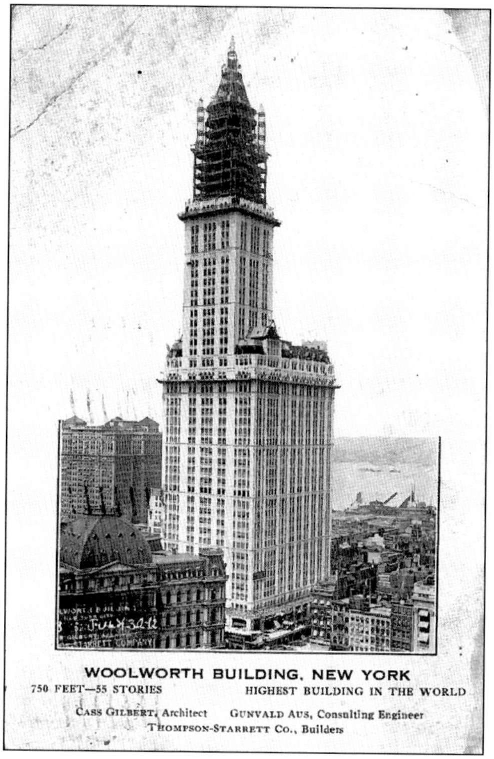

Frank W. Woolworth, who aspired to own the world's tallest building, succeeded and created one of the most revered office towers. The neo-Gothic building, designed by Cass Gilbert, rises 792 feet at No. 233, the block between Barclay Street and Park Place. Desiring a corporate symbol, Woolworth attained an immediate landmark, one hailed as the Cathedral of Commerce. Toch Brothers, the paint supplier, sought to hail its participation with an advertising card prior to completion. A printed message on the back touts their "R.I.W." paint.

Woolworth occupied only one floor upon completion, regarding rental income as a better accompaniment to corporate icon. An observation deck on top attracted crowds and photographers alike, but it closed long ago, joined in recent years by another loss. Visitors once stood in awe in the richly decorated lobby, but it too is effectively closed. A sign outside the building (loosely paraphrased) warns, "Tourist Get Lost." The seemingly once-ubiquitous Woolworth's possesses a lore and stamp on the collective memory like no other failed retailer. Its story is best told in Karen Plunkett-Powell's 1999 *Remembering Woolworth's.*

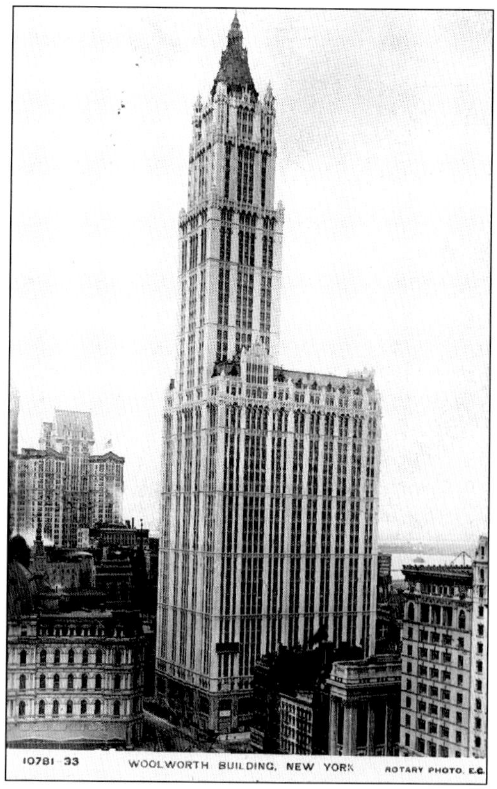

The Transportation Building at No. 225 became Woolworth's southern neighbor in 1928 when the 44-story, 542-foot tower was completed. Its architects, York and Sawyer, had recently designed the widely praised nearby Federal Reserve Bank, but the pictured office was criticized for its awkward proportions and unskilled application of setbacks, prompted by the 1916 zoning law. Comparison with its neighbors did not help, both the outstanding Woolworth and the 1926 Barclay-Vesey Building in the background at 140 West Street, the latter one of the best of setback style.

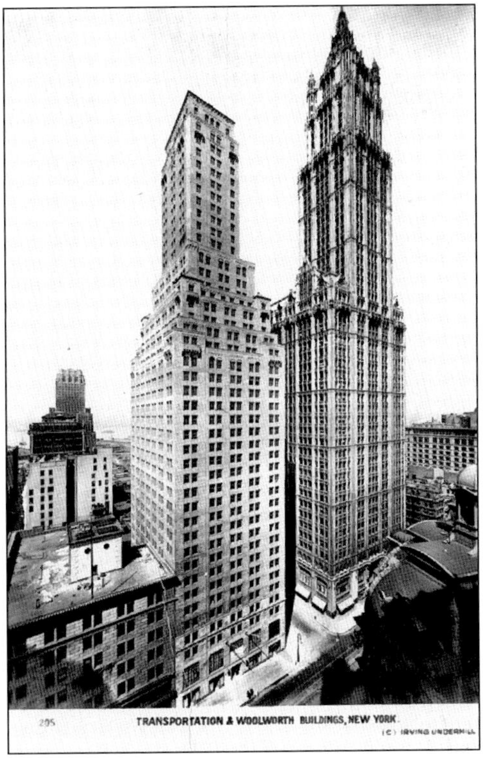

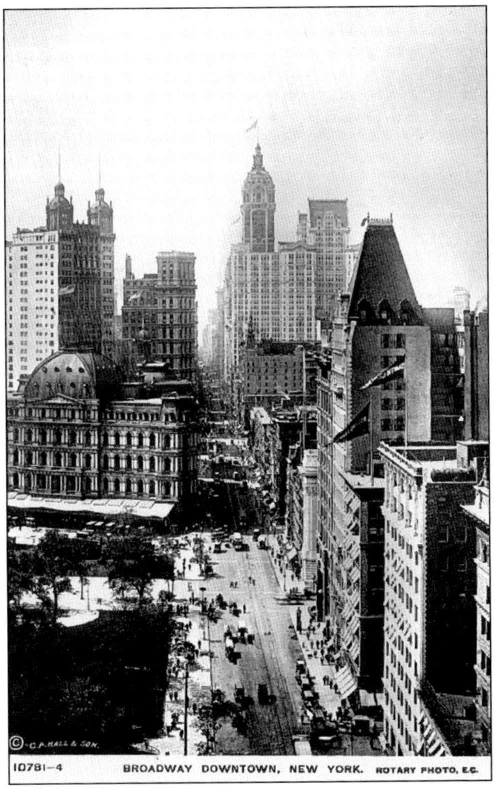

The view south, probably from the roof of the former A. T. Stewart store/Sun Building on the northeast corner of Chambers Street, shows four former world's tallests. In addition to the previously pictured, from left to right, the Park Row, St. Paul and Singer Buildings, there is the 1894 titleholder, the 287-foot, 16-story Home Life Insurance Company Building at the right, the one topped by the steep mansard. The 480-foot City Investing Building, under the Singer tower, was never in the running. Having the morning sun on the west side was of appeal and rental worth when lower Broadway was a retail center. The early glow gave rise to its nickname of "the dollar side," while the shadowy east side was "the shilling side," an illusion to disparaged English currency.

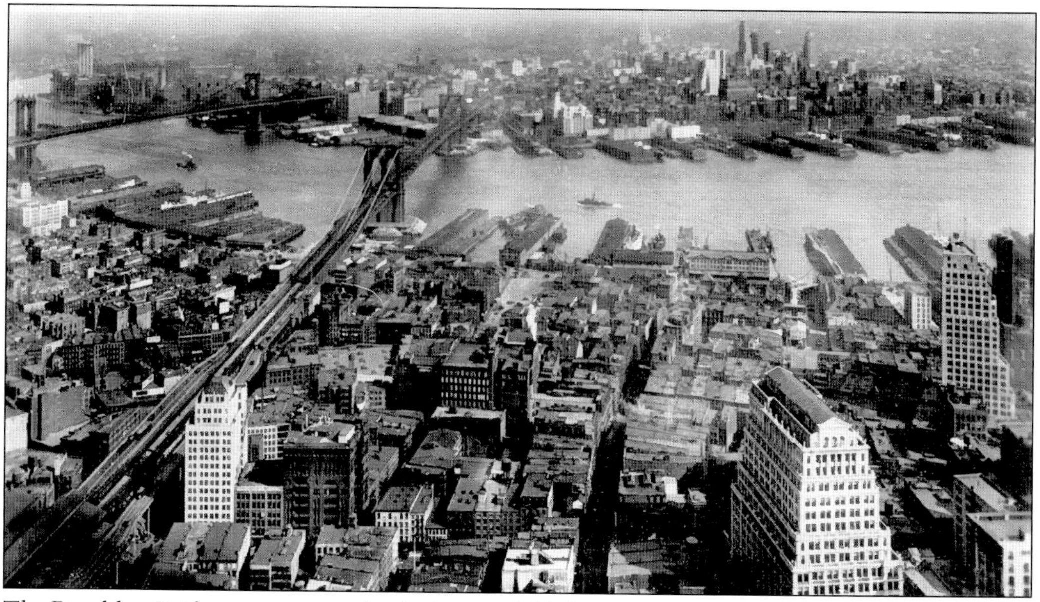

The Brooklyn Bridge tower, once the city's second-highest structure, was vantage for photographers even prior to the bridge's 1883 opening but never rivaled Broadway. It overlooked a seamy residential quarter, left, and the shoe, leather, paint, varnish, drug, and chemical industries, right. The latter, in time, moved, pushed by an expanding insurance district and prompted by increasingly congested, narrow streets. The appealing but rarely seen top of Royal Insurance's headquarters at the northeast corner of William and Fulton Streets, is in the foreground, while a center for insurance firms at 116 John Street is at right. The South Street Seaport's East River location is a direct line from the Royal building.

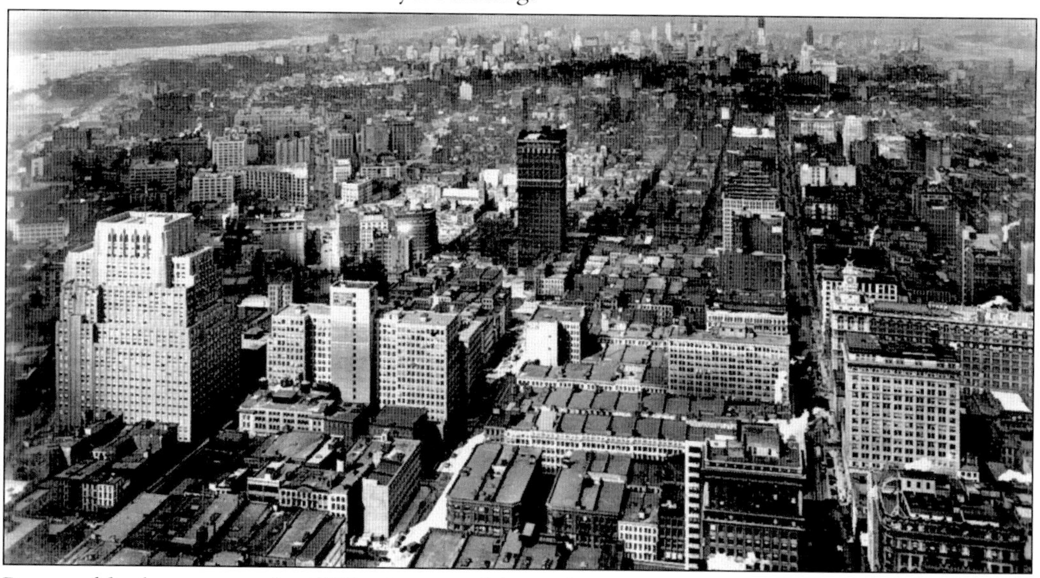

Presumably these two early-1930s photographic cards were among those sold at the observation deck souvenir stand. This view from Woolworth's north depicts the wholesale and apparel districts that were in a state of change in the decade after the tower's completion. New York Life, the site of the clock tower at right, departed for Madison Square in 1928. Dry goods were also on the move.

Four

Chambers Street to Union Square

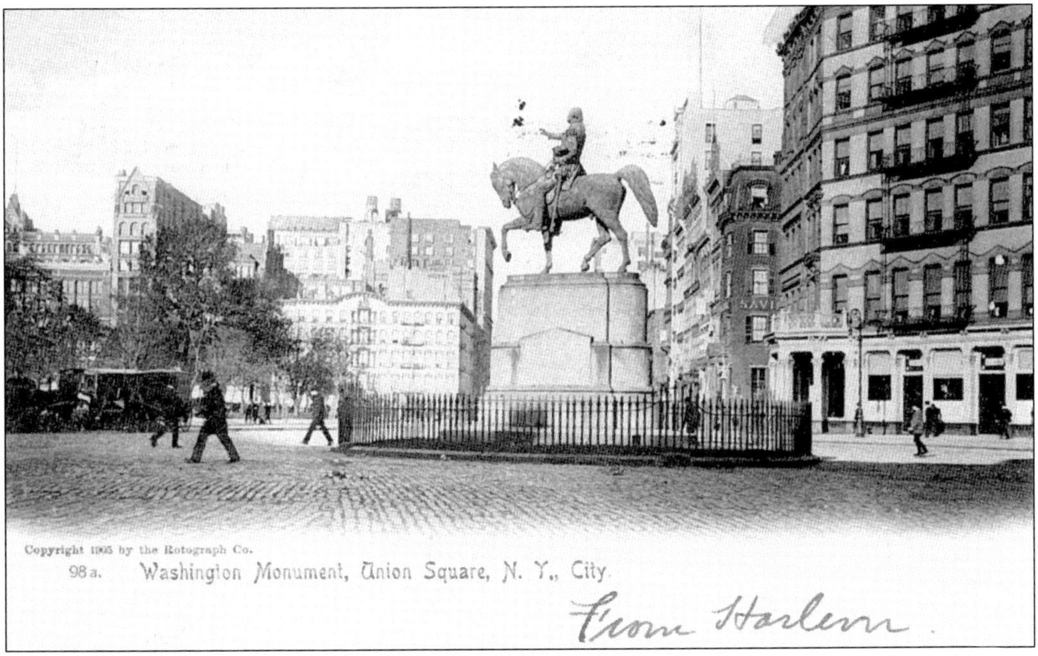

New York's earlier monuments were placed at Broadway but were often later relocated. Washington on 14th Street could not cope with increasing traffic. Washington's horse appears to be pointing to the 17th Street Everett House, the building with the curved cornice, a hotel razed in 1908, replaced by the 15-story Everett Building. The former Union Square Hotel is at right.

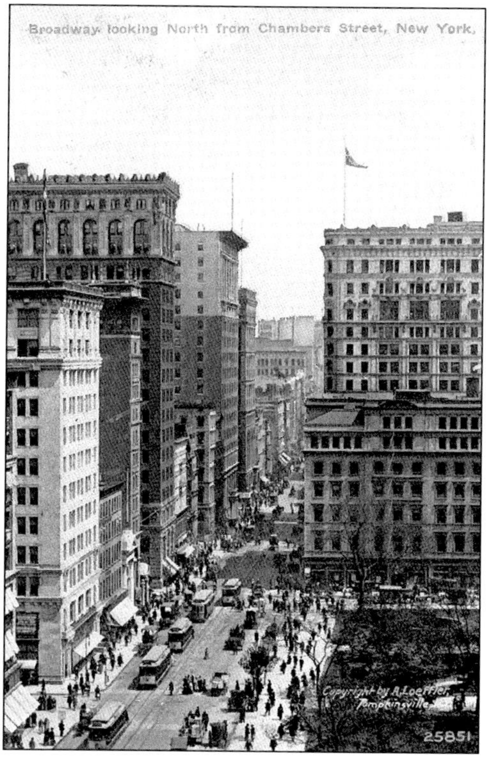

The wholesale district emerged at Chambers Street northward. Federal offices now impinge eastward, removing the 223-foot, 15-story Dun Building by Harding and Gooch on the northeast corner of Reade Street pictured around 1912 over the Stewart/Sun Building. The 18-story Cass Gilbert–designed Broadway Chambers is the tall building at left; the stem to its south is pictured/described on page 47. Three doors north is the East River Savings Institution, 18-stories, built 1910–1911 to Clinton and Russell's design.

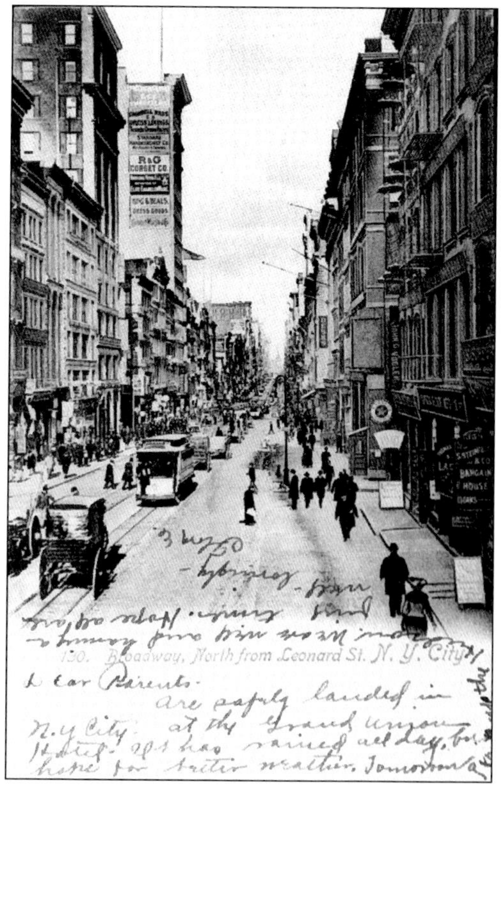

Rows of five- and six-story buildings lined both sides of Broadway north of Leonard Street around 1905.

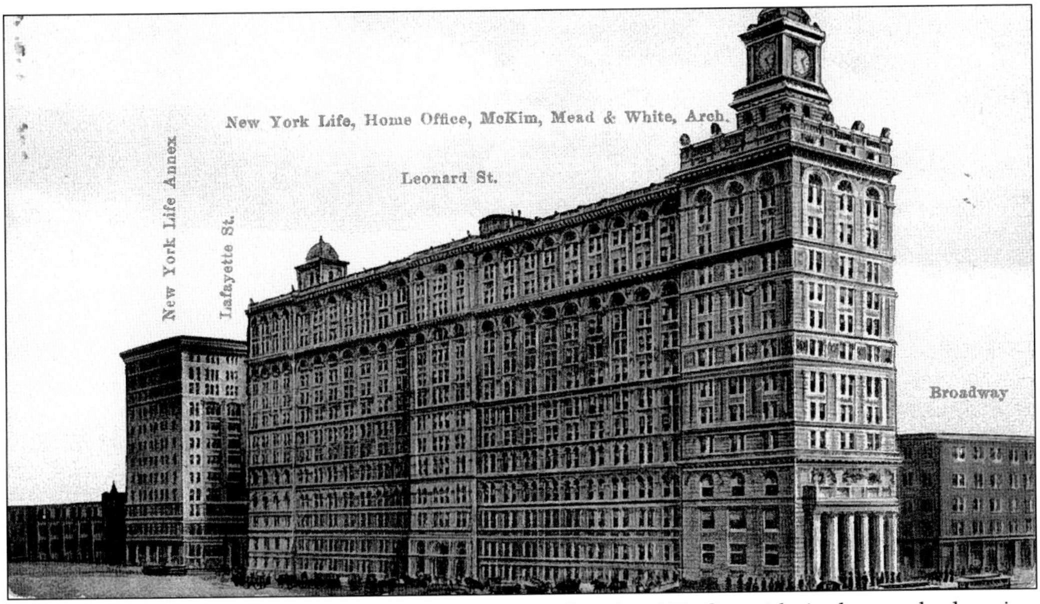

This *c.* 1910 card describes the location but omits that the 400-foot side is the north elevation of former New York Life Insurance building at No. 346. McKim, Mead and White raised a four-story 1870 building and extended it to the rear in an 1896–1899 project. The annex was also constructed then. The extant clock is by the Howard Clock and Watch Company; the Philip Martiny sculpture was removed. The City of New York acquired the building in 1968, 40 years after the builder moved to Madison Square.

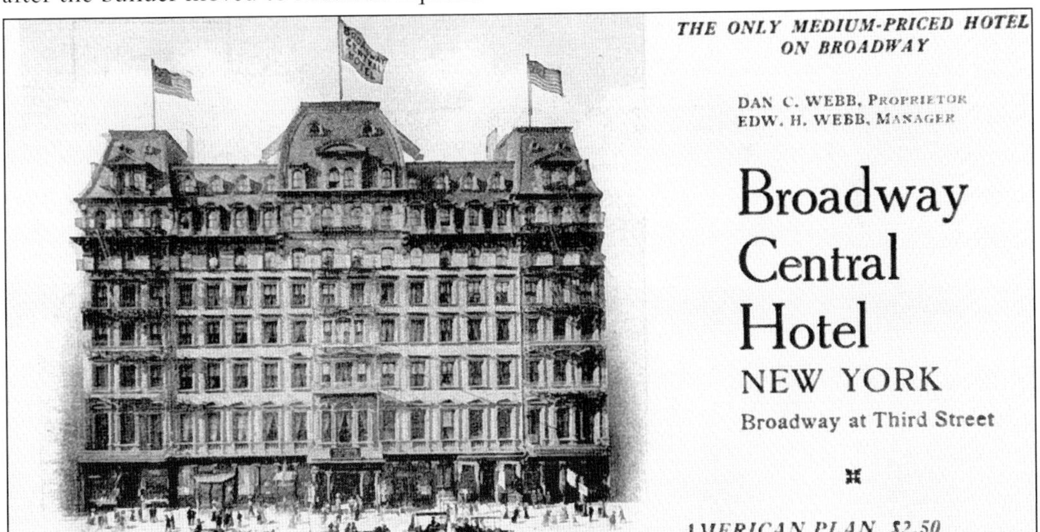

The Broadway Central Hotel, which literally collapsed in the mid-1970s, included historical details in the rubble. Three hotels filled the west side block south of the 3rd Street corner. The Tremont and Southern, each 25 feet wide, were on either side of Grand Central, "A Monster Hotel," headlined the *Times*, the day after the hotel's opening on August 25, 1870. Waxing enthusiastic over Central's size, comfort, and elegance, the reporter recounted the site's history, including the March 1867 fire that devastated the block and destroyed the Winter Garden Theater. The name was changed by the 1880s. Once a great hotel, Central advertises price on this *c.* 1910 card. (Courtesy of Joan Kay.)

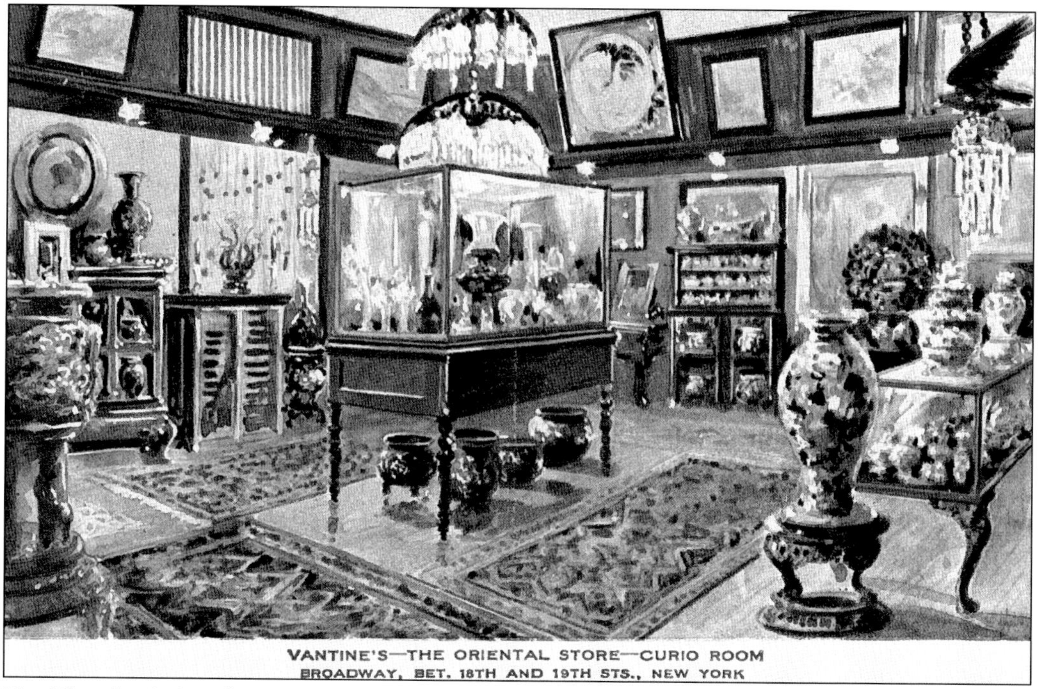

Van Tine the Oriental Store sold a variety of novelties and other Asian imports in a Broadway store that used postcards extensively to tout its wares. One writer exclaimed in 1894 that the visitor "feels that he has passed in a moment from New York to the furthurmost parts of the world."

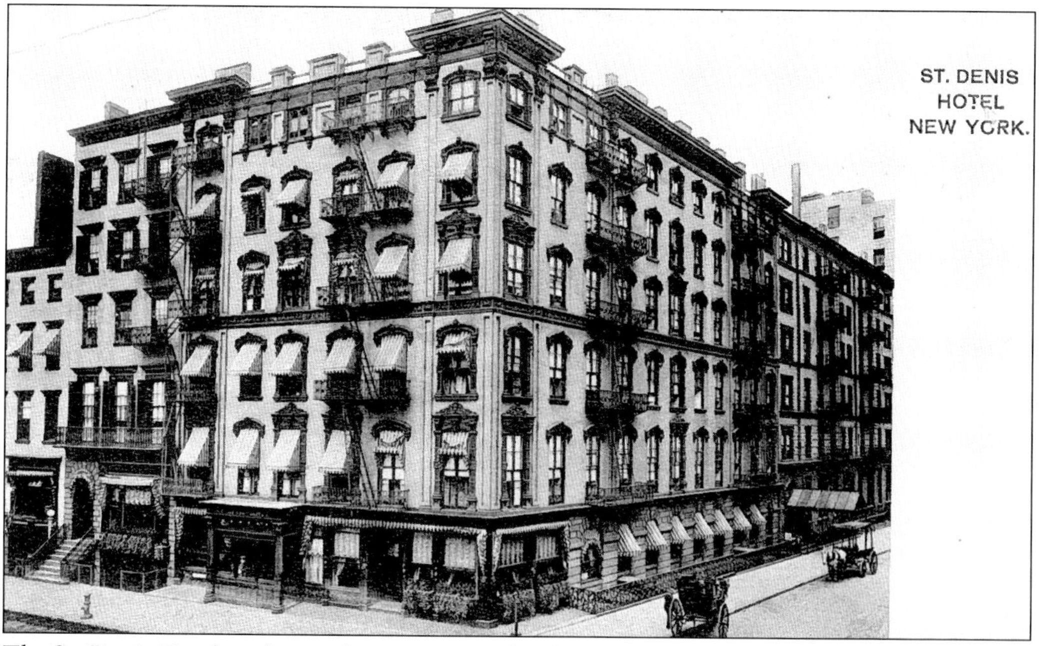

The St. Denis Hotel, at the southwest corner of 11th Street and designed by James Renwick Jr., opened in 1853 when the area was in the height of fashion. The place was rebuilt in 1875 following an 1873 fire. The St. Denis endured longer than expected, boosted by a locale halfway between downtown business and uptown residential districts.

Grace Church was built in 1843–1846 on the northeast corner of East 10th Street where Broadway curves west. The Gothic edifice, designed by James Renwick Jr., was a house of worship to the socially prominent, possessing substantial social stature in its own right. The congregation, which moved uptown from 1808 origins downtown, became a leader in the Episcopal Low Church branch, dedicated to social action.

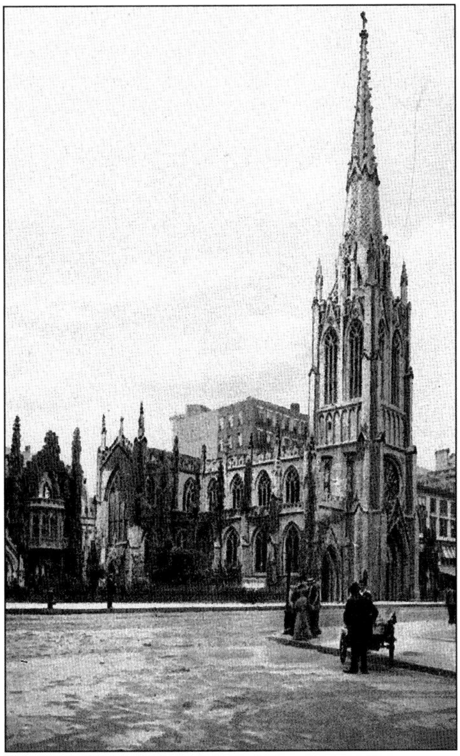

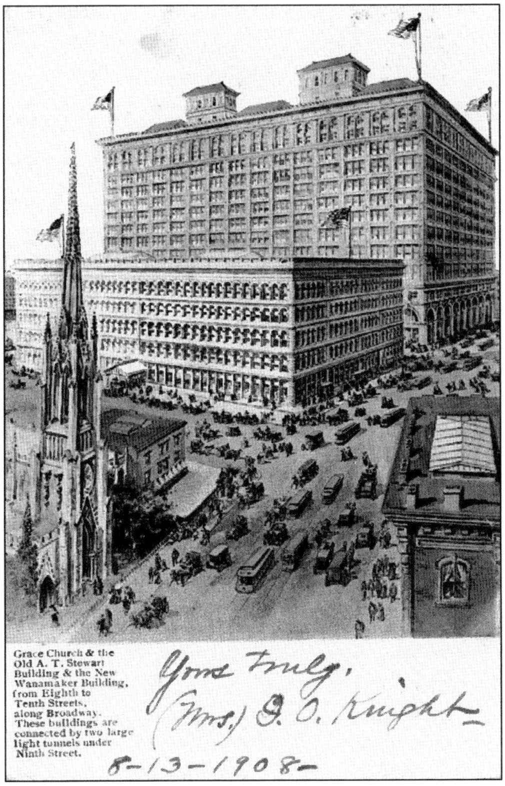

John Wanamaker arrived at the East 10th Street location in 1896, taking the former A. T. Stewart store, then erected the 13-story building on the 9th Street block, designed by D. H. Burnham and Company and completed in 1910. The two were connected with a tunnel. After retailing ceased in 1954, the older store was destroyed in a spectacular fire on July 14, 1956.

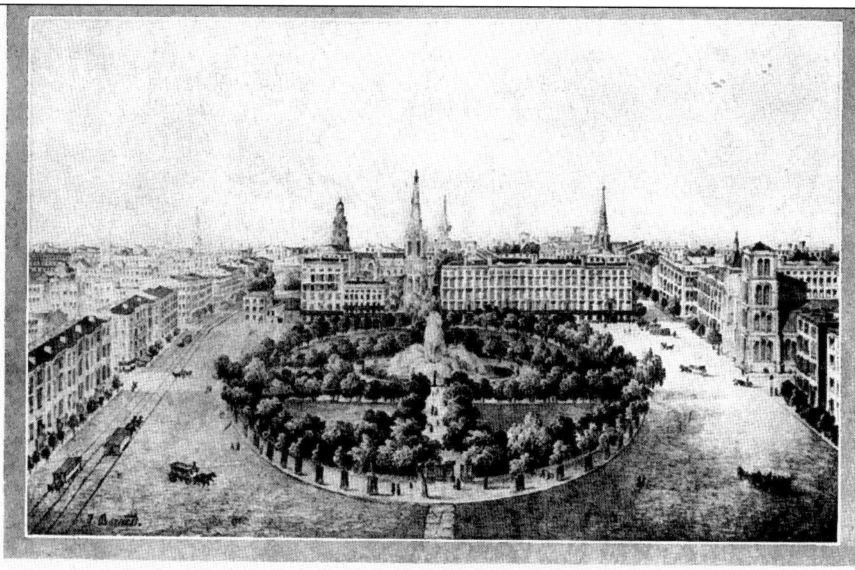

Avenues near Union Park, as it was called, lined with trees. Reservoir on 13th Street, near Fourth Avenue. Four-horse car on Fourth Avenue. Lithograph by J. Bornet. One of *Views of New York* issued by H. Hoff. From proof in Eno Collection, The New York Public Library.

UNION SQUARE IN 1850

Union Square, earlier Union Park, was formed at the juncture of Bloomingdale and Bowery Roads. The once hilly terrain was graded by 1834 and opened to the public by 1839 when it was designed for urbane dwelling in a city "moving uptown." D. Willis James presented the fountain by Donndorf where the supply of public water from the Croton Reservoir was celebrated on October 14, 1842.

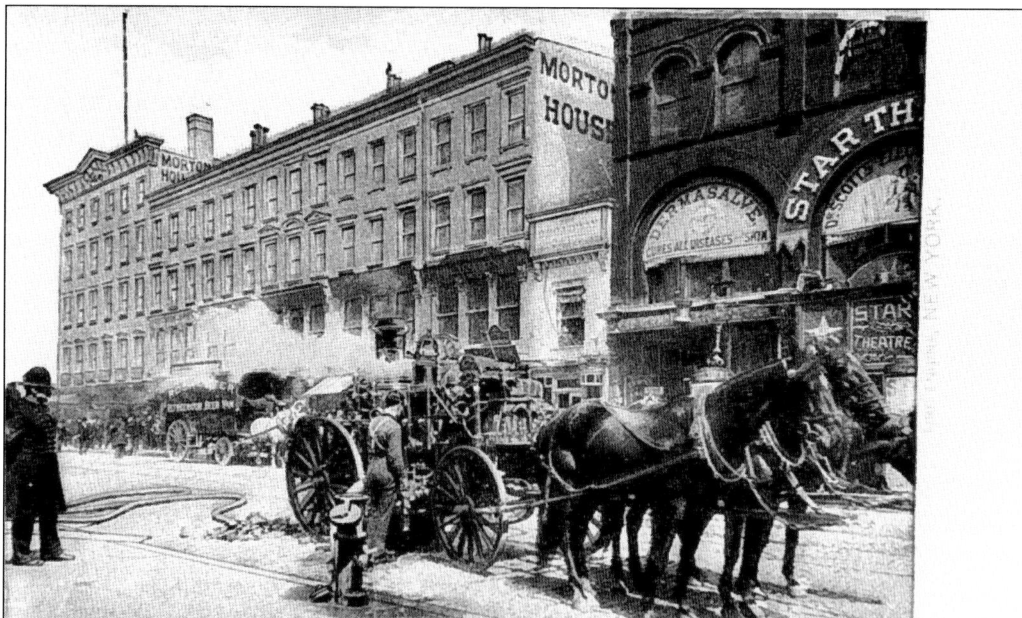

The card depicts the January 2, 1902, blaze that damaged the stores and basement but spared the theater. Morton House, originated around 1850 as Union Place Hotel, expanded several times and was named for the Morton Brothers, operators from 1868 to the 1880s. It was demolished around 1926. The Star was known as Wallick's when the area, pictured on the 13th Street block, was the theater district.

"The Union Forever! Immense Population in the Streets," the *Times* headlined the day after the April 20, 1861, gathering in Union Square rallying support for the Union cause. Union Square as rallying center for public outcry, whether a single soapbox orator or large-group demonstration, often radicals, is long rooted in city tradition. That day set a standard, the 100,000 there constituting the "largest meeting ever held on this continent." The image is Anthony Stereograph No. 910. (Courtesy of Robin Kaller.)

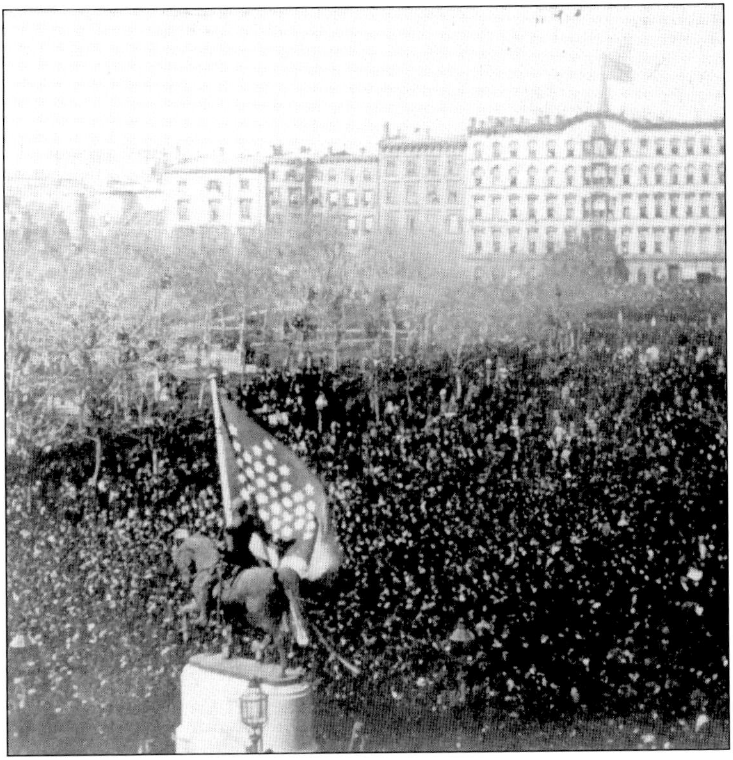

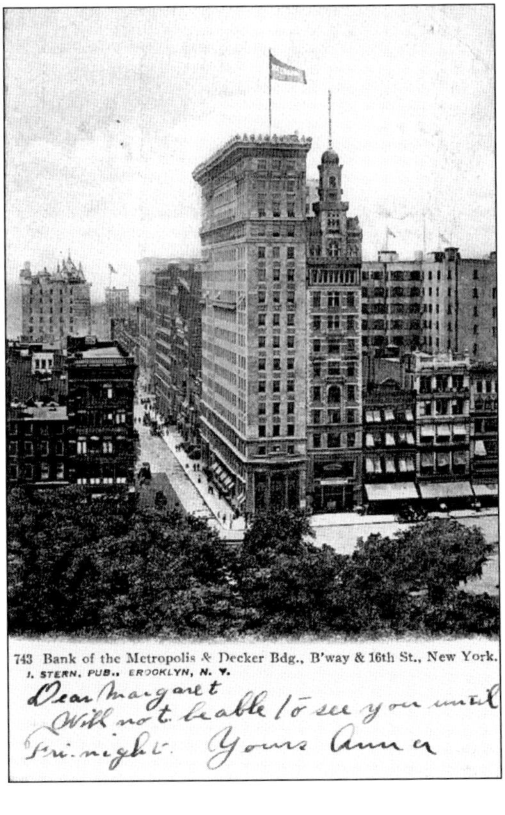

The Decker Building possessed an Islanic-style minaret when completed in 1893, when it towered over its neighbors. Arthur Zucker was traditionally credited as the architect, but Prof. Paul Sprague's research, recounted by Christopher Gray in the *Times* on December 18, 1994, indicated the design was by John H. Edelmann while in Zucker's employ. In 1903, the 17-story Bank of Metropolis obscured Decker, which lost its minaret by 1944. The two buildings stand on a block that has since grown up.

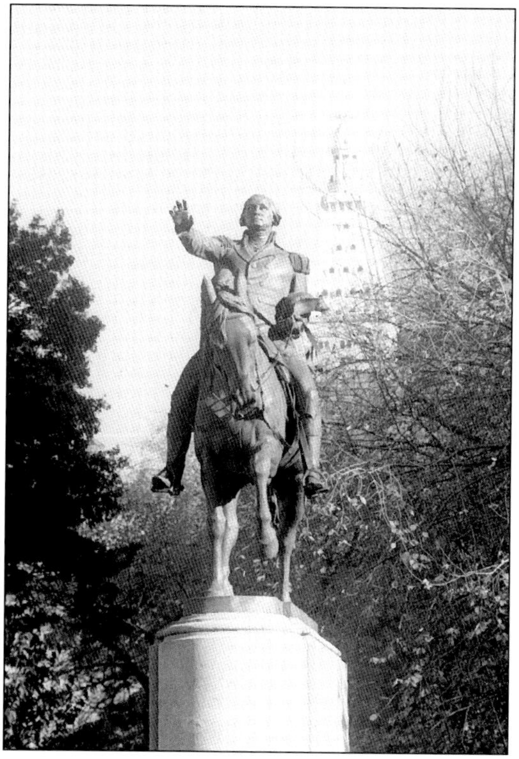

Henry Kirke Brown's Washington was modeled at his Brooklyn studio and cast by Ames Manufacturing, Chicopee, Massachusetts, in a rich bronze, 88 parts copper, 9 tin, 2 zinc, and 1 lead. The triumphant Washington symbolizes his 1783 New York arrival as the British left on November 25, an event long celebrated as Evacuation Day. Unveiled on a rainy July 4, 1856, and placed near where George Washington was thought to have been greeted, the statue was moved inside on July 10, 1930. The work is huge, with statue and base each measuring 14.5 feet.

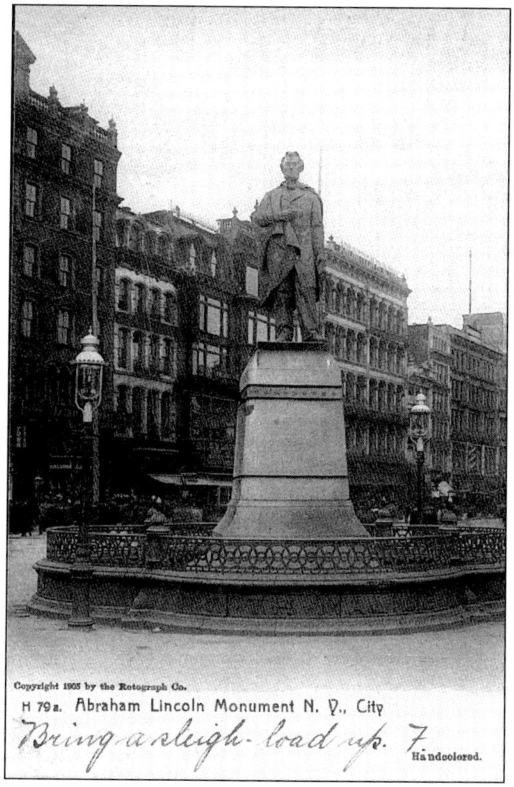

Henry Kirke Brown's Lincoln, sponsored by the Union League Club, was installed without ceremony on September 16, 1870. Eleven feet tall and cast a year earlier by Philadelphia's Wood Bronze Company, Lincoln was kept from view in a bonded warehouse until the base was ready. One of three pieces of Dix Island, Maine, granite base was claimed as the largest stone ever quarried in America. Lincoln, initially on 14th Street facing the park, was moved northward in the 1930s.

Frédéric-Auguste Bartholdi's Lafayette represents the general as the 20-year-old who joined the Revolutionary forces, presenting his sword. This 1876 gift from France, unveiled on September 6, was a token of gratitude for support in the Franco-Prussian War. The pedestal was a gift of French residents in New York. Initially placed in the center of the park at 14th Street, Lafayette was moved in 1929 to the east side opposite 16th Street.

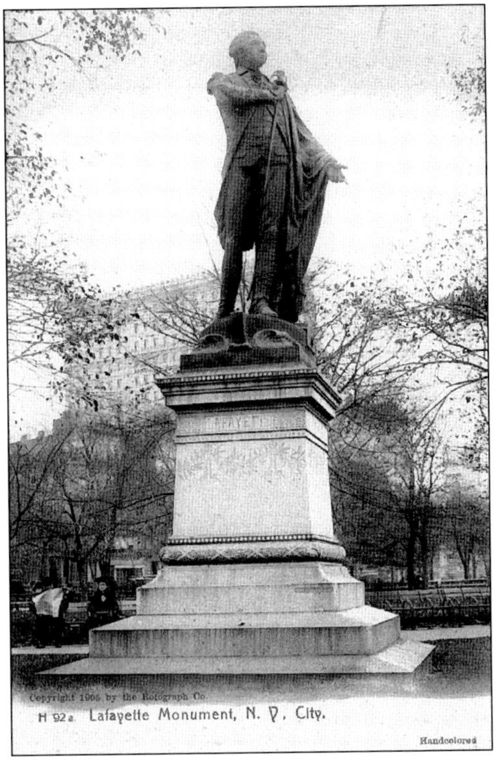

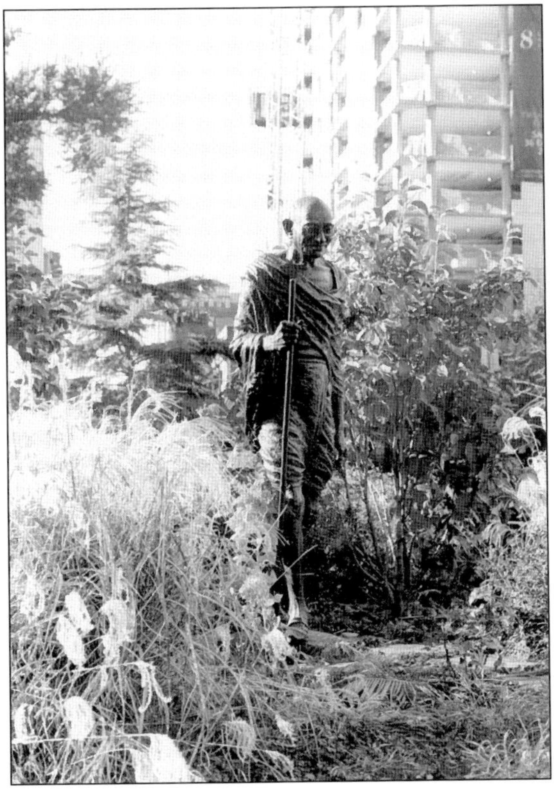

Kantilal Patel's 1986 Mohandas Gandhi seen looking southwest appears in a garden. The statue was a gift to New York from the Gandhi International Memorial Fund.

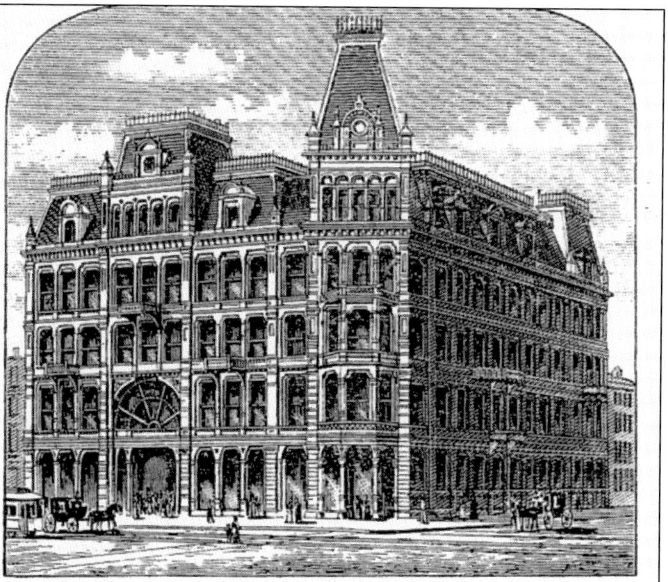

Lord & Taylor, founded in 1826, moved uptown to this cast-iron-clad Second Empire building at the 20th Street northwest corner. The James H. Giles–designed store opened on November 28, 1870, to instant critical acclaim. This image from Rand McNally's 1895 guide is still recognizable, although the building, subject of recent preservation work, was extensively rebuilt nearly a century ago. Lord & Taylor moved in 1914 to Fifth Avenue.

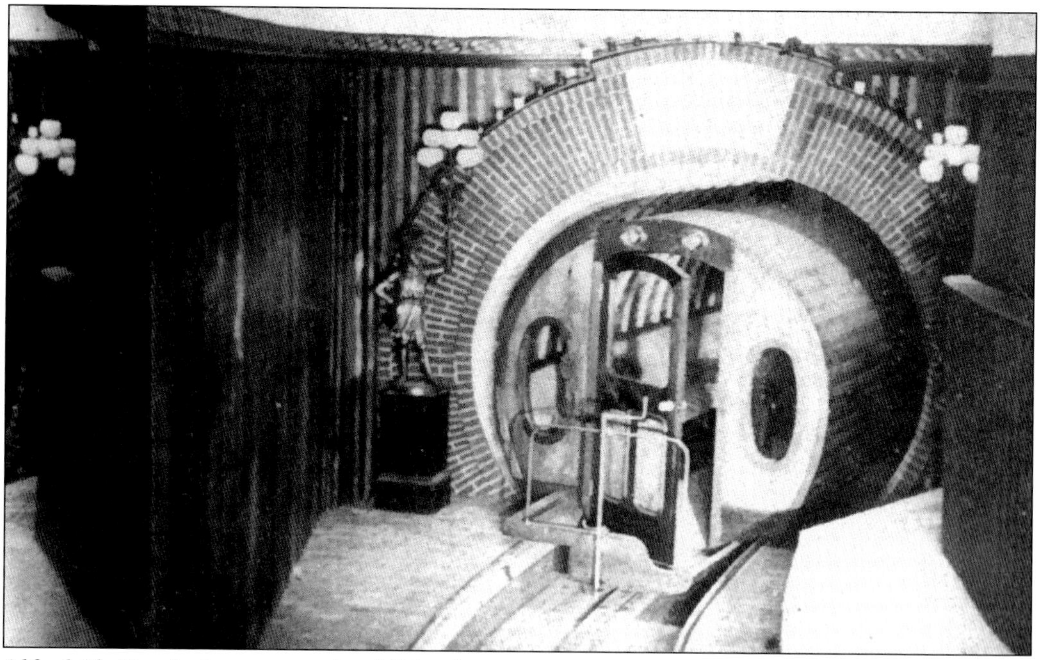

Alfred Ely Beach, inventor and publisher born in 1826, proposed remedying street congestion that plagued Broadway. In 1860, he began building at night, in secret, an underground pneumatic tube, finishing a segment between Warren and Murray Streets. Absent a franchise, favorable political environment, and public preparedness, the project was doomed and covered up. Beach's successful inventions included pneumatic tubes for mail and tunneling shields. Beach died in 1896, eight years prior to the subways' opening, for which his tube is considered a prototype. (Courtesy of Robin Kaller.)

Five

MADISON AND HERALD SQUARES

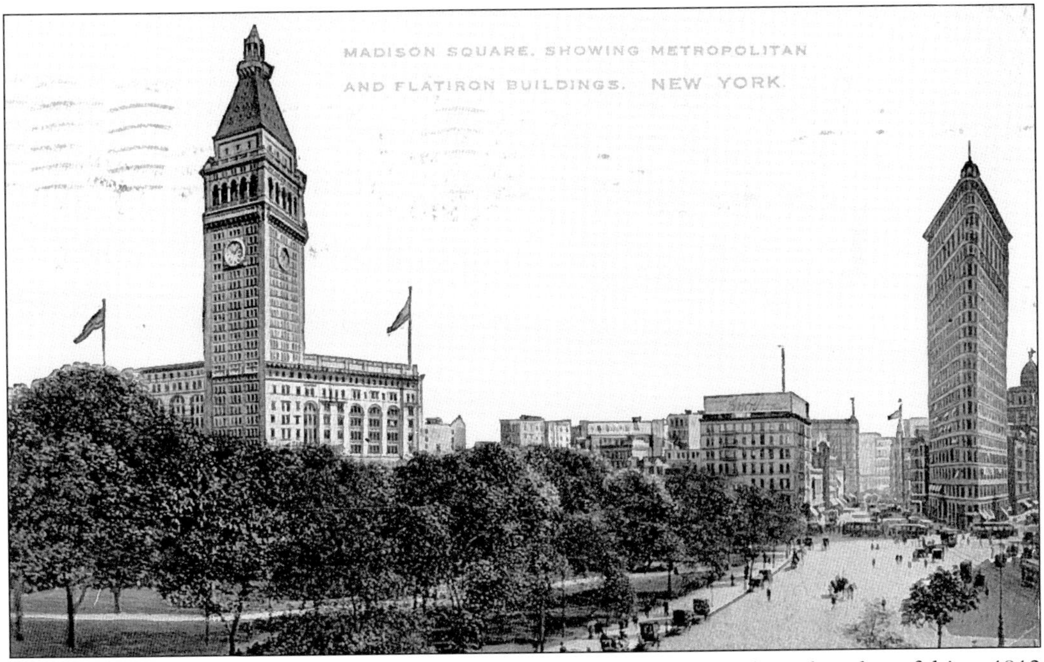

Broadway, crossing Fifth Avenue at Madison Square, proceeds westerly at the edge of this *c.* 1912 card. This break in the grid creates a famed city pie-shaped lot, filled by the iconic Flatiron Building. Madison Square opened in 1847 at the juncture of Bloomingdale Road, a predecessor of Broadway, and Eastern Post Road. Prior incarnations include the parade, a huge military drill field, the 1807 United States Arsenal, later the House of Refuge for juvenile delinquents, and a potter's field.

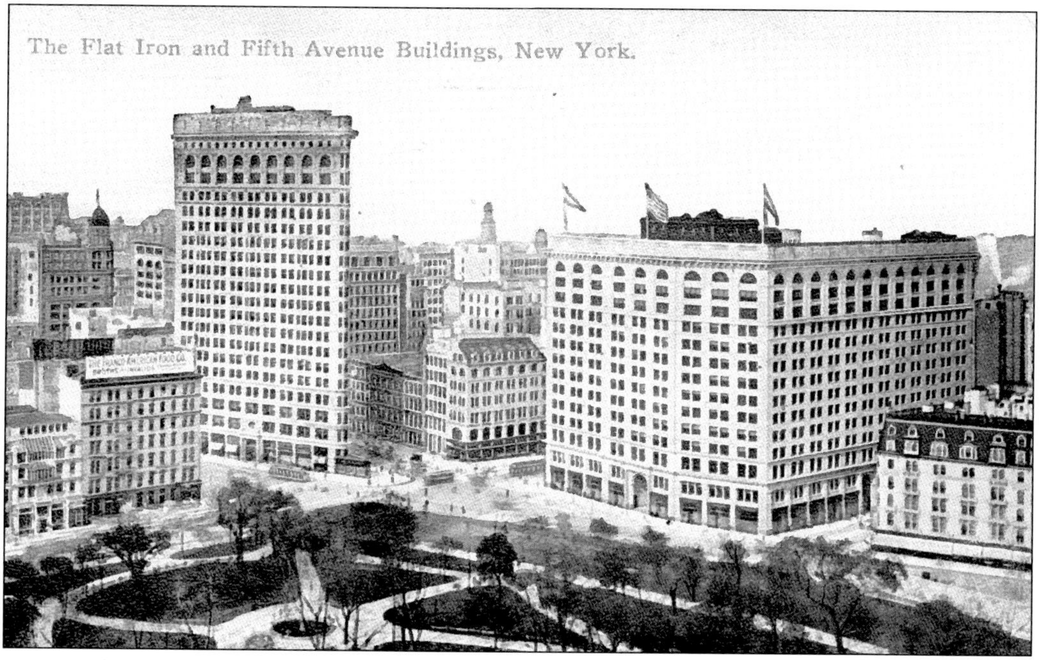

Franconi's Hippodrome occupied the Fifth Avenue juncture from 1853 to 1855, while the arsenal grounds began at the right of this *c.* 1912 card. The Hotel Bartholdi, left, reminds that the Statue of Liberty arm was exhibited at the park from 1876 to 1884, while funds for the base were raised. Walks and lawns were changed periodically. Recently Madison Square Park took a new role, exhibition space for large artwork.

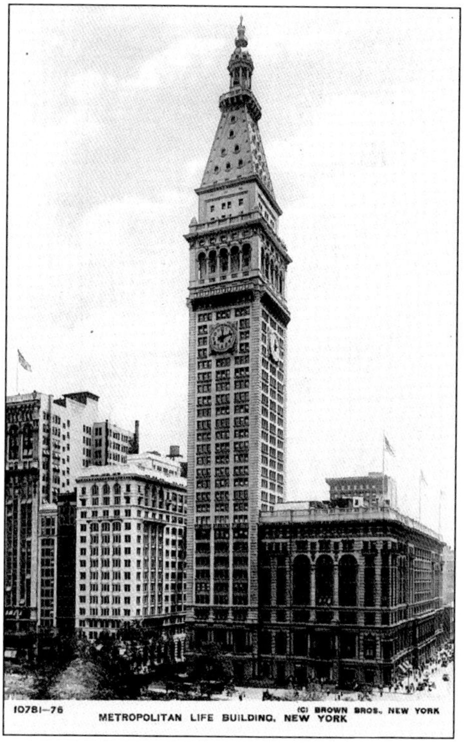

Metropolitan Life, first occupying the 10-story corner in 1893, expanded along 23rd Street. Its architect, Napoleon LeBrun, later designed the 700-foot-tall tower, completed in 1909. Based on Venice's St. Mark's Campanile, the Met was for four years the world's tallest. Even after losing its tallest stature to the Woolworth Building, its headquarters, with the image of a powerful beacon atop, provided an enduring symbol. The four-faced Metropolitan clock at 26.5 feet in diameter is the city's largest.

The 51-foot obelisk honoring Maj. Gen. William Jenkins Worth (1794–1849) was designed by James Goodwin Batterson and erected in 1857 at the northerly intersection with Fifth Avenue. It is surrounded by a fence of pickets modeled after a commemorative sword awarded Worth, who is buried here. Of the background, the *Times* of March 8, 1896, "Eyesores on Broadway," noted, "On the triangular plot at Broadway, Fifth Avenue, and Twenty-third Street are some of the worst eyesores along the way." The plot was long known as the "flatiron block," a name later embedded in city lore. (Courtesy of Robin Kaller.)

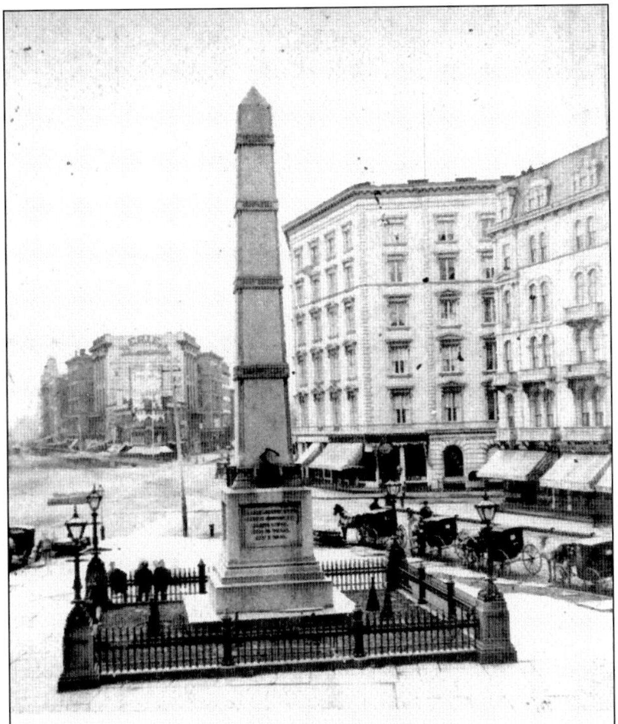
Worth's Monument, Madison Square.

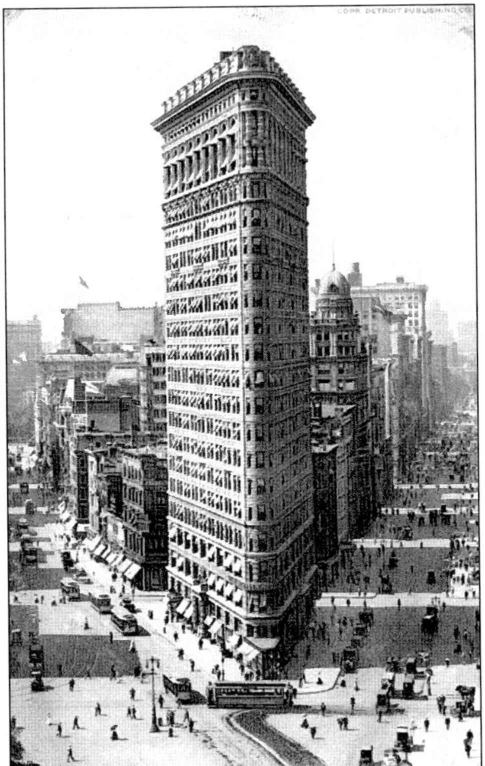

5745 FLAT IRON BUILDING, NEW YORK.

Chicago's Daniel H. Burnham designed the 21-story Fuller Building, initially named for its builder. However, the fabled tower soon took its triangular plot's identity, which resembled a hand iron, like lots wherever streets bisect grids on an angle. New York's Flatiron Building became an instant landmark for the tall, unusual shape rising at a prominent open space, then at the head of the city's major retail district. The lore of the Flatiron was blown up by the effects of wind at the vast open space. Gusts not only wreaked havoc with ladies' attire but could be dangerous.

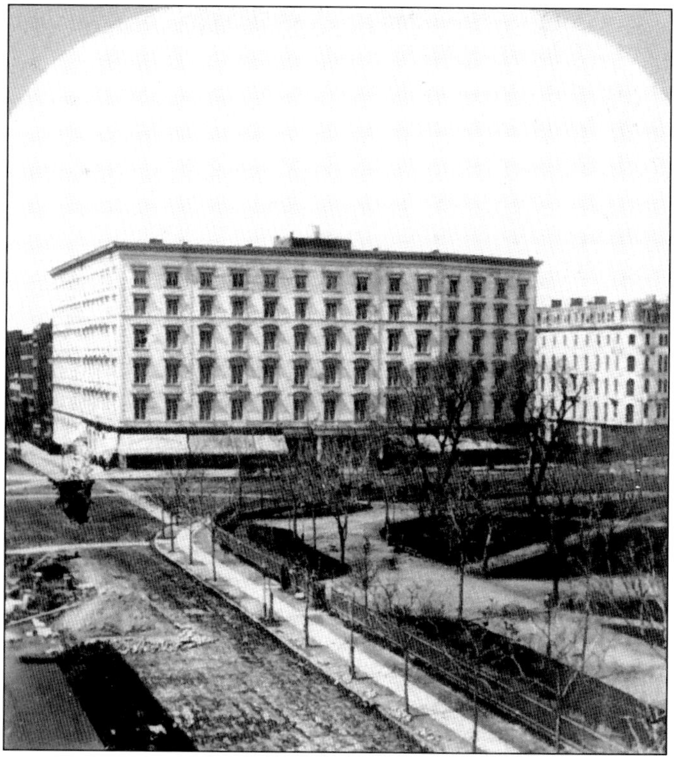

Abram R. Eno began construction of the Fifth Avenue Hotel in June 1856 on the block between 23rd and 24th Streets, where Broadway meets Fifth Avenue. The Italianate-style building, designed by William Washburn, was called, when opened on August 23, 1859, "an immense structure of white marble"; its entrance hall spanned 165 feet. From a facilities standpoint, it was the "best specimen we can offer of the possibilities of hotel luxury." It remained so for some while, but taste, neighborhood fashion, and lodging expectations moved up. The hotel, which closed on April 4, 1908, was soon demolished, replaced by the building below.

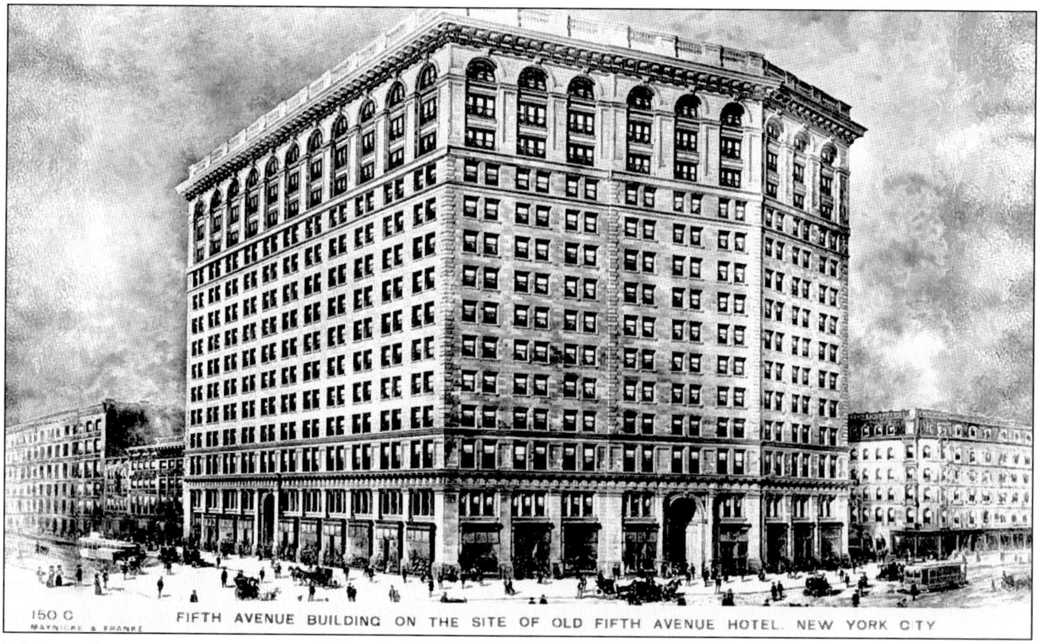

This card, postmarked 1909, features a rendering of the Fifth Avenue Building, known as the Toy Center, built then on the Fifth Avenue Hotel's site. The 15-story office designed by Maynicke and Franke has an appealing balustrade over its three-story arcade, while its facade bends to fit Broadway's arc. The Hotel Albemarle is the structure at right. Completed in 1860, it was replaced in 1915 by the 16-story Albemarle Building.

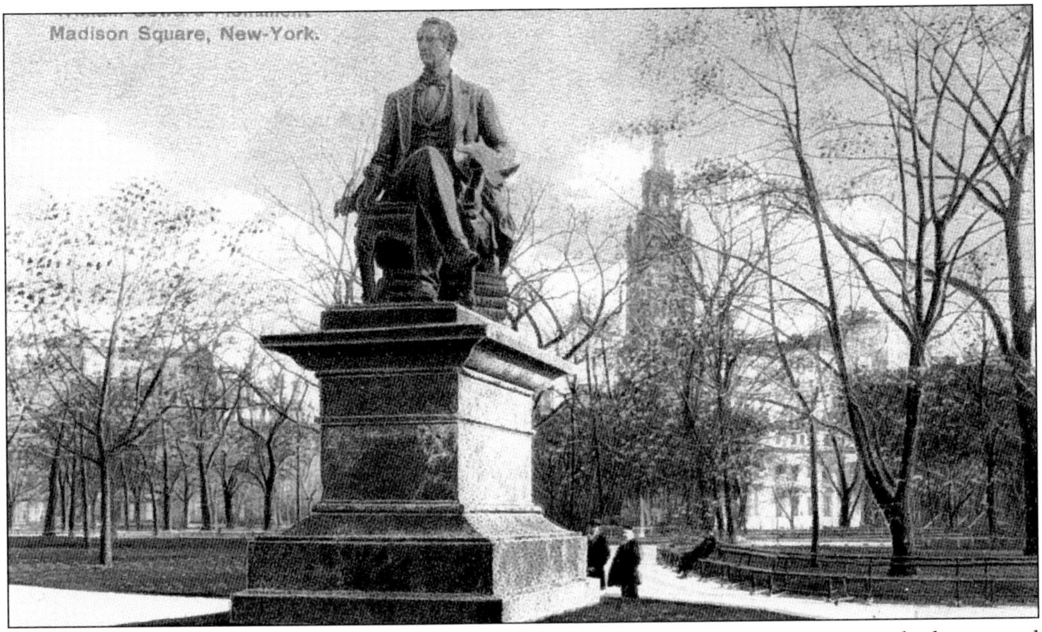

William H. Seward's monument is pictured around 1910, facing 23rd Street, with the second Madison Square Garden behind. It was unveiled on September 27, 1876, when Alaska, Abraham Lincoln's secretary of state's bargain purchase from Russia, was known as "Seward's Folly." Sculptor Richard Rogers's work was commissioned by 250 subscribers contributing $100 for its $25,000 cost. The pedestal's base is New England granite, while Spezzia marble is above. The inscription denotes New Yorker Seward's other offices, governor and United States senator.

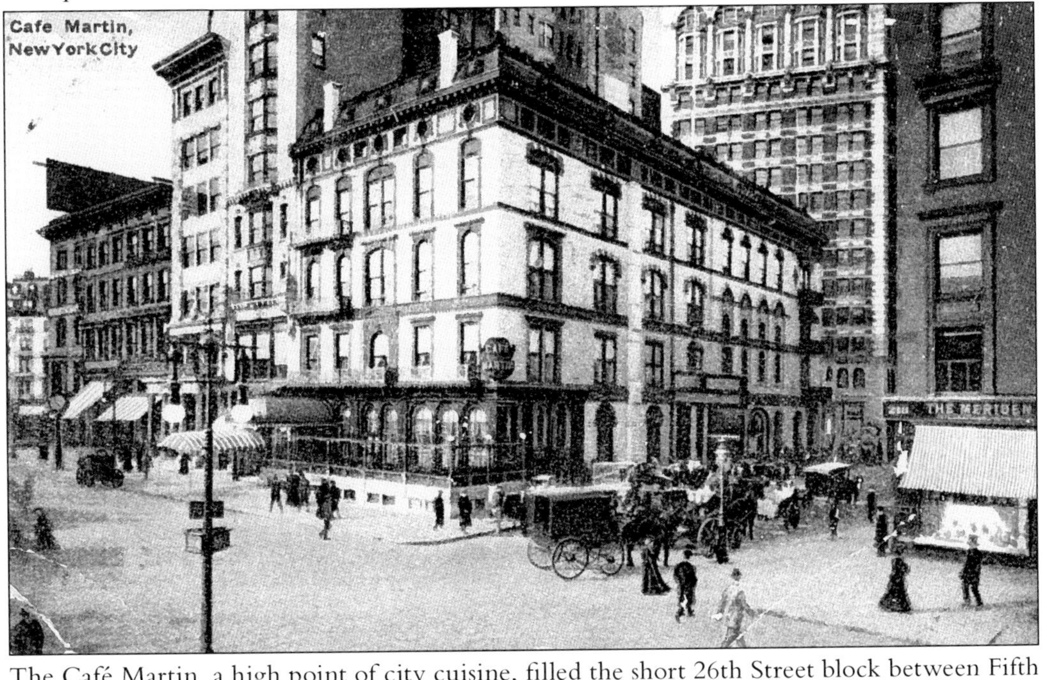

The Café Martin, a high point of city cuisine, filled the short 26th Street block between Fifth Avenue, in the foreground, and Broadway. The 16-story St. James Building designed by Bruce Price, built in 1897 on St. James Hotel's site, looms over Café Martin's Broadway corner.

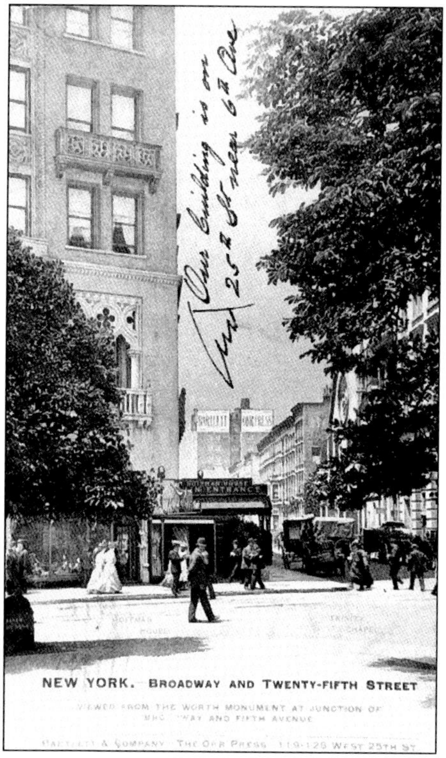

The writer fortunately found some representation of the mid-block location as side streets were not often postcard subjects. The Hoffman House is left, while amid the trees is the former Trinity chapel. (Courtesy of Joan Kay.)

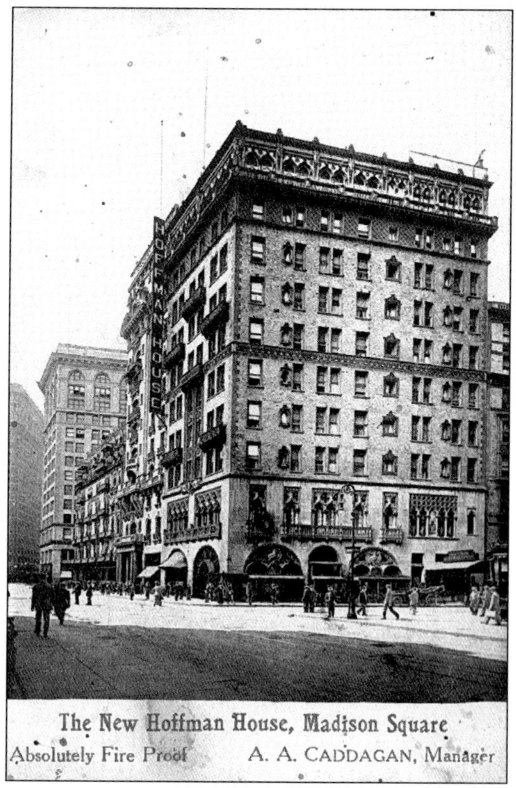

The "New" Hoffman House had the dubious distinction of being new for all its short existence. Hoffman, built in 1864 at the square's peak of fashion, was enlarged in 1882 and 1896, but when the 12-story section at 25th Street opened in 1908, lodging in the square was dying. Removing 2,000 tons of steel was a daunting challenge for the wreckers in 1915, but the site was more valuable for the modest 12-story office replacement at Nos. 1115–1117.

Quick! Who was the 21st president? Chester A. Arthur, obscure chief executive, was a prominent New York lawyer and civil rights activist who was given the 1880 Republican vice presidential nomination as concession for losing his customs-collector post. He ascended following the September 1881 death of the assassinated James Garfield. Arthur served admirably but failed at renomination in 1884. This 17-foot bronze by George Edwin Bissell was installed in 1899 near the park's northeast corner on a base designed by James Brown Lord. Arthur died on November 18, 1886.

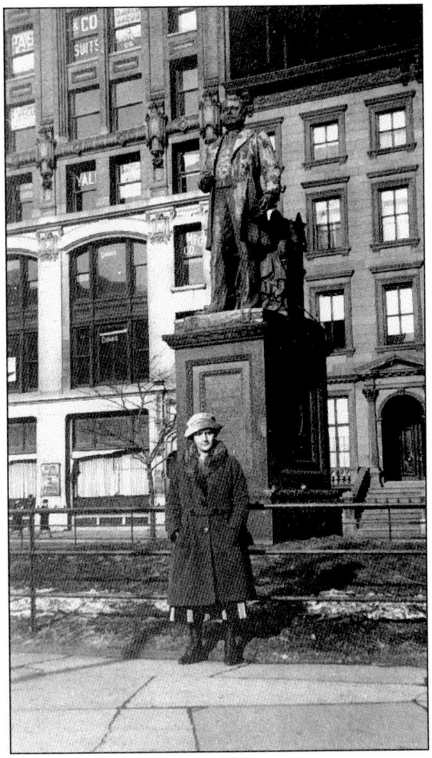

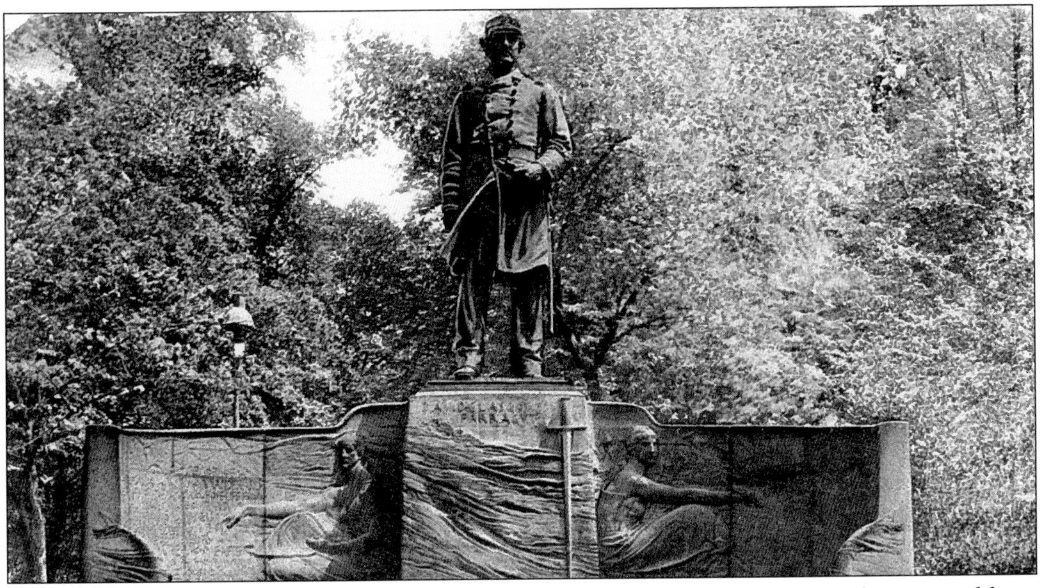

The young Augustus Saint-Gaudens, chosen for the monument to honor Civil War naval hero David Glasgow Farragut shortly after his 1870 death, collaborated with architect Stanford White for one of New York's greatest public sculptures. Over the latter's black granite pedestal embracing a bench with maritime motifs in relief stands an over-life-size bronze figure appearing lifelike in naval uniform. The New York Farragut Association–sponsored monument, initially standing in the park's northwest corner opposite the Worth monument, a commanding spot overlooking Fifth Avenue, was moved to the north-central section in the 1930s, a diminished site.

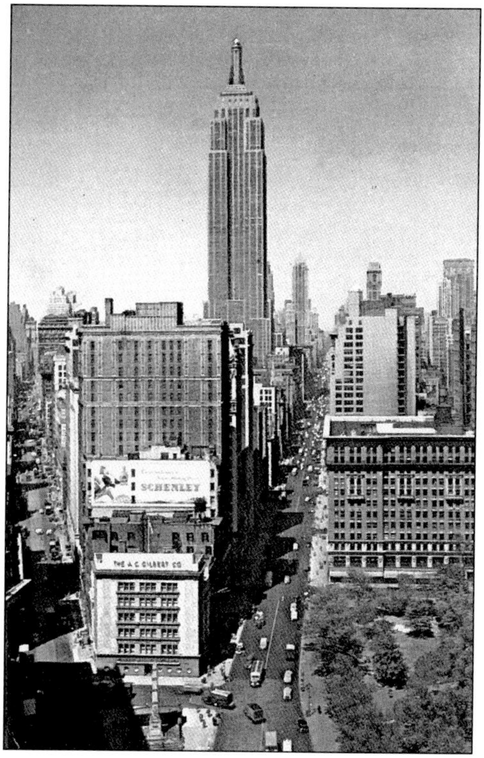

Broadway, left, is pictured around 1950 where it passes Fifth Avenue at Madison Square. The Empire State Building at 33rd–34th Streets is in the background. The Worth monument top is in the foreground; above is the 1918–1919 Thomas Cushman Company Building, designed by Ely Jacque Kahn.

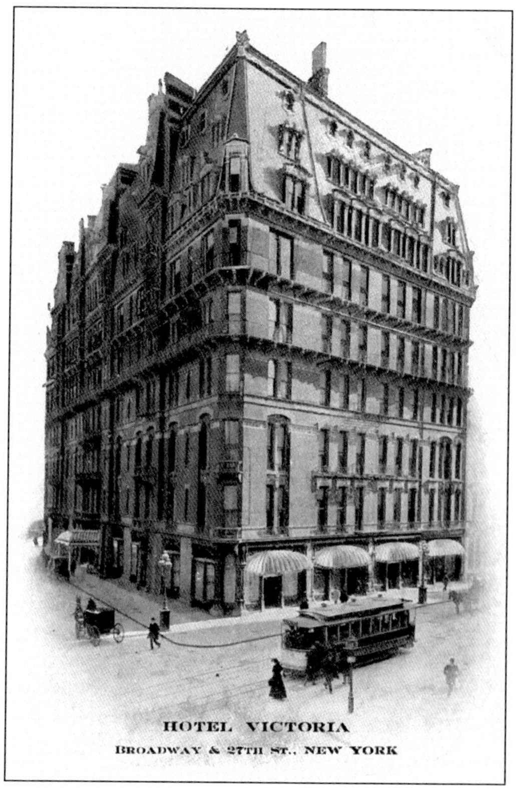

Paran Stevens, who operated the Fifth Avenue Hotel, built the Hotel Victoria on the southeast corner of 27th Street in 1872. The Richard Morris Hunt design is unusual for its three-story mansard.

Carpet merchant Elias S. Higgins built the Grand Hotel at No. 1238, the southeast corner of 28th Street, in 1868. Architect Henry Engle Blert's Second Empire design embraced a slate with cast-iron tip dormered mansard floor. The "New Grand" reflects an unspecified renovation. The place, later the Milner, slipped out of fashion along with its surroundings and fell to single-room-occupancy status in the latter 20th century. Landmarked in 1979, the hotel was the subject of late-20th century preservation projects.

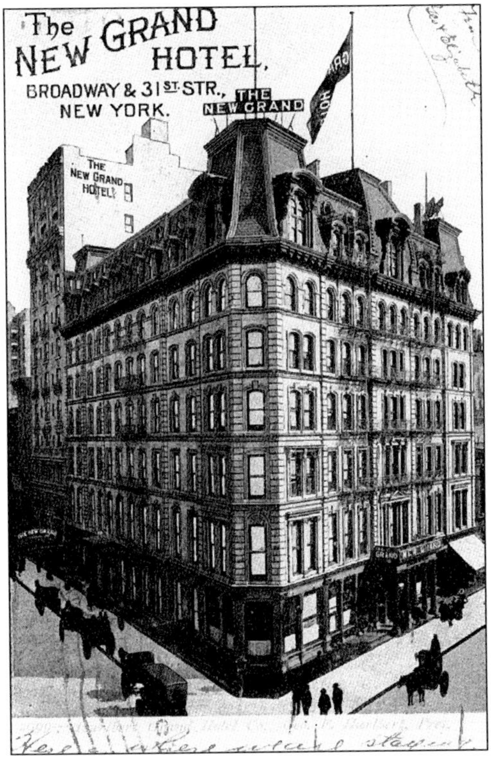

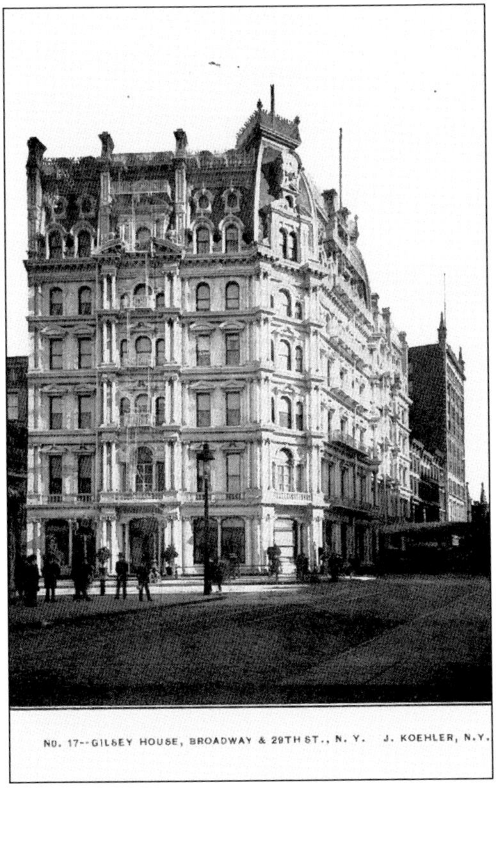

NO. 17--GILSEY HOUSE, BROADWAY & 29TH ST., N. Y. J. KOEHLER, N.Y.

"Another Monster Hotel," exclaimed the *Times* of March 25, 1871, reflecting a largeness trend. This hotel of 275 rooms, on Old Anderson Farm's site, was the Gilsey House when completed in 1872. The Second Empire–style hotel, designed by Stephen D. Hatch, is pictured around 1905 shortly before conversion to loft occupancy. The richly decorated building survived relatively intact to be preserved and converted to cooperative apartments in 1980, while additional restorative work was carried out in the 1990s. Although windows were changed and projecting columns removed ages ago, the landmark at No. 1200, the northeast corner with 29th Street, is recognizable in its special formulation of white paint.

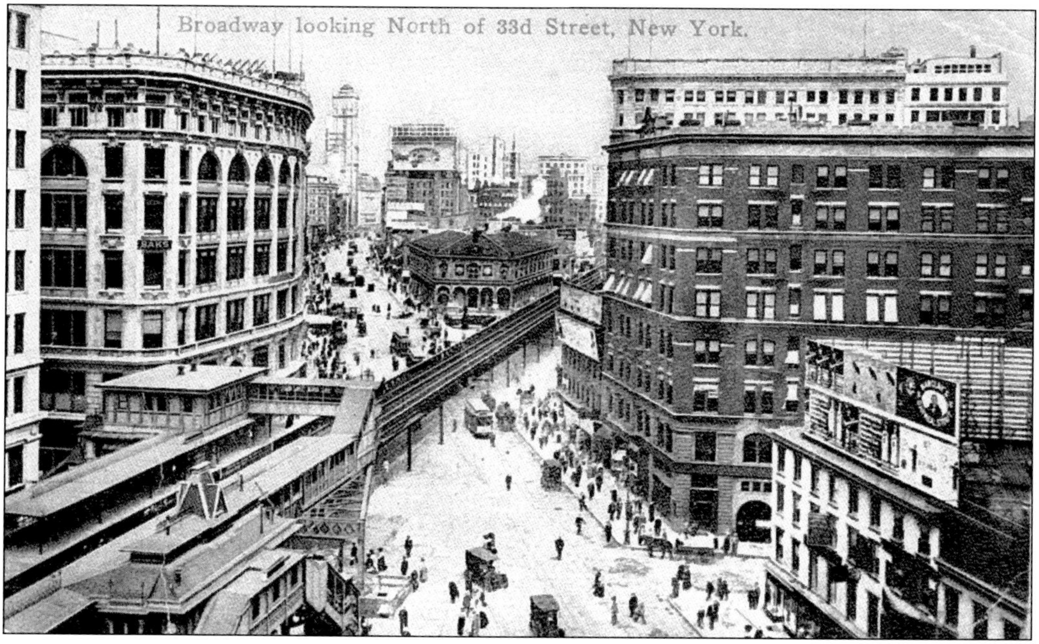

Broadway's crossing of Sixth Avenue at 34th Street created Herald Square north and Greeley Square south, an area enlivened by the 1879 arrival of the Sixth Avenue Elevated. Apartment houses, right, fill the future McAlpin's site. The Renaissance Revival Saks and Company store, left, completed in 1902, is pictured around 1907 as designed by Buchman and Fox. Its latest incarnation is a blue reflective glass box housing multiple retail tenants in Herald Center.

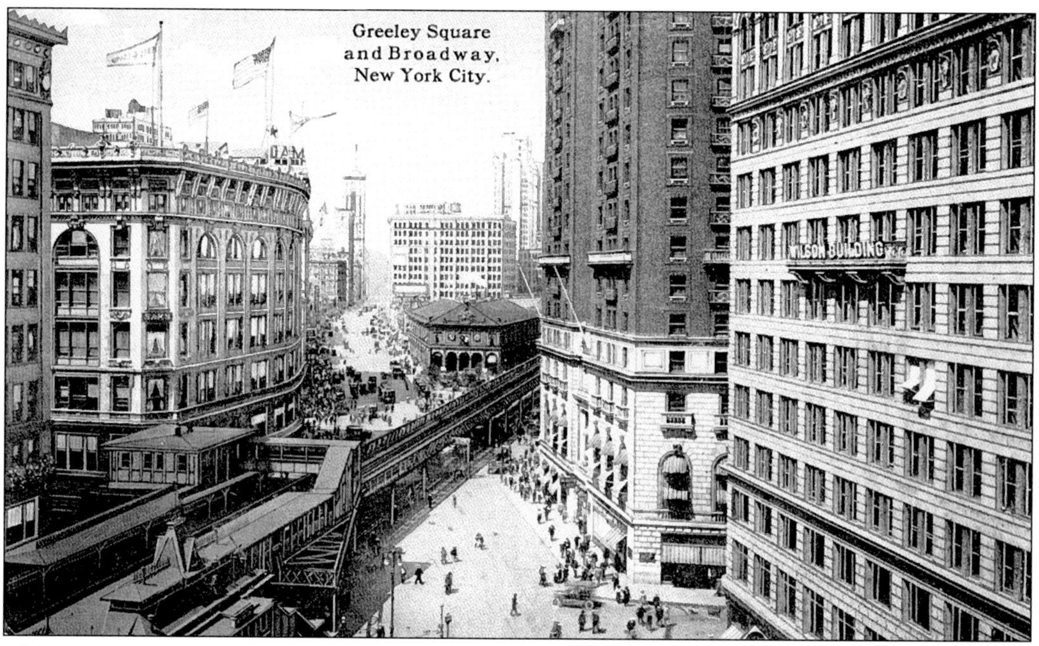

This *c.* 1915 Greeley Square view replicates the top perspective. The Wilson Building was built in 1911–1912 to Rouse and Goldstone's design, on the southeast corner of 33rd Street.

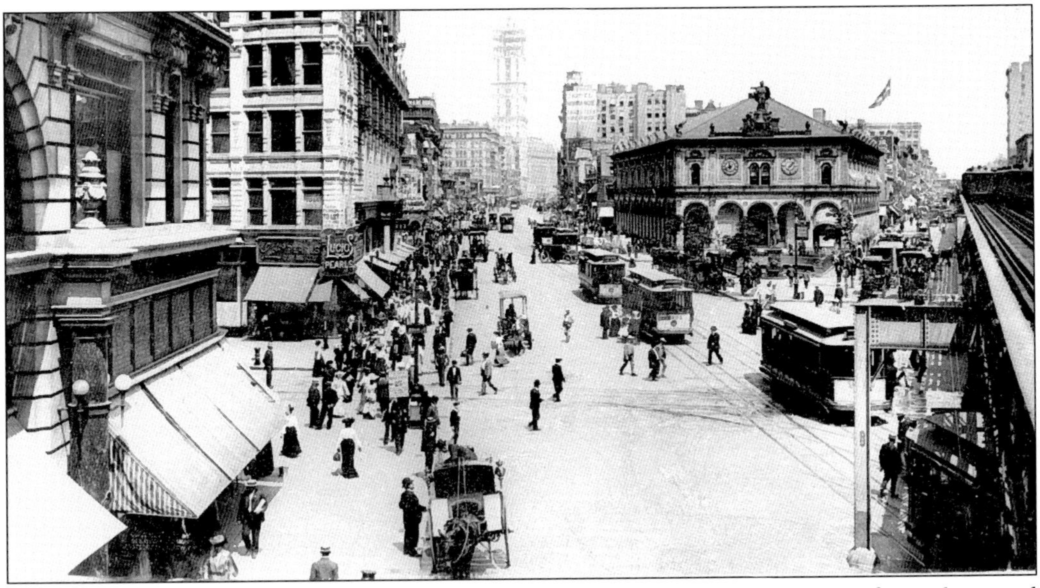

Horace Greeley, *New York Herald* publisher, built this headquarters at the apex of Broadway and Sixth Avenue, completed in 1894 to an Italian Renaissance Revival design by McKim, Mead and White. The publishing house, an enduring namesake to the intersection, resembled a Venetian palace, but not for long. The Herald Building was demolished in 1921. Macy's is pictured on the left edge, around 1903 by the construction of the Times Tower. The John Quincy Adams Ward statue of William Earl Dodge, in front of the building, was relocated to Bryant Park.

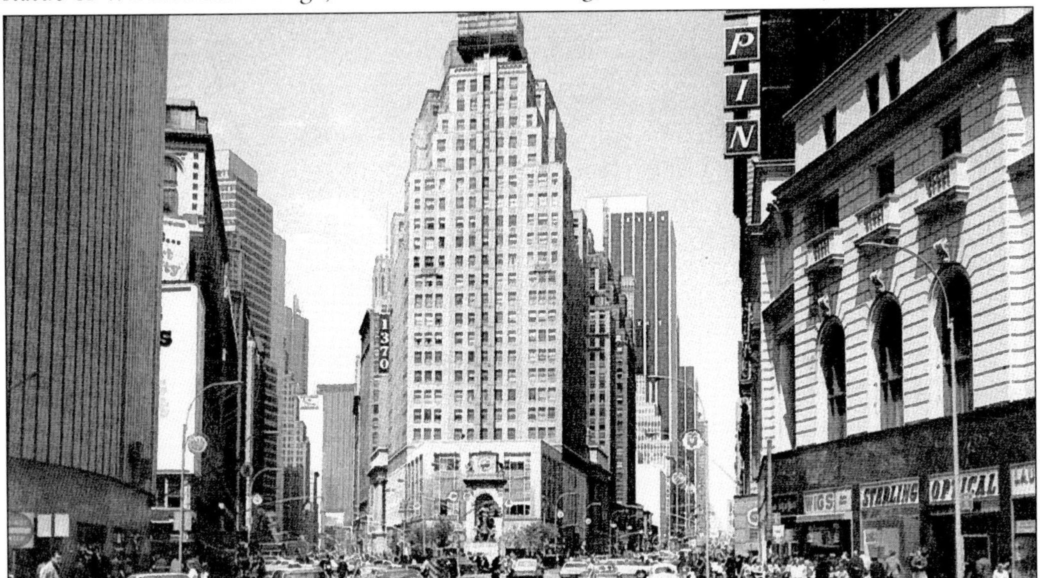

The sad little limestone box is a four-story annex of the 24-story 1930 Herald Square Building, designed by Clinton and Russell. Removal of the Third Avenue Elevated in the 1950s spurred prompt building there, but the 1940s demolition of the Sixth Avenue Elevated took longer before construction took off. Later metal and glass towers are visible at right around 1970. Note the lamppost plaques of the nations, signifying the street's official name, Avenue-of-the-Americas. If one hears that name spoken in New York, one is likely listening to a tourist.

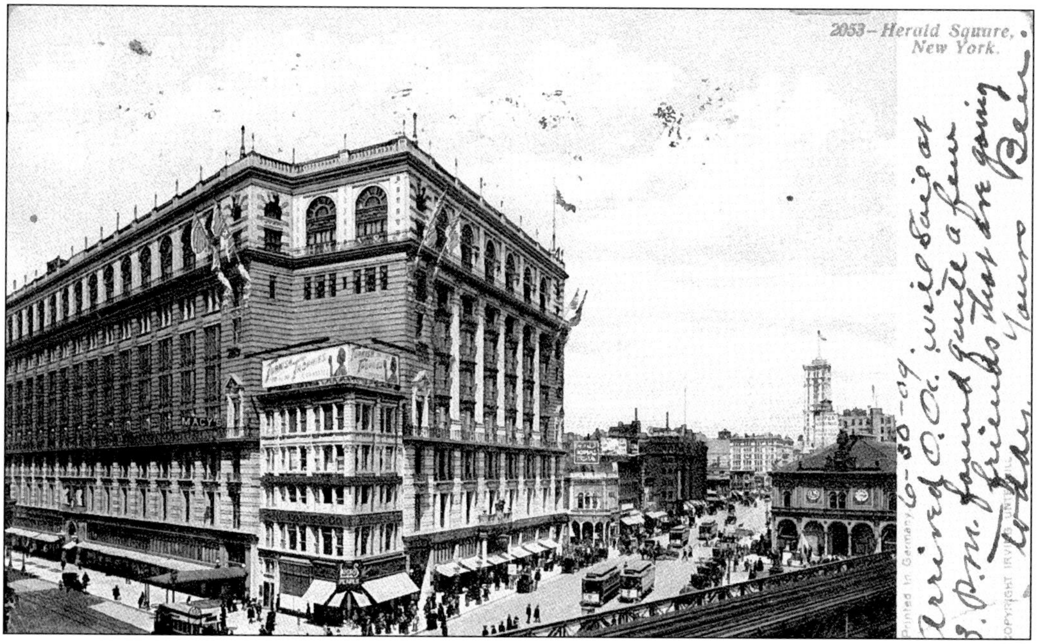

Macy's 1890s decision to move north would take it to the 34–35th Street block, but it was unsuccessful in securing the corner. The DeLemos and Cordes–designed store, built around the now-famous holdout, opened in 1902. The next year the tiny five-story Beaux-Arts building in the notch, designed by William H. Hume, opened. Once a thriving retail outpost, the structure is now substantially a sign for Macy's.

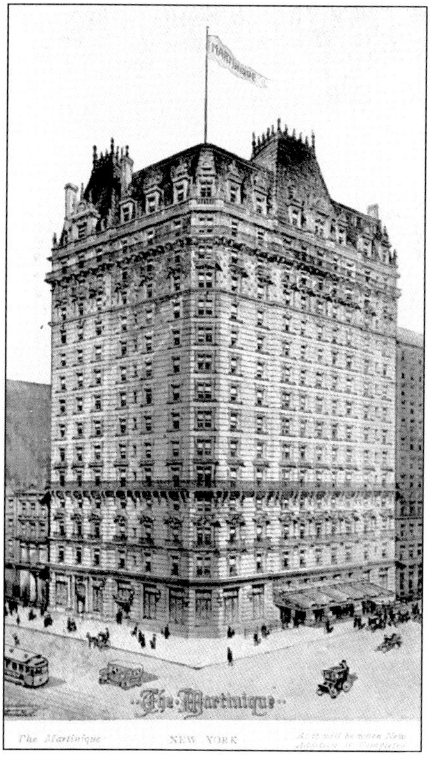

The original 10-story Hotel Martinique filled an L-shaped lot from mid-block locations on Broadway and 33rd Street. William R. H. Martin expanded in 1910 with a 14-story addition on the northeast corner of 32nd Street, pictured as a rendering of Henry J. Hardenburgh's design. The Beaux-Arts hostelry enjoyed a spell of fashion but faded as theater and hotel districts moved into Times Square. The Martinique reached nadir in the 1970s as a homeless shelter but was revitalized and reopened for hotel purposes.

The Hotel McAlpin's 1,500 rooms made it, when completed in 1913 on the southeast corner of 34th Street, the city's largest. The 27-story, 322-foot building, designed by F. M. Andrews and Company, was located on the McAlpin state. The two facade breaks for light courts suggest the building's shape as the letter *E*. The backgrounds around 1915 show a glimpse of the Martinique, right, and underdeveloped 34th Street, left, while the Sixth Avenue Elevated runs along the bottom.

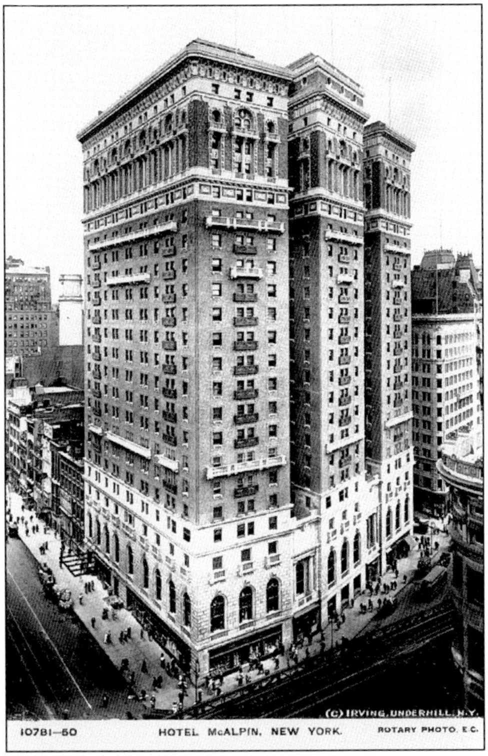

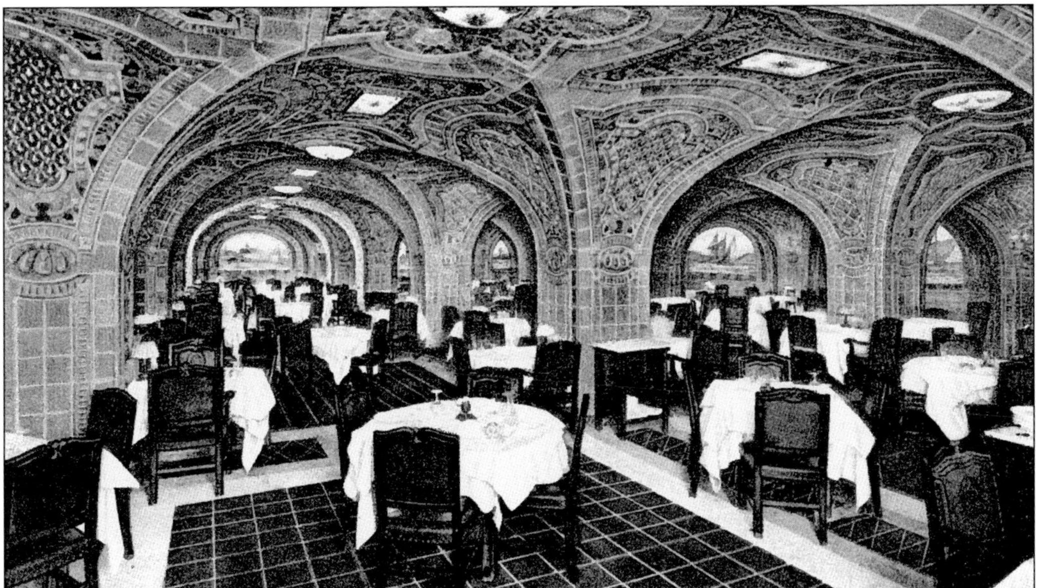

The basement Marine Grill, McAlpin's signature decorative public space, was richly finished in colored terra-cotta, which, extending upward and outward from the many posts, formed the great, pictured curved vaults. Barely visible in the background are some of Fred Dana Marsh's tile murals depicting scenes from the city's maritime history. The murals were discarded at the restaurant's 1989 closing but were literally rescued from the trash. Around a decade later, they were installed in the Broadway–Nassau Street subway station.

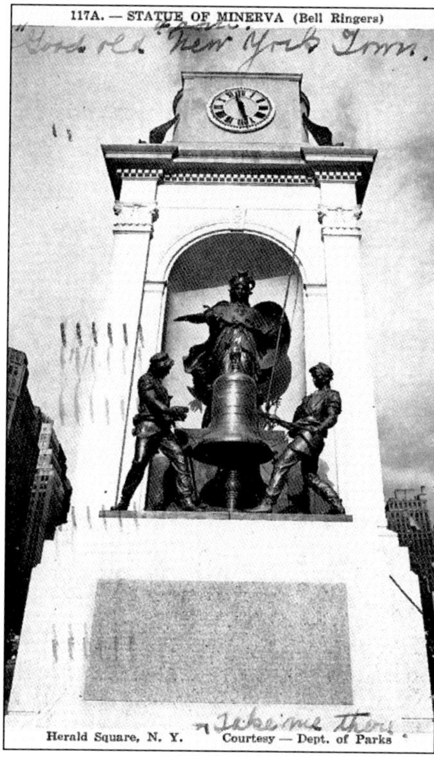

James Gordon Bennett commissioned French sculptor Jean Antonin Carles to create his monument to wisdom and work, *Minerva and the Bell Ringers.* Note her ever-present owl on the bell, once rung hourly by the blacksmiths nicknamed "Scuff" and "Guff." The monument, removed to New York University after the Herald's 1921 razing, was reinstalled after the 1945 redesign of Herald Square. The clock, once requiring three hours to wind manually, now operates electrically.

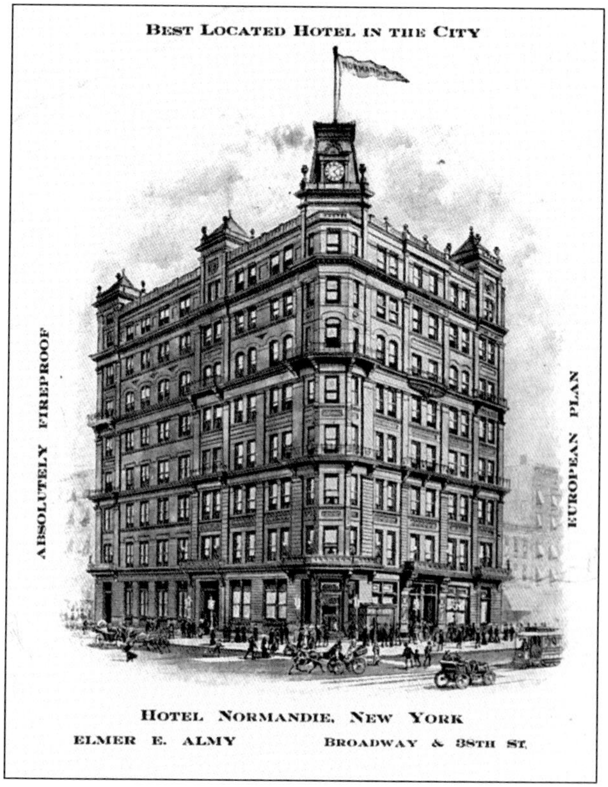

The Hotel Normandie, designed by William H. Hume, was built in 1887 of gray stone on the southeast corner of 38th Street. It was reported as one of the first city fire-resistive hotels, was rented at a premium, and was patronized by a prestigious clientele. The Normandie was demolished in 1928 to make way for the 1929 Lefcourt-Normandie Building, a 25-story showroom-office marketed to the needle trades.

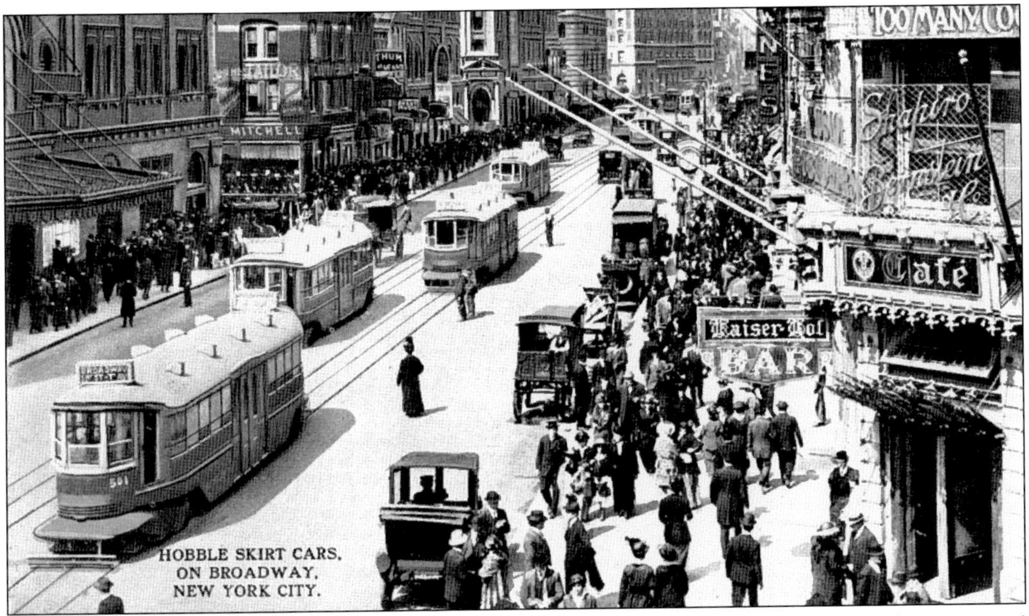

Progress was delayed on Broadway's stem between Herald and Times Squares when the vanguard of development "jumped" from the former to the latter following the 1904 opening of the Times Tower. The scene runs from the 40th Street corner of the Metropolitan north to the Astor. The hobble-skirt streetcars were the publisher's focus. First used 1914, their steps were only six inches above ground.

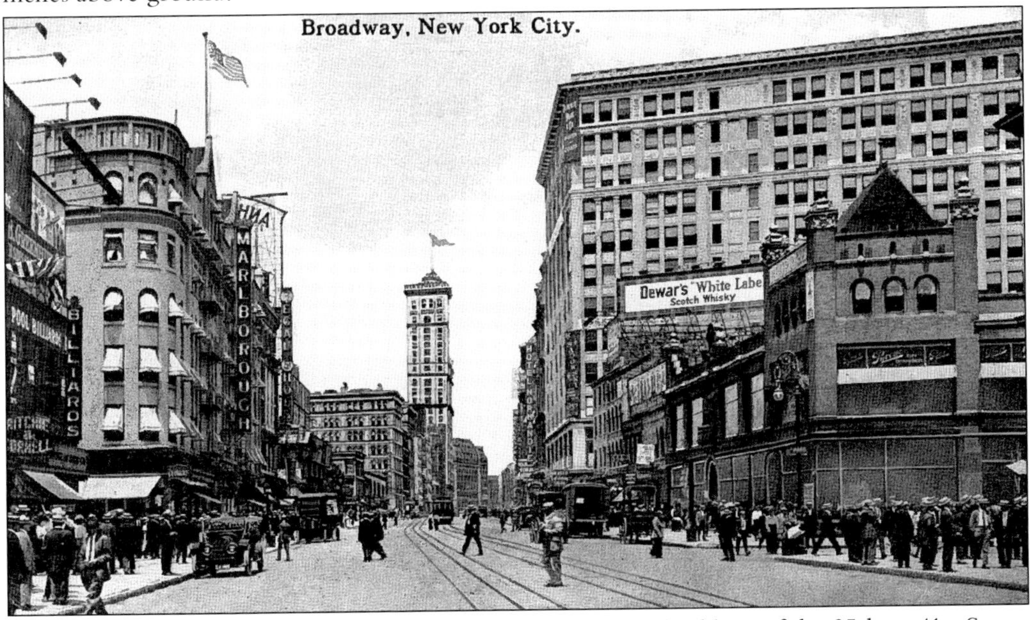

Abraham Lefcourt accounted for an almost single-handed rebuilding of the 35th to 41st Street area, erecting in the 1920s many tall buildings serving needle trades relocating there. The Hotel Marlborough was demolished in 1923, replaced by the Lefcourt-Marlborough Building at No. 1359. Lefcourt's simple naming practice gave new structures names combining his surname with the site's former hotel. The National Tower at No. 1372, the tall structure at right, was built in 1914, designed by George Keister.

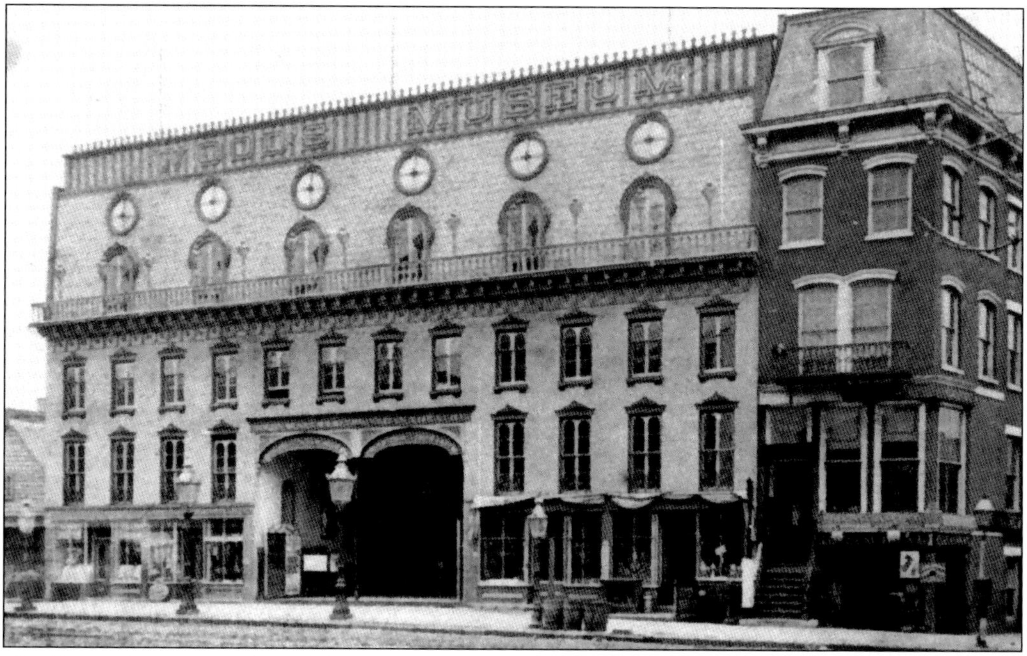

The Barvard Museum, founded in 1867 at the southwest corner of 30th Street, was altered in 1868 by manager John Wood and reopened as Wood's Museum and Metropolitan Theater. Augustin Daly took over in 1877, disposed of the curiosities, and ran what was strictly Daly's Theater. The exhibition of oddities and designation as museum both amused theatergoers and elevated the calling's raffish stature. The place was demolished in 1920. (Courtesy of Robin Kaller.)

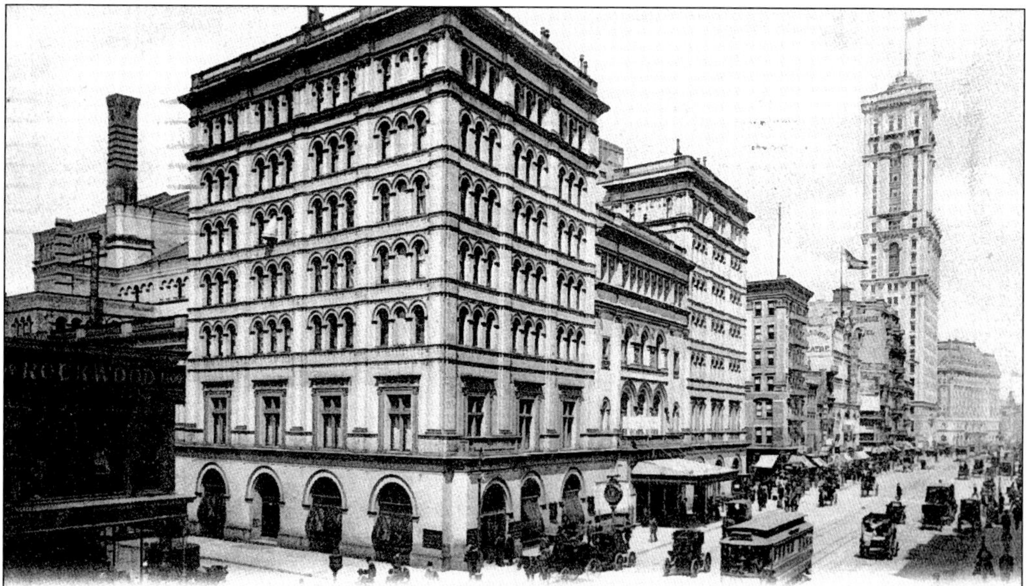

Broadway at 39th St. Showing Metropolitan Opera House, N. Y. Times Building and Hotel Astor. New York

The Metropolitan Opera filled the 39th–40th Street block between Broadway and Seventh Avenue. The 1883 opening of the house, designed by Josiah Cleveland Cady, marked a jump northward for New York's musical center. Inadequate offstage facilities doomed the Met; the company moved in 1966 to Lincoln Center. A 1969 office tower now fills the site.

Six

Crossroads of the World

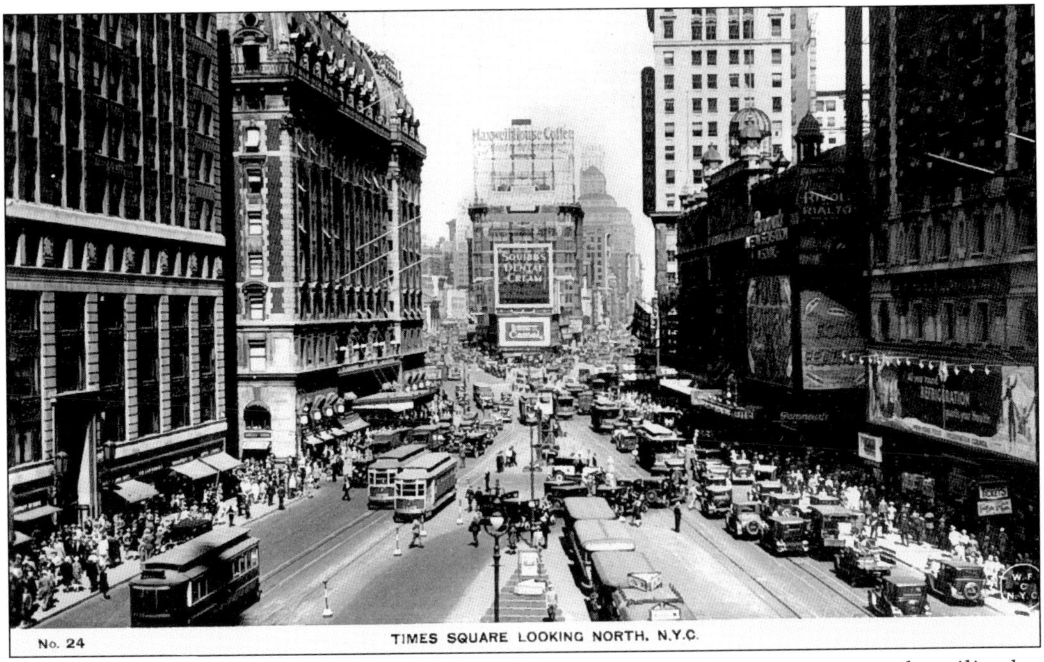

The crossing of Seventh Avenue with Broadway, then Longacre Square, an area underutilized at best, dismal at worst, was morphed into the Crossroads of the World following the Times Tower's 1904 completion. This building stirred the northward move of the hotel center, the theater district, and the entertainment industry. They made the square the city's pulsating hub, day and night. In the dark, the colorful lights of spectacular advertising signs made the place glow. The square's renaming for the *Times* became an icon of the city, instantly recognizable worldwide.

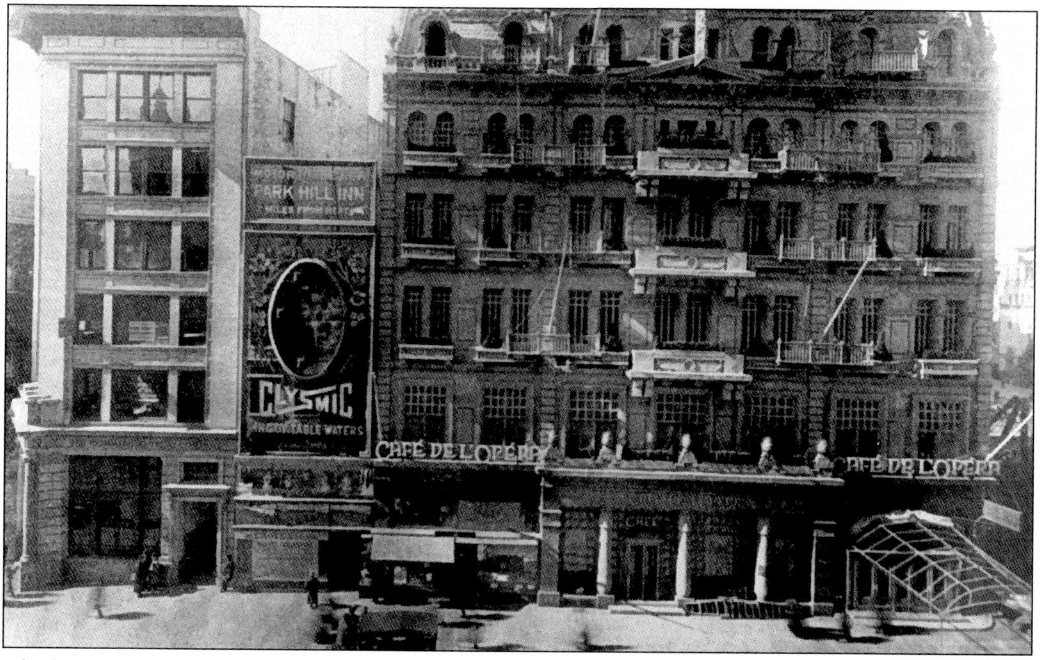

The hotel industry's northward march up Broadway is chronicled herein. "North" was established by the Rossmore in 1875, a Second Empire design by John B. Snook, built by George Ross. Renamed the Saranac (among others), the place was sold several times in the early 1900s, its price a benchmark for the emerging square's hot real estate market. The Café De L'Opera was a 1909 lavish, but failed restaurant makeover. Demolition began in February for replacement by the Brokaw Building.

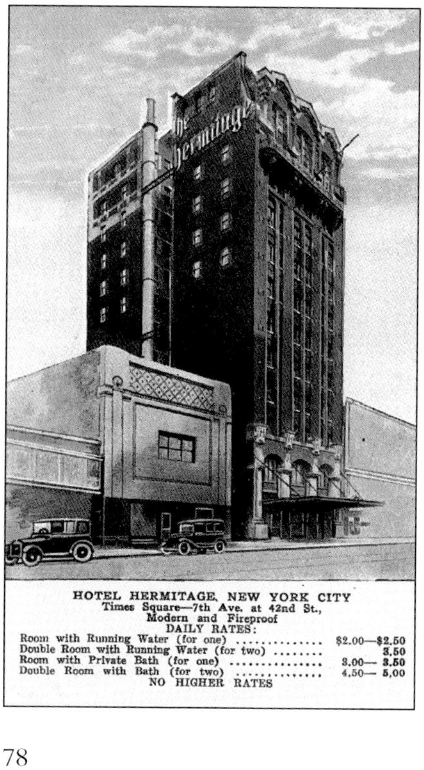

The 14-story Hermitage, a hotel opposite Broadway on Seventh Avenue, opened around 1907. The Beaux-Arts design by Robert D. Kohn makes effective use of tall Tuscan columns and a three-story capital set off by a balcony. Timing and location in the shadow of the Knickerbocker and Astor diminished the Hermitage from the outset, a standing also suggested by the 1920s price promotion. Later the National, the place was demolished around 2000.

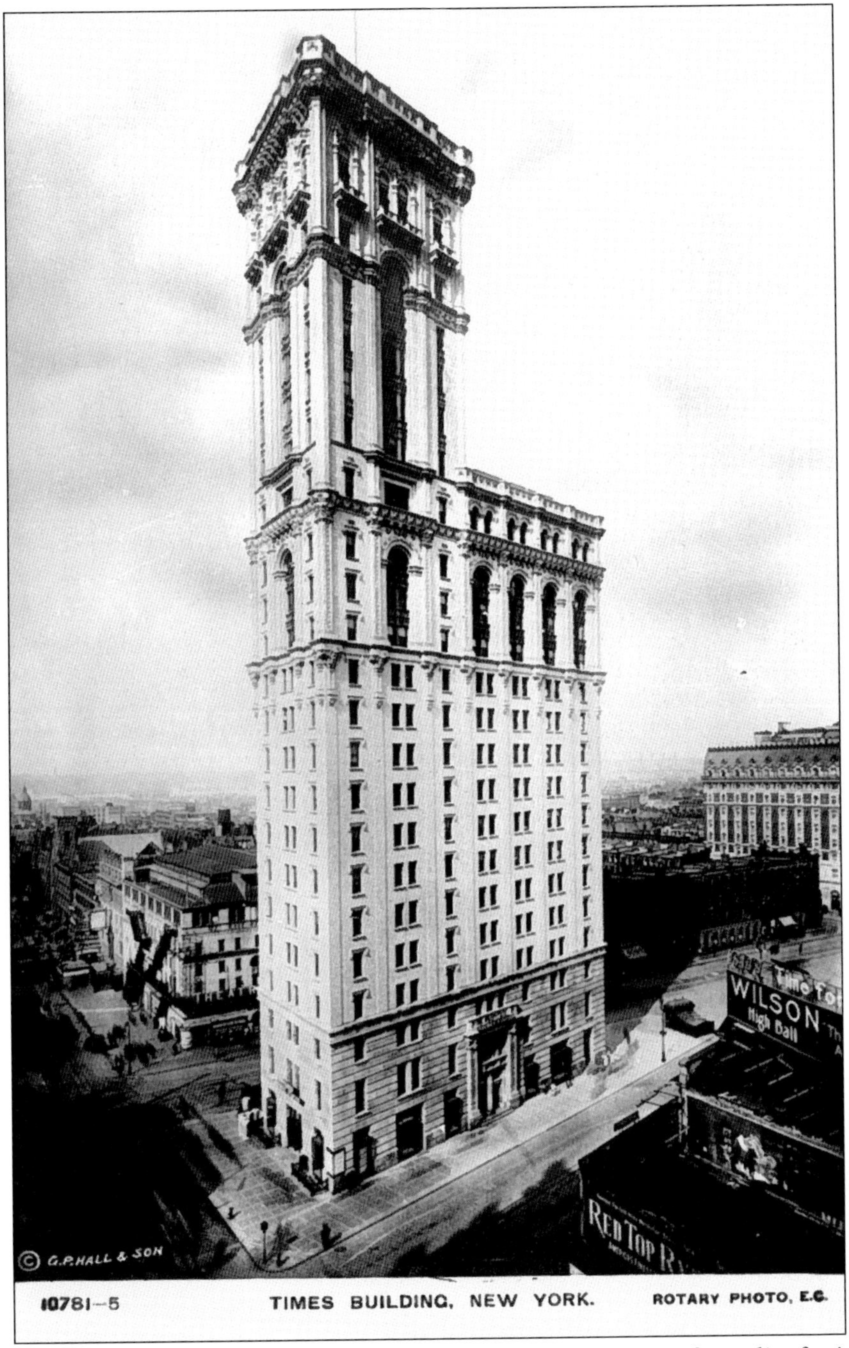

The Times Tower deserves prominence on New York's 10 most significant list for impact in propelling Longacre Square from the carriage industry's center to the east's entertainment and lodging capital. The site's prior occupant, the Pabst Hotel, existed only from 1899 to 1902. *Times* publisher Adolph Ochs desired an infrequent New York irregular-shaped block. The Astor is an early sign of a maturing Times Square. The brownstones across the street were replaced by the Putnam and later the Paramount Building. The Longacre Building came in 1912 on the lower right corner. The 42nd Street theaters soon multiplied.

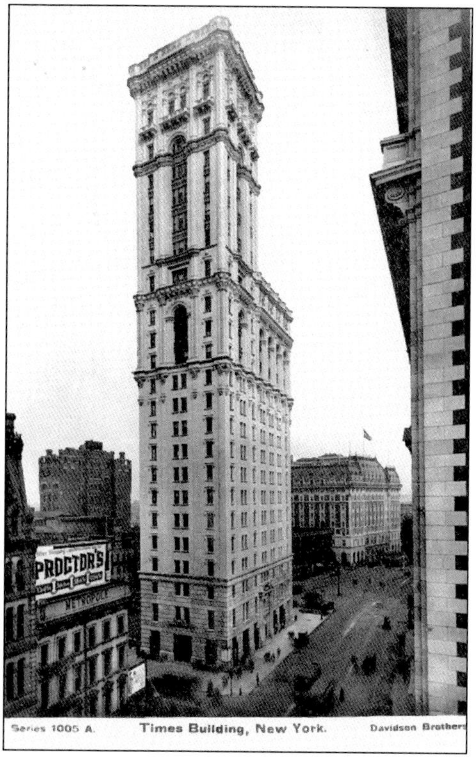

Cyrus L. W. Eidlitz and Andrew C. McKenzie designed the 362-foot-tall Times Building, a height then exceeded only by the Park Row Building's 380 feet. The newspaper's production facilities, contained in subsurface floors, prompted an outrageous superlative claim. The *Times* claimed that measuring buildings from the lowest subbasement floor should be standard, a measure that would have made its building nine feet "taller" than Park Row. The *Times* soon outgrew this facility, building in 1912 a new headquarters nearby on 43rd Street.

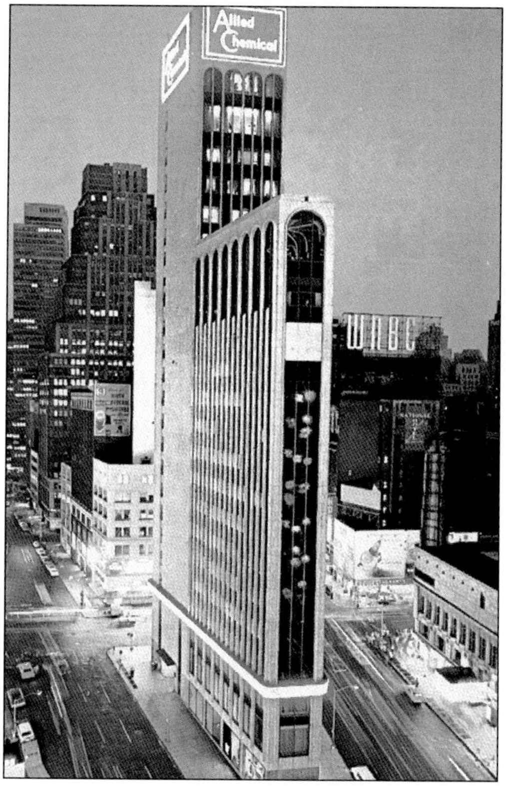

Douglas Leigh, master sign creator, bought the Times Tower in 1961, later selling to Allied Chemical. The new owner stripped the building to its skeleton, hiring Smith Smith Haines Lundberg and Waehler to design this marble-clad structure. Allied moved to New Jersey, and the building changed hands several times and was emptied above grade, becoming more valuable as a towering billboard, totally enveloped with signs. The 1935 Rialto, a theater, store, and office designed by Rosario Candela, at right, was demolished for 4 Times Square.

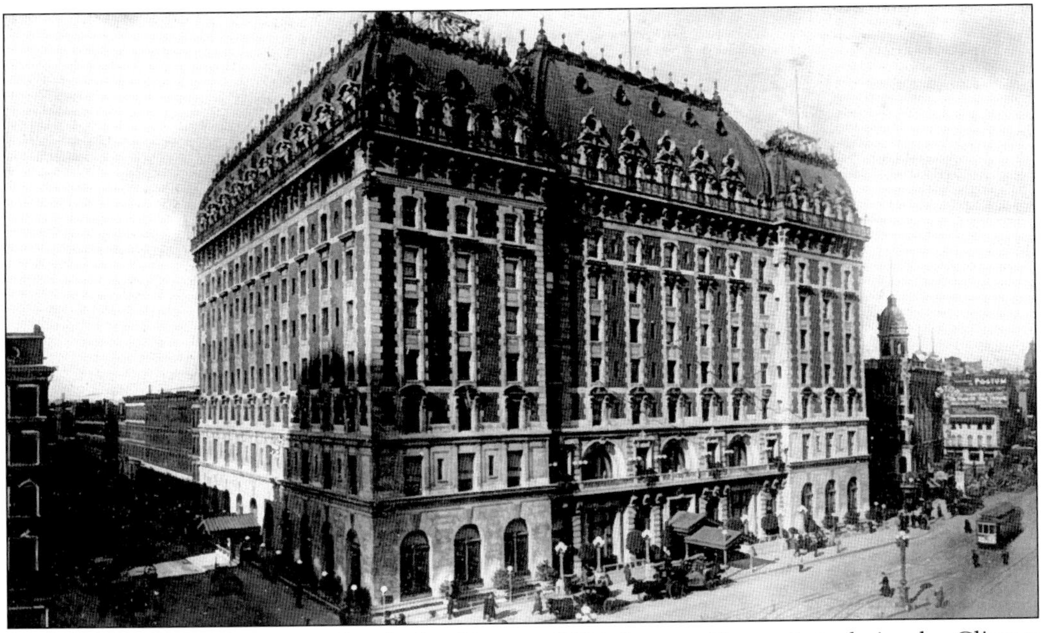

The first Times Square major hotel, the 11-story 1904 Astor, a Beaux-Arts design by Clinton and Russell, was an immediate success. Spanning the full block from 44th to 45th Streets, the hostelry soon demolished the residences behind, adding six bays around 1909. The Astor Theater on the 45th Street northwest corner, right, opened in 1909. The Astor, sold in 1954 to Sheraton, changed with the times and endured into the 1960s. However, well past its prime, it was razed in 1967–1968.

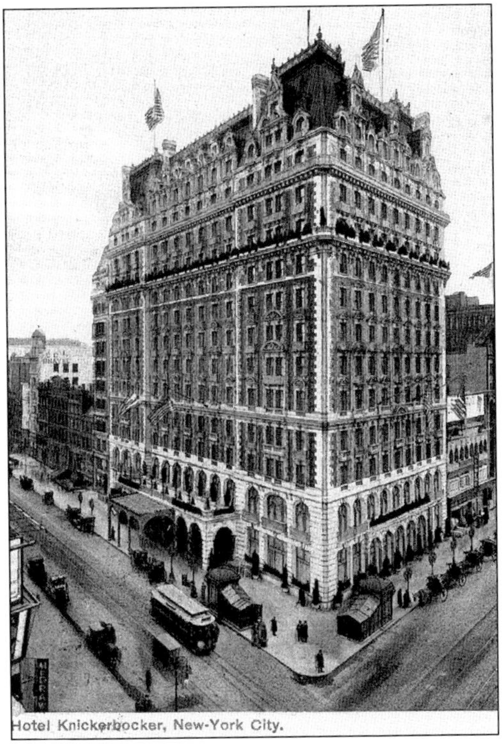

The Beaux-Arts Knickerbocker, designed by Bruce Price, demonstrated the rapidly changing demands on hotels. Construction was halted in 1905 as the rising stature of Times Square required amenities beyond those anticipated three years earlier. Trowbridge and Livingston planned a massive interior modification that raised the Knickerbocker's cost 50 percent by the 1906 opening. The Knickerbocker was fading a decade later and in 1920 was remodeled as offices. That role endures, although plans to reconvert to hotel use have surfaced.

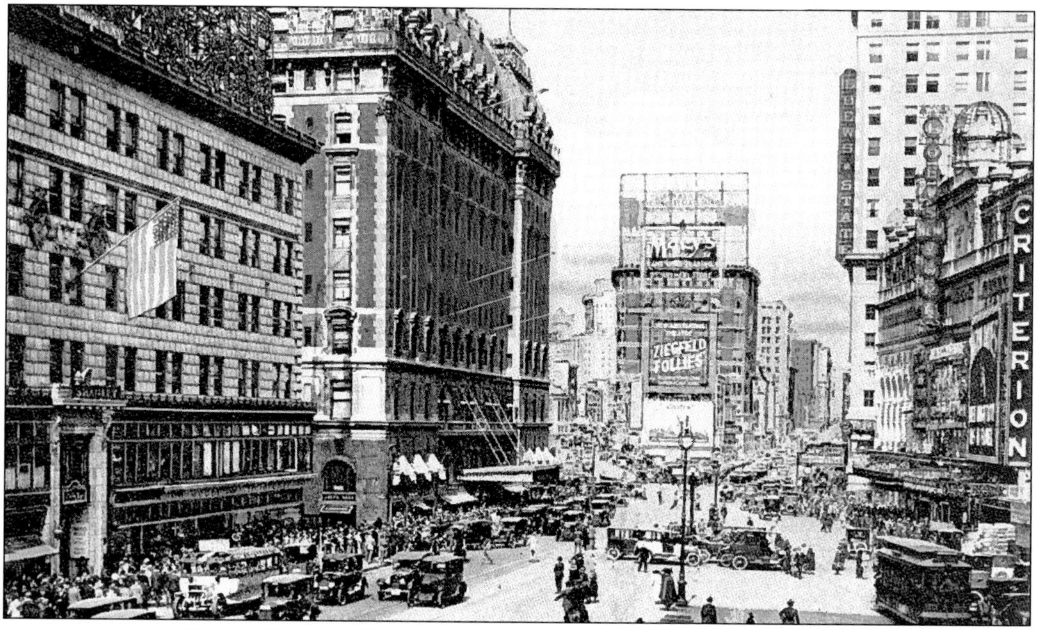

The Putnam Building, left, seemed appropriate there when completed in 1909 by Col. John Jacob Astor, replacing the Barrington Hotel. The site was celebrated for a meeting of Gen. George Washington and Gen. Israel Putnam on September 15, 1776, after the debacle Battle of Brooklyn. Rapidly rising values underscored underutilization of the block; the Putnam fell in 1925 for the Paramount. Oscar Hammerstein's 1895 Olympia Theater, designed by John B. McElfatrick, filled the east side block between 44th and 45th Streets. It was demolished in 1935.

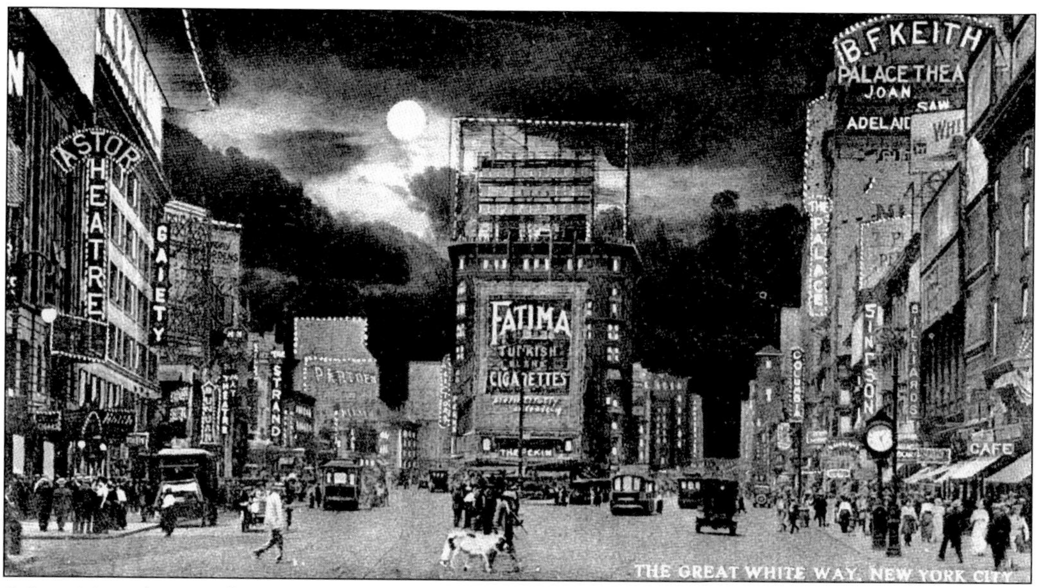

Advertising signs making Times Square "the Great White Way" are so well rooted that early alarms are historically curious. The *Times* of September 10, 1910, headlining "New Electric Signs Offending the Eye," examined the issue and compliance with zoning regulations but noted there was no bar to the erection of signs or freak buildings to hold them. The significance of signage was clear by century's end when regulations required new buildings to display signs.

The dramatic impact of Times Square lit at night is perceived around 1931 even when the built environment appears little more than a silhouette.

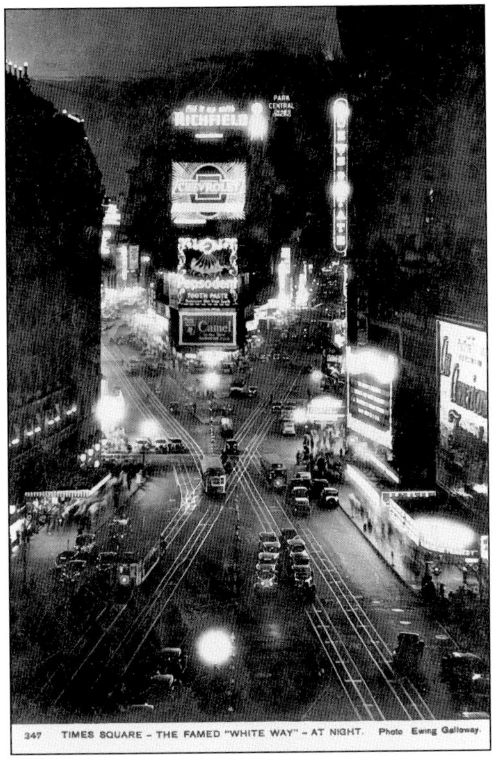

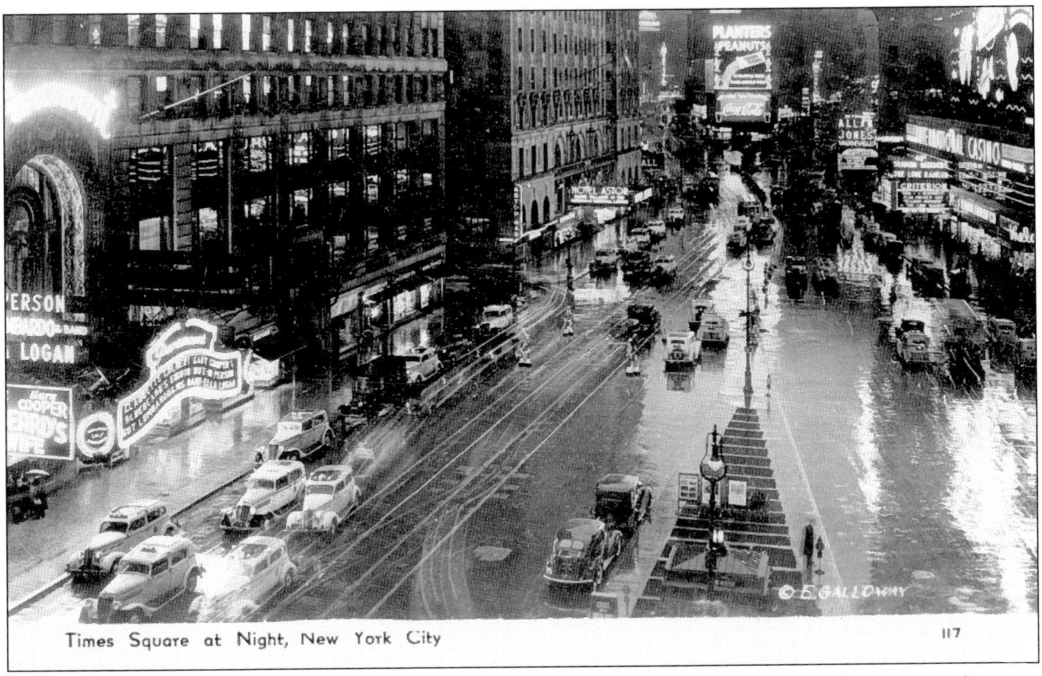

The huge 4,000-seat theater in the 1927 Paramount Building included top live entertainment in its prime. The first sign on the International Casino is visible at right, a Wrigley's gum packet with colorful fish. First lit on March 28, 1936, the 75-by-192-foot sign was the country's most awe-inspiring advertisement. Note two-way traffic in 1938, unimaginable now.

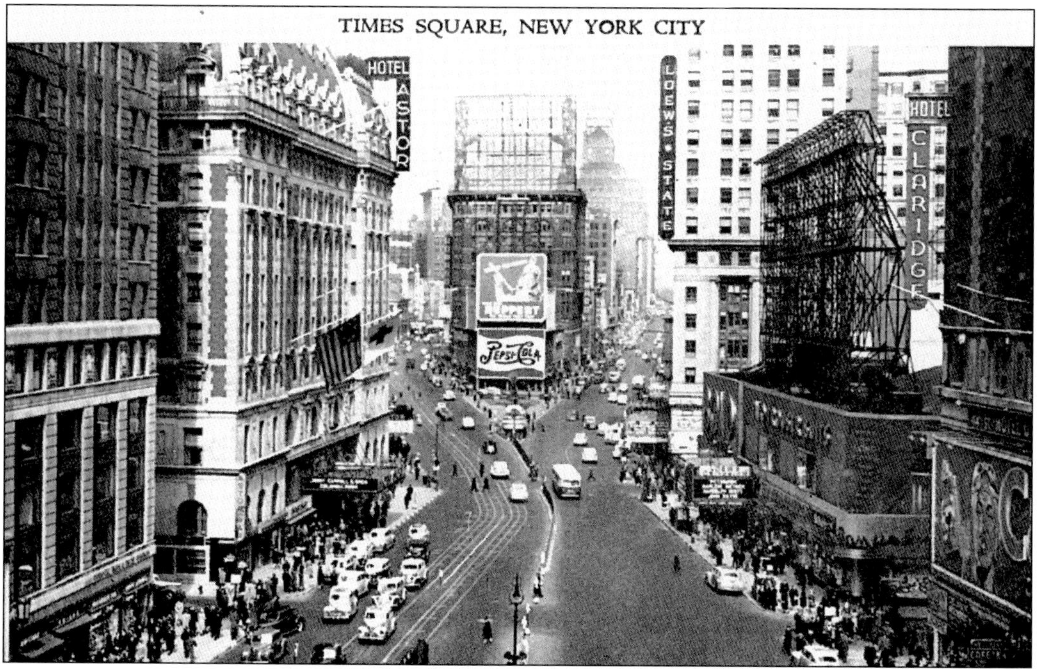

Wartime lighting restrictions dimmed the night, occasioning dismantling of the Wrigley sign where only its structure is seen. The sign's 29,508 lamps and 1,084 feet of neon tubing cost an estimated $10,000 monthly. The building, designed by Acock and Lloyd, replaced the Criterion and New York Theaters in 1935. It stands, signage concealing its appealing art moderne lines.

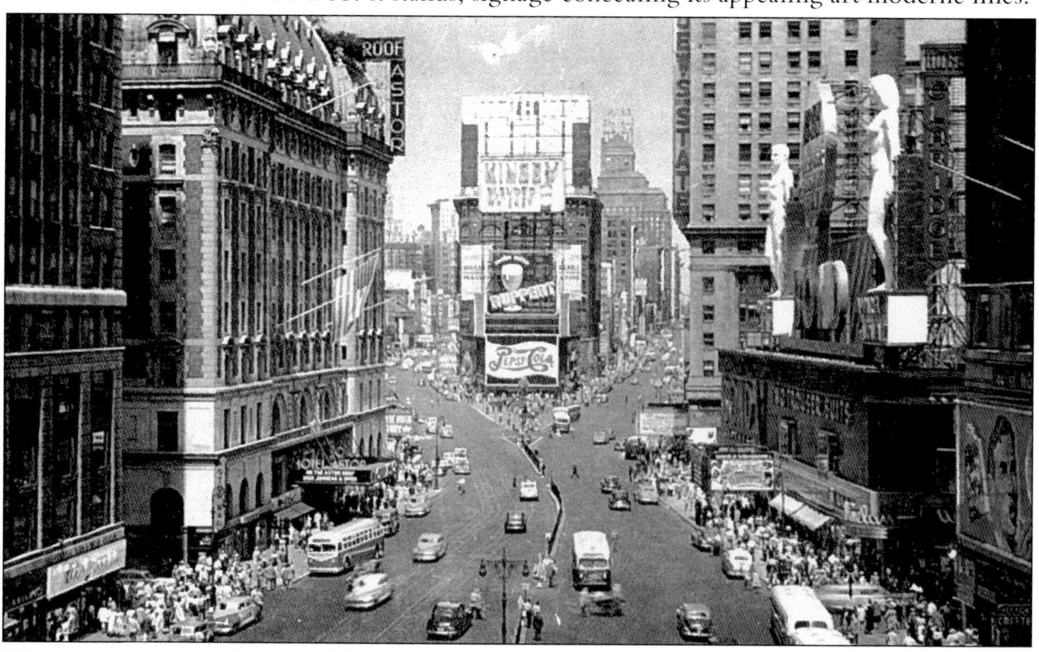

Theater marquees and automobiles date Times Square images. However, the word over "Astor" provides broader timing classification. Early ones specified "Hotel," later replaced by "Roof," in turn replaced by "Sheraton" following its purchase in 1954. Are those figures nude? See the top of page 91 for the bare truth.

Where does Seventh Avenue, clearly a straight, north–south street running from bottom left to top right around 1947, go when it crosses Broadway? It "disappears" from 42nd to 47th Streets, a stem where both sides of the crossroads have Broadway addresses. As new addressing practices use numbers preceding Times Square, without suggesting locale, maps will be needed for the short distance.

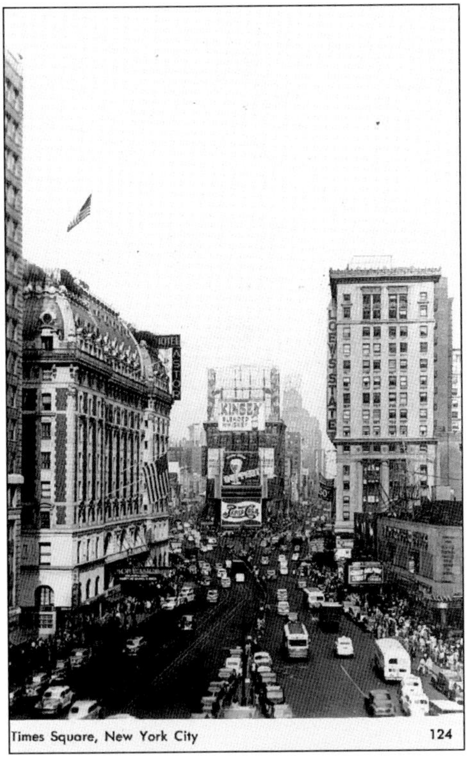

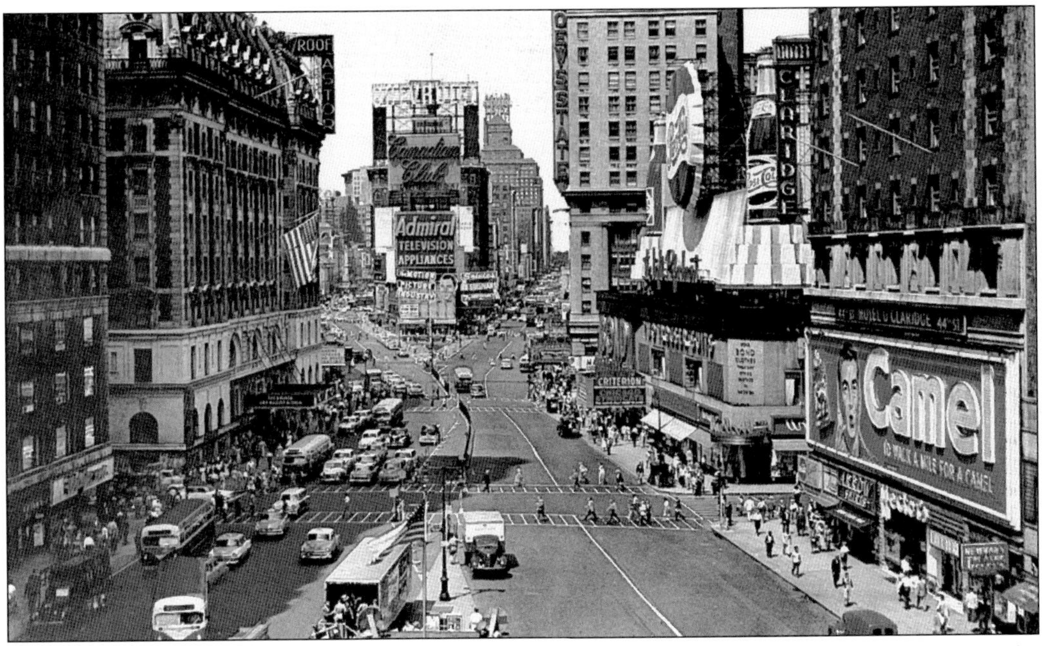

Two gigantic Pepsi bottles replaced the Bond figures in 1955. Wartime exigency inspired the Camel sign at right. Wanting an impact not necessitating lights, master sign developer Douglas Leigh recalled a parlor trick involving blowing smoke in a cellophane wrapper, then tapping the wrapper to cause smoke rings to emerge. Employing a similar principle, the pictured figure on the sign, a soldier during the war, blew two-foot-wide smoke rings every four seconds.

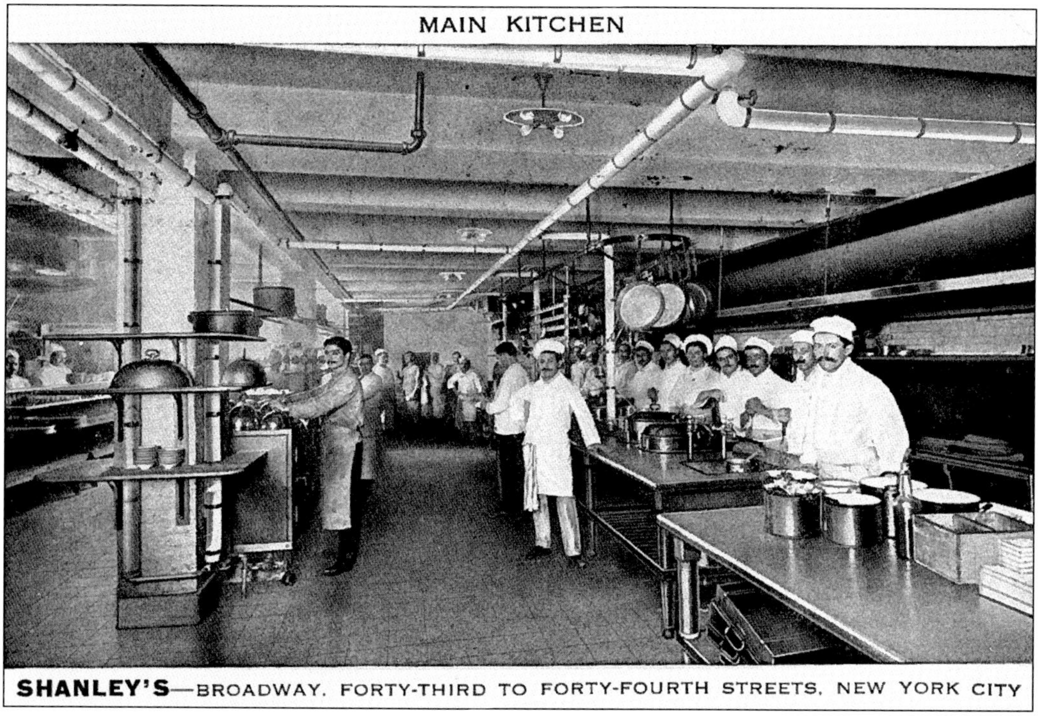

The Shanley brothers, initially Bernard and Thomas, Irish immigrants, opened their first restaurant on 23rd Street in the 1880s, moving to Broadway and 30th Street and later to the Longacre Building. This Putnam Building restaurant was their largest. Shanley's introduced cabaret-style entertainment to eating places. Labeled "lobster palace" for a principal viand, but alcohol dependent, they suffered from Prohibition's effects, which in 1922 killed them.

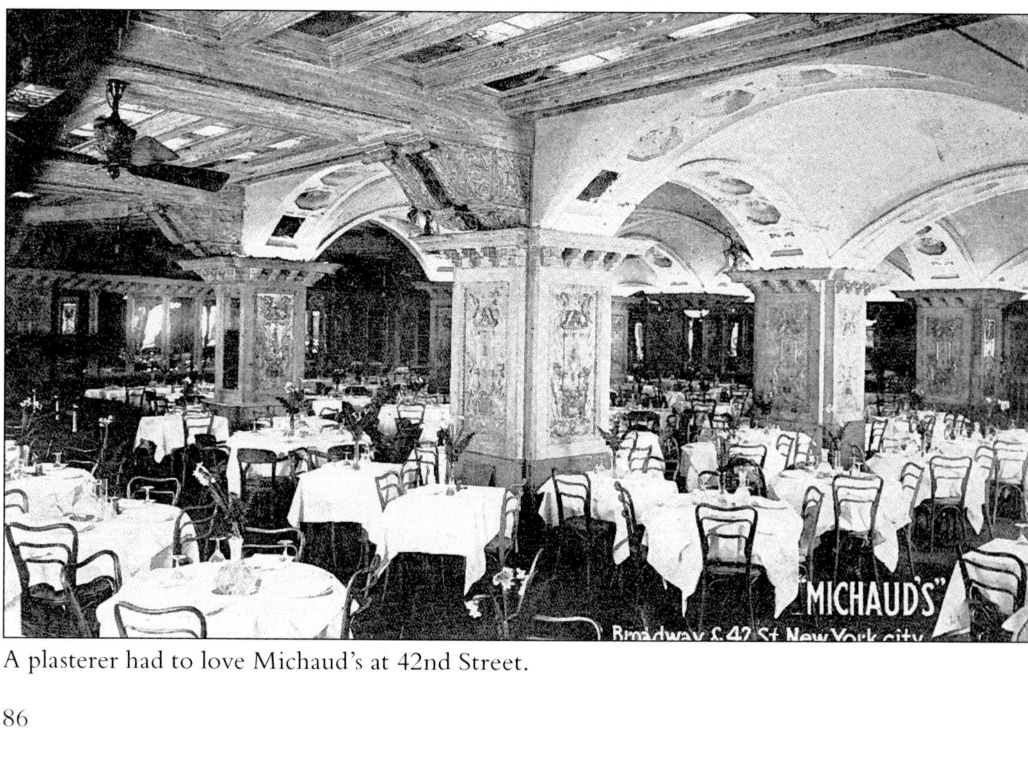

A plasterer had to love Michaud's at 42nd Street.

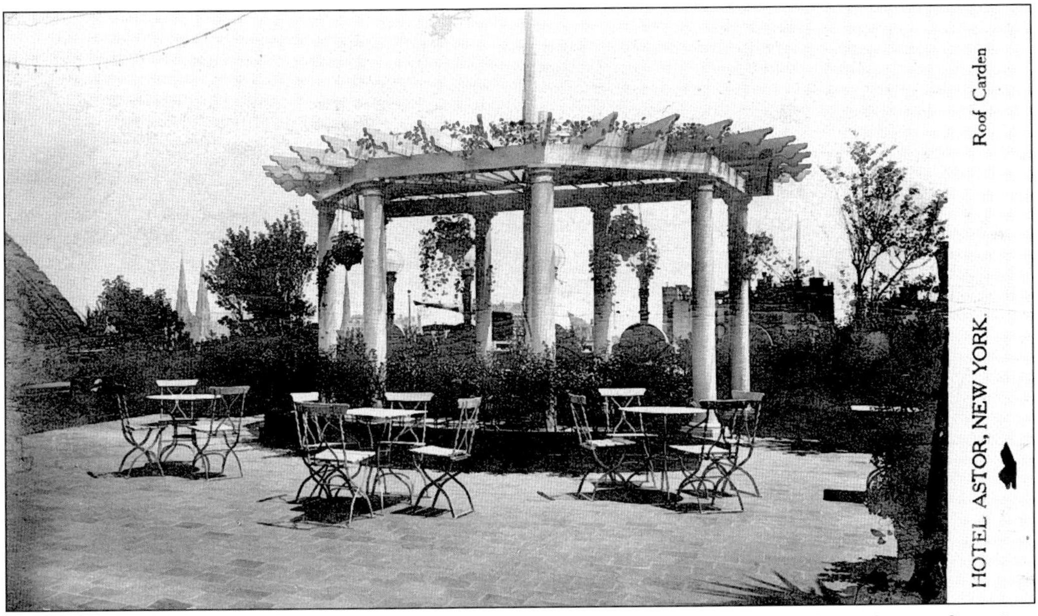

The Astor Roof Garden was the most prominent of the aboveground rooftop places of respite, which offered chances for cooling breezes before air-conditioning. Beverages, light food service, musical entertainment, and dance floors provided sustenance and amusement. Early Astor proffered Italian landscape effects, such as geranium-clad metal cupolas around 1906, the pictured pergolas hung with vines, and cleverly contrived mountain cascades. Over time, changing character included air-conditioning and soundproofing.

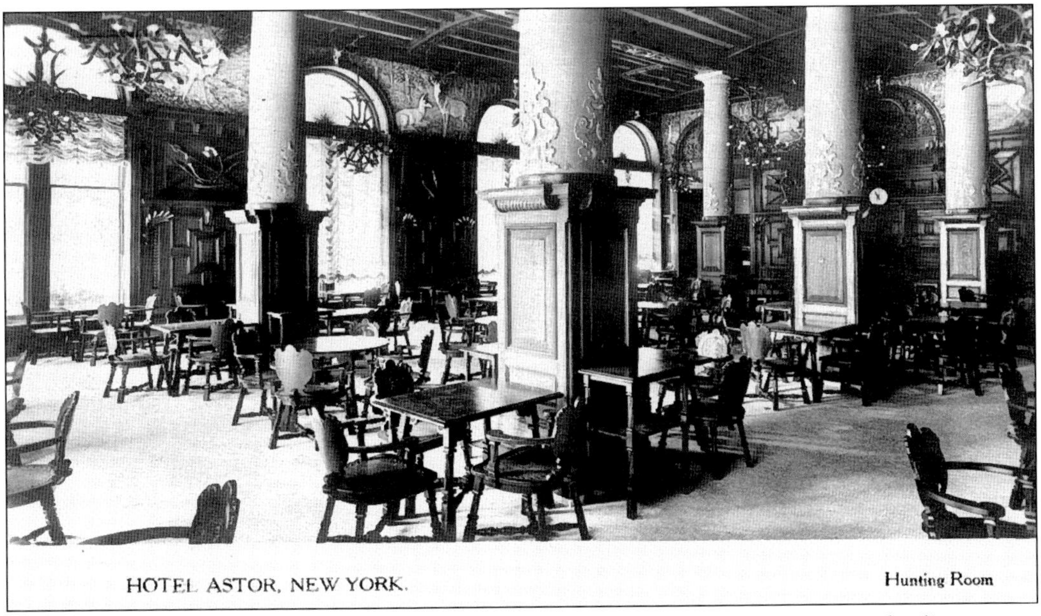

The skilled management of Fred and William Muschenheim made the Astor a leading venue for dining out. Indeed, "Meet me at the Astor" became a byword among the New York smart set, a place where diners were assured fine food served with grace in halls with varied ambiance and decor, such as this dark, richly decorated wood of the Hunt Room, around 1905.

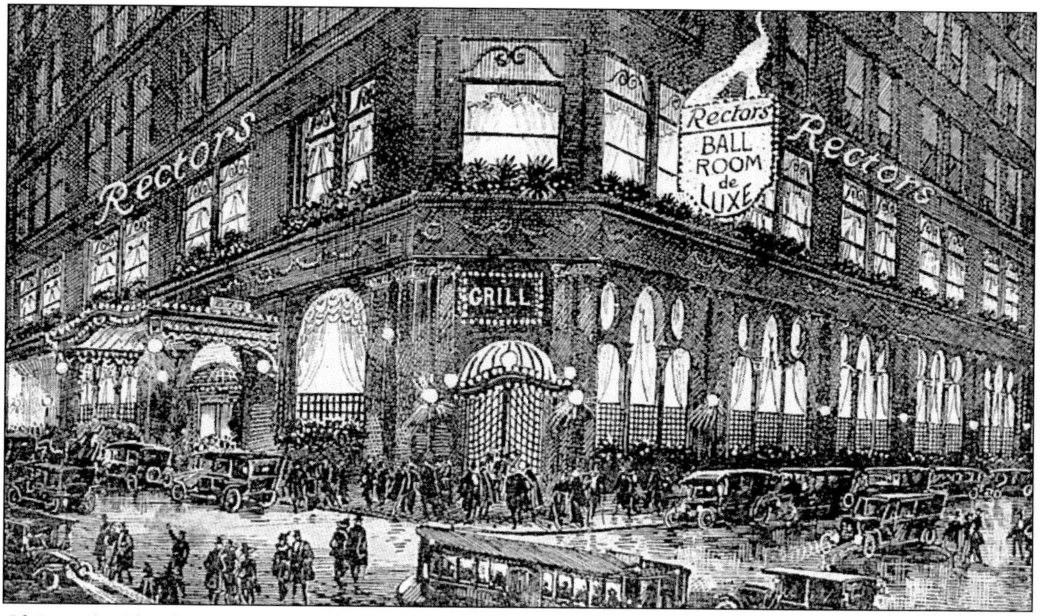

Chicago's Charles Rector, honing culinary skills at the 1893 World's Columbian Exposition, opened a lavish restaurant between 43rd and 44th Streets. Later the Hotel Rector was built there, the restaurant relocating to 48th Street. Rector's fall from the pinnacle of New York dining out was as rapid as its rise. Financial reverses led to its January 1, 1919, closing.

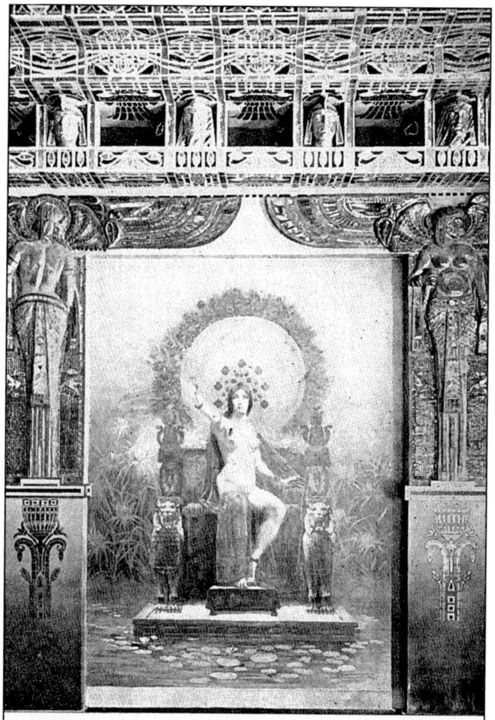

MURRAY'S, 42nd ST., NEAR BROADWAY
CIRCE IN PEACOCK ROOM

John Murray's Roman Garden, a lavishly decorated restaurant designed by Henry Erkins on 42nd Street just west of Broadway, combined entertainment with food for a new dining experience. Mirrored rooms, statuary, and other art filled the place, along with, perhaps unique among its genre, a revolving dance floor. The place could not survive Prohibition and closed in the 1920s.

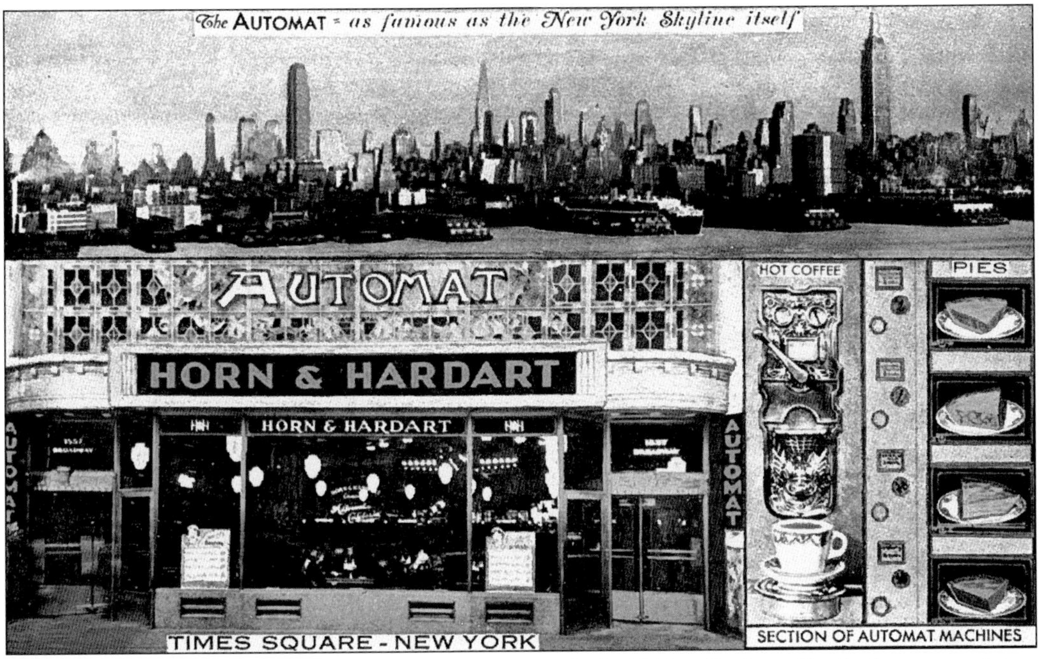

New York's first Automat opened at No. 1557 on July 2, 1912, offering a limited menu, pricing each item 5¢, enabling customers to vend food by dropping nickels in slots. Gargoyle-dispensed hot beverages were a trademark. Pictured in the 1930s, the chain started a slow decline in the 1960s, closing its last outlet in 1991.

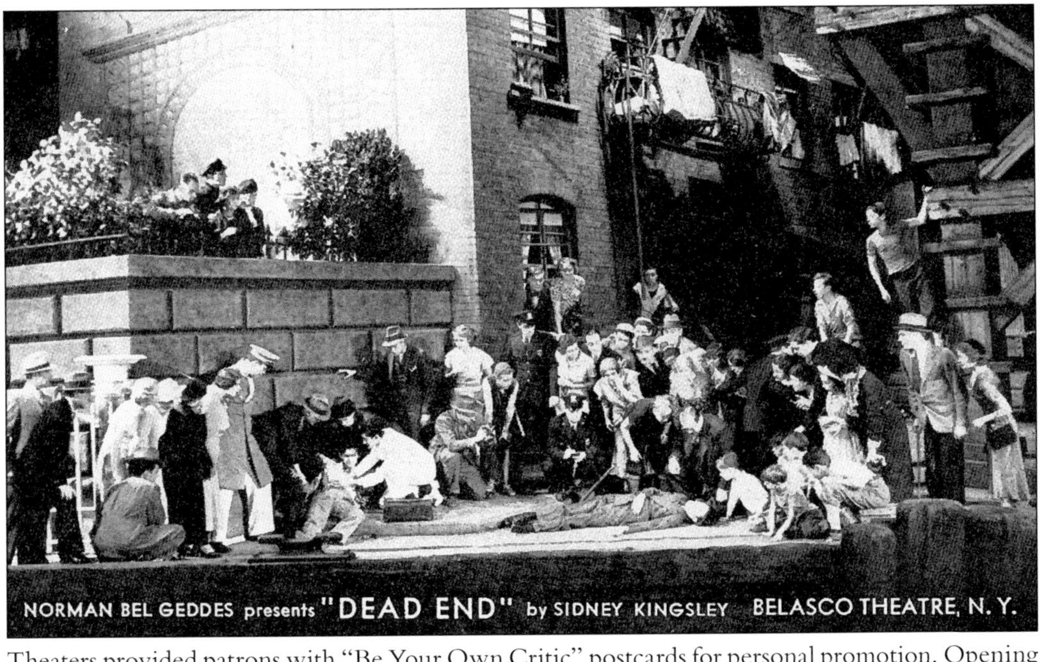

Theaters provided patrons with "Be Your Own Critic" postcards for personal promotion. Opening on October 28, 1935, *Dead End* ran for 684 performances. The house, the Stuyvesant when opened in 1907, was renamed for David Belasco following its rebuilding to his specifications. One wonders if management mailed critical comments.

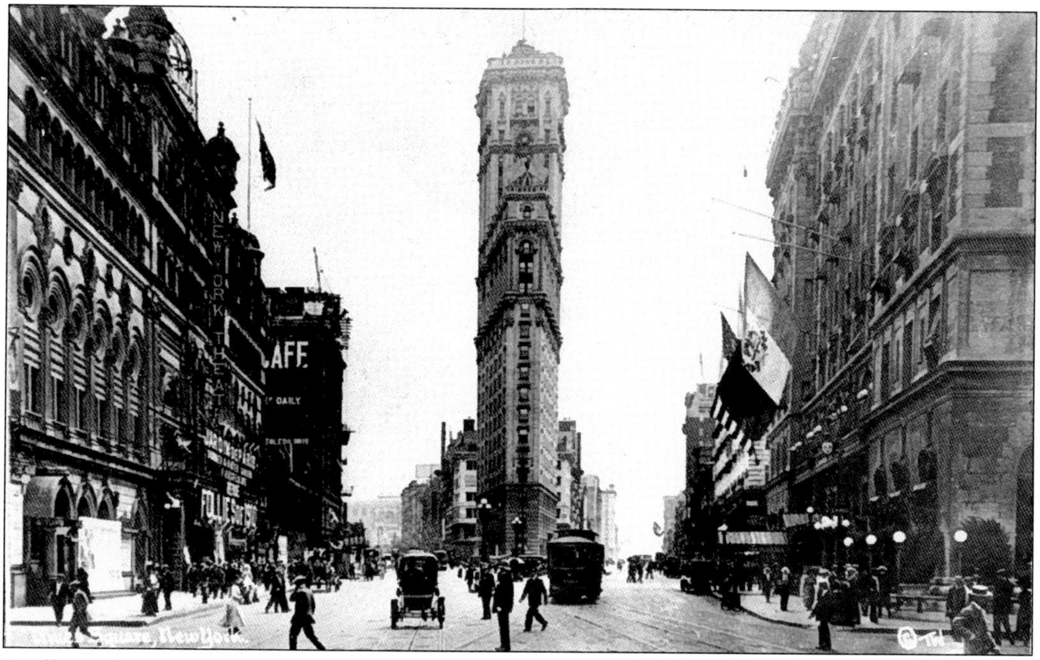

"Follies of 1910" dates this photographic card of Thaddeus Wilkerson, taken from 46th Street with the New York Theater at left and Astor at right. However, the pictured progress of the 1912 Longacre Building in the left background may suggest a date a year later. The photographer's prolific output centered on the Upper West Side. The former Hindenburg Building, behind the Times, was also under construction. (Courtesy of Joan Kay.)

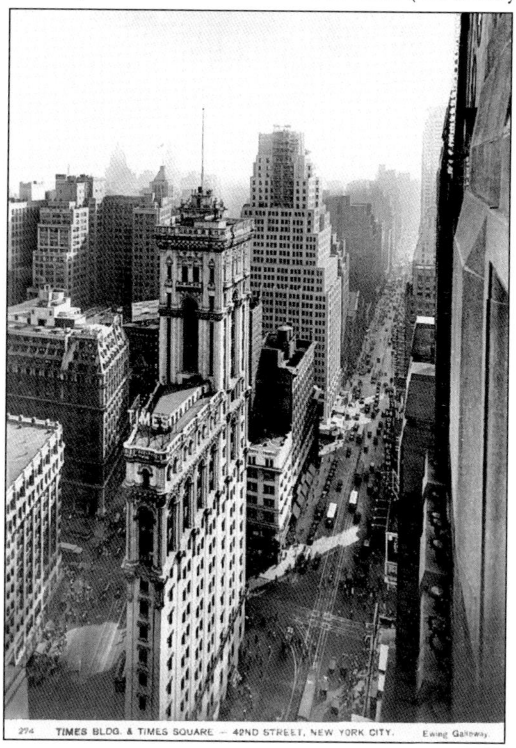

Looking down at rooftops is arguably the best standard for appreciating the height of nearby buildings. The Knickerbocker mansard is at left, the Longacre Building under it. The photographer leaned out the Paramount Building to show the Times roof close up, revealing the staff from which New Year's balls dropped. Down Seventh Avenue, the short blocks west to Broadway near the square are typically filled by a single building.

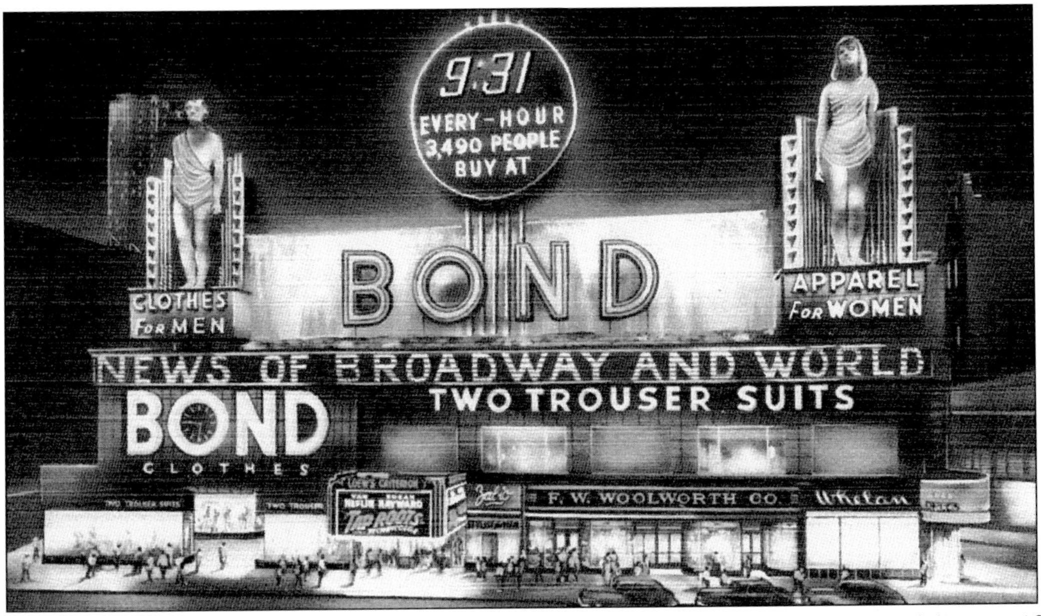

Bond Clothes was the provocative classic sign. These enormous plastic figures depicted discreet, if minimal, clothing at night. However, they appeared nude viewed in daylight, as on page 84. The sign, first lit on June 17, 1948, enjoyed a six-year run prior to demolition at the year-end in 1954. Bond's advertisement merits its own card, as it was then the largest and costliest sign ever.

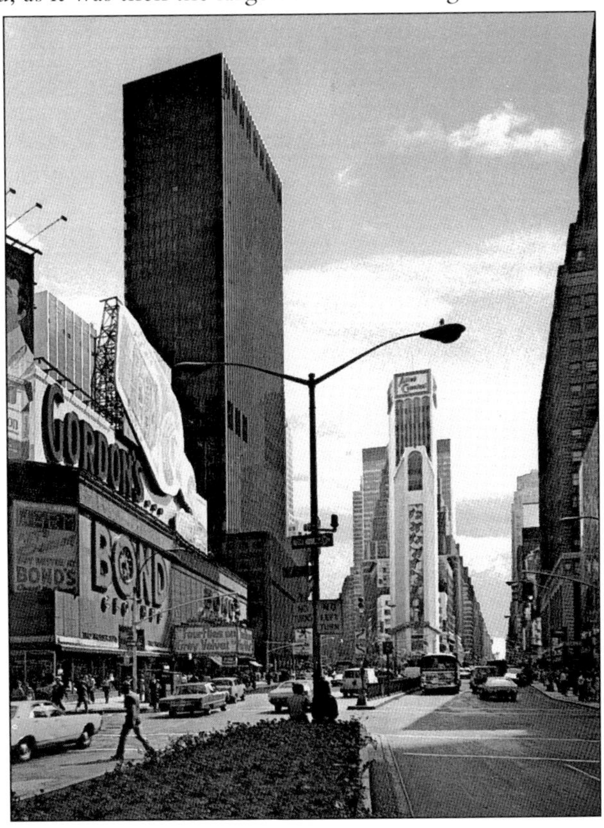

The 33-story glass tower at No. 1500, designed by Leo Kornblath, is depicted around its 1973 completion. Built on the Rector Hotel 43rd Street block, this office was the west side's vanguard of rebuilt Times Square, albeit undertaken well prior to the area's reaching rock bottom. Bond thrived, while a gin bottle took its roof in 1966, pouring constantly.

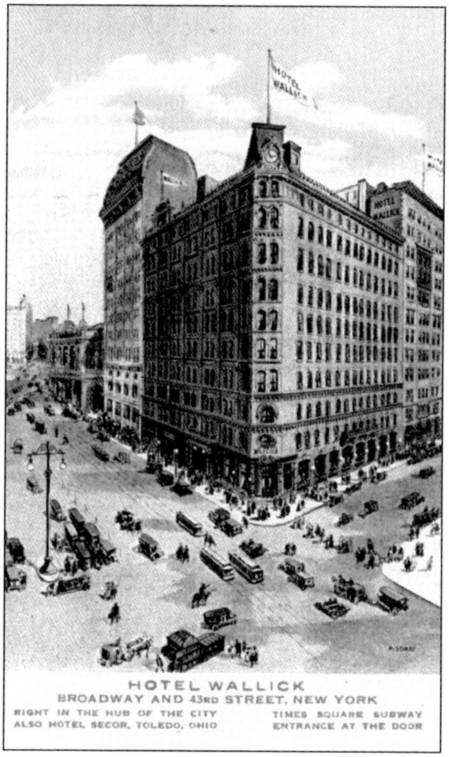

The Barrett House, built on the northeast corner of 43rd Street in the 1880s, changed to the Hotel Cadillac around 1898, and to Wallick around 1914. This crude white border dates from around 1915, prior to Wallick's large roof sign. The place, which retook the Cadillac name in the 1930s, was razed in 1940. One is getting old if he remembers "Cadillac" as a superlative.

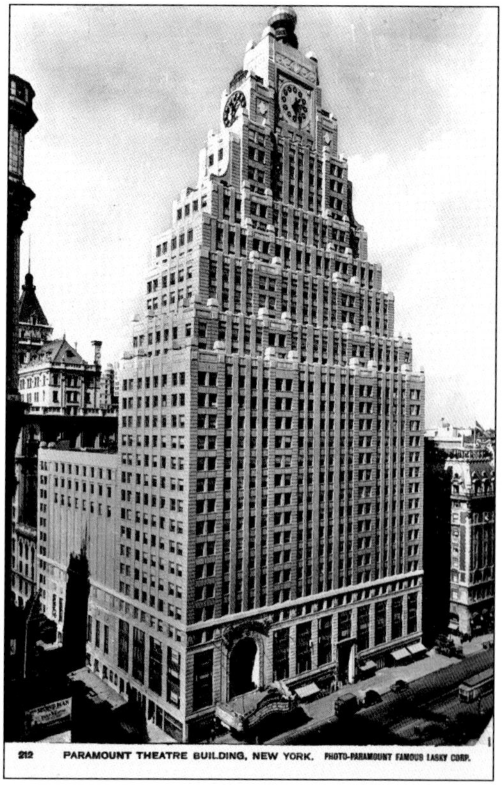

The 455-foot, 31-story Paramount Building, erected by Famous Players-Lasky Corporation, filled the 43rd–44th Streets block of the Putnam Building and the Westover Court houses. Designed by C. W. and George L. Rapp and completed in 1927, the buff-brick building's series of eight setbacks was a literal interpretation of the 1916 zoning law. The clock's 26-foot-diameter face was one of the country's largest, while different flashes from the globe marked each quarter hour. The Paramount marked the last major Times Square construction prior to World War II. The Times Annex is in the left background.

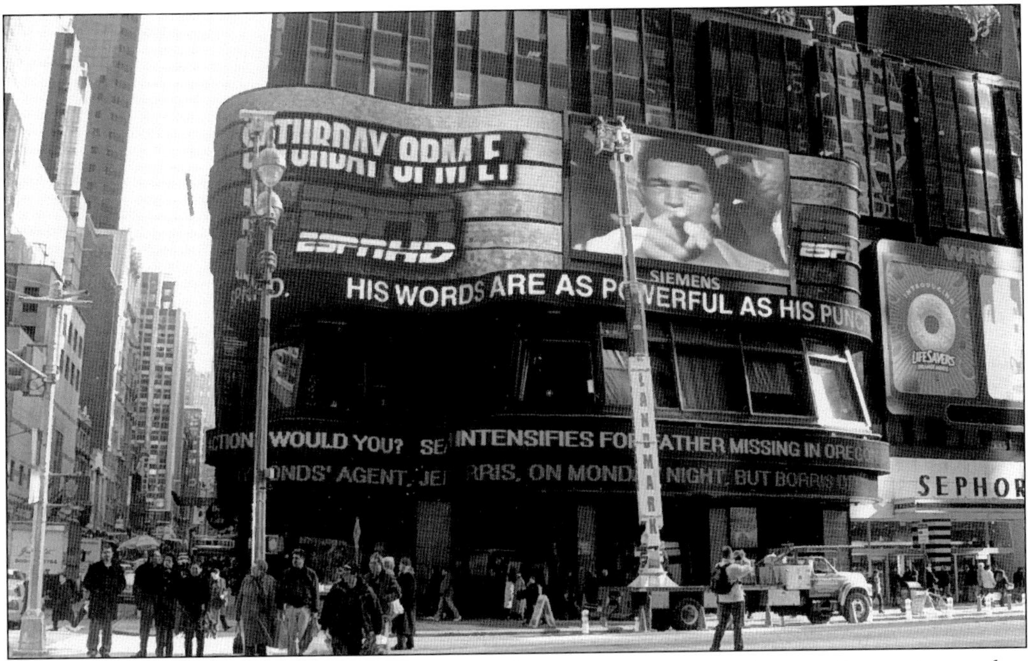

From the single row of lights in the "zipper" that circled the Times Tower, Times Square has turned into a light show, with multiple lines of text and changing pictures. This scene may be familiar from the American Broadcasting Company. The author took the photograph, initially believing the pictured words referred to himself, but then thought better of it.

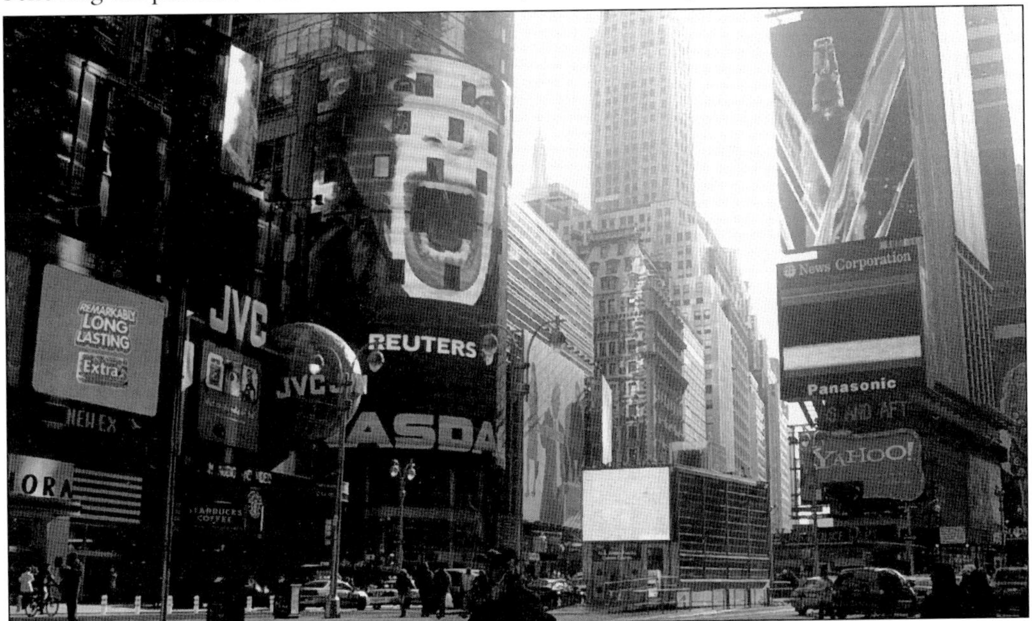

The flashing, changing NASDAQ sign on the Conde-Nast Building was caught in 2006 with a mouth-agape face, perhaps mimicking a bedazzled tourist. Is old Times Square visible? Yes, spot the words "and aft" on the Times news "zipper." The building, empty above grade, is totally covered by signs, usage that produces greater rental income than office occupancy. Note the Knickerbocker's mansard.

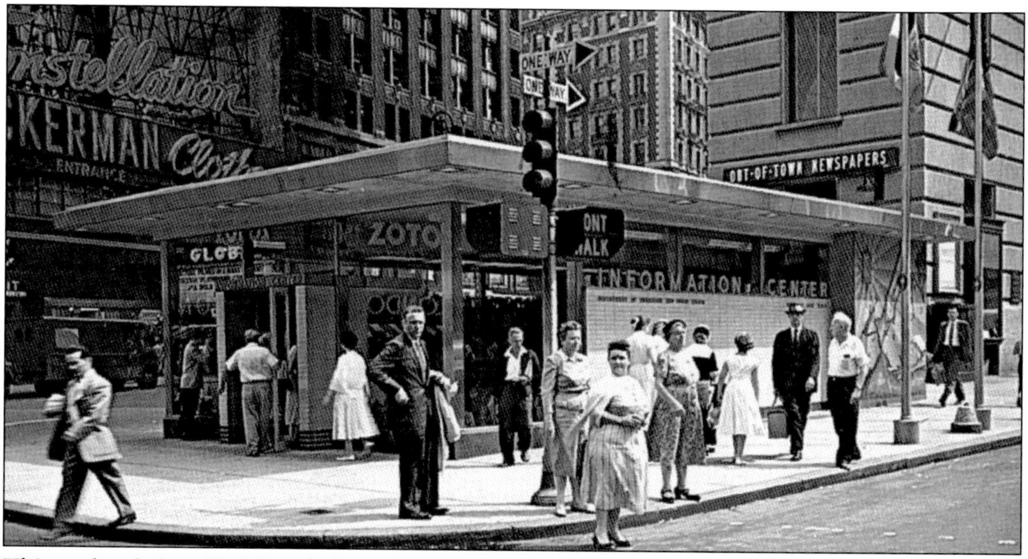

This steel and glazed brick and glass information center designed by the New York City Department of Public Works was erected on the Times Tower's edge in 1957. It began operating in November but was "officially" opened on March 18, 1958. The police department, which previously staffed an information kiosk on the site, sought replacement to better use its forces. The roof was since raised, while a military recruitment center is in the building now, euphemistically called an "Armed Forces Career Center."

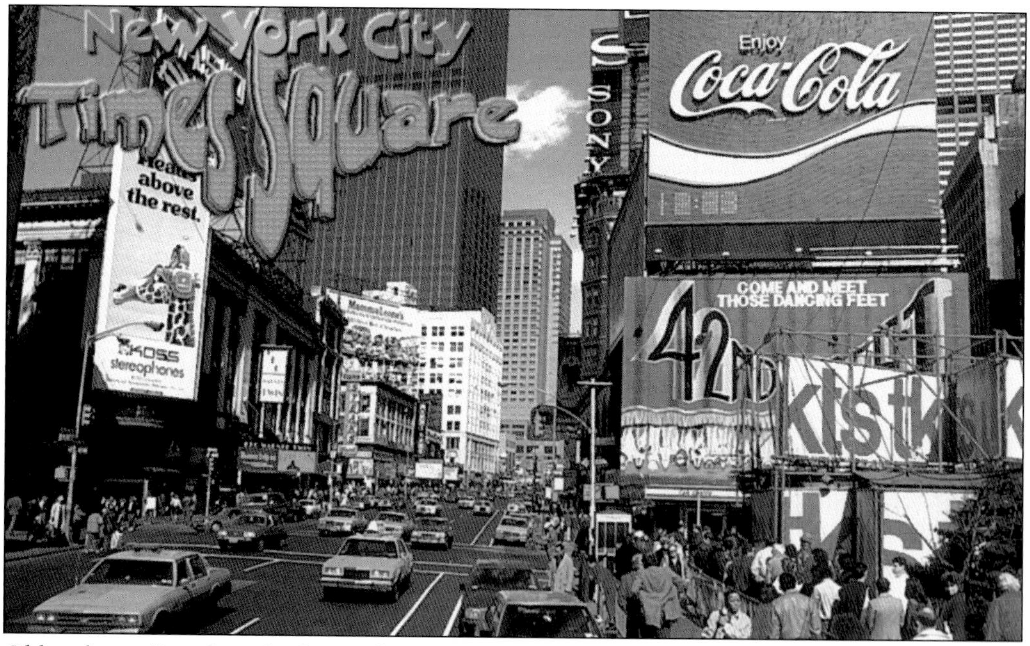

Old and new Broadway looks north around 1986 from 47th Street just prior to the demolition of the Strand (later Warner) Theater at left and as No. 1675, background, was rising. Between the two are the former Churchill's Restaurant (later a theater), demolished that year, the 1931 Brill Building, and a piece of the 48-story, 1972 Uris Building at 50th Street. The TKTS booth, which opened in 1973 to promote theater attendance, sells an enormous number of discounted tickets on the day of performance.

Seven

The Duffy Square Region

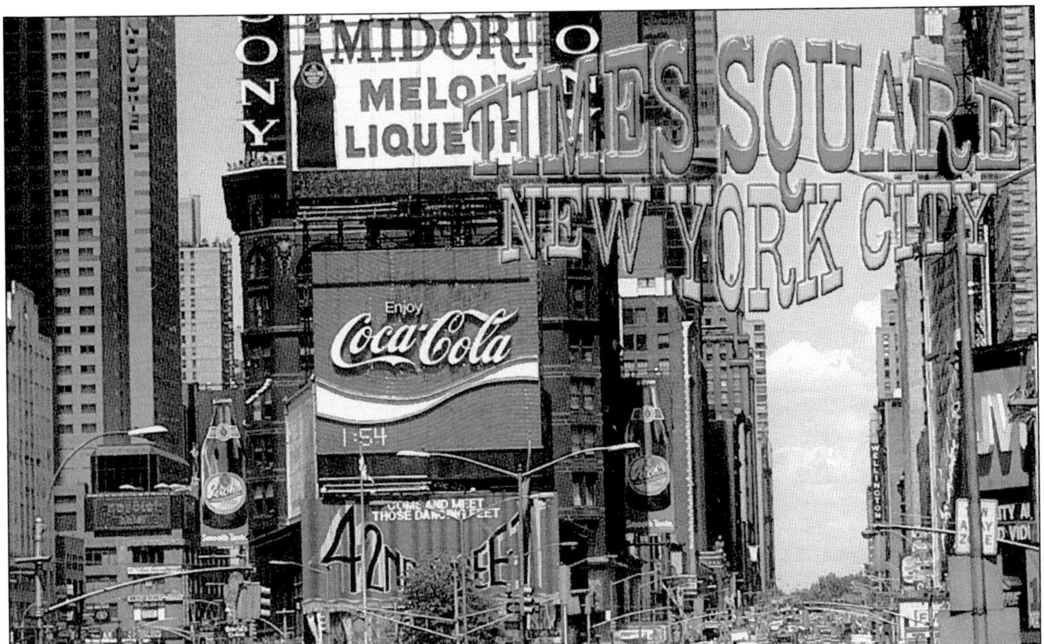

Studebaker's 1902 erection of its 10-story carriage building at 1600, the block between 48th and 49th Streets, appears poorly timed, but who knew the industry would soon depart Longacre Square. It, too, left in nine years. The sign-laden James Brown Lord design was obscured in its later years. Indeed, the building was an early indicator of signage revenue potential when Kellogg paid a then-huge near-$25,000 annually in 1910 for a rooftop touting of cereal. Studebaker's was visually obliterated by the 1990s construction of a hotel on the site of the Coke sign, and it too fell in 2004, replaced by a 26-story residential condominium.

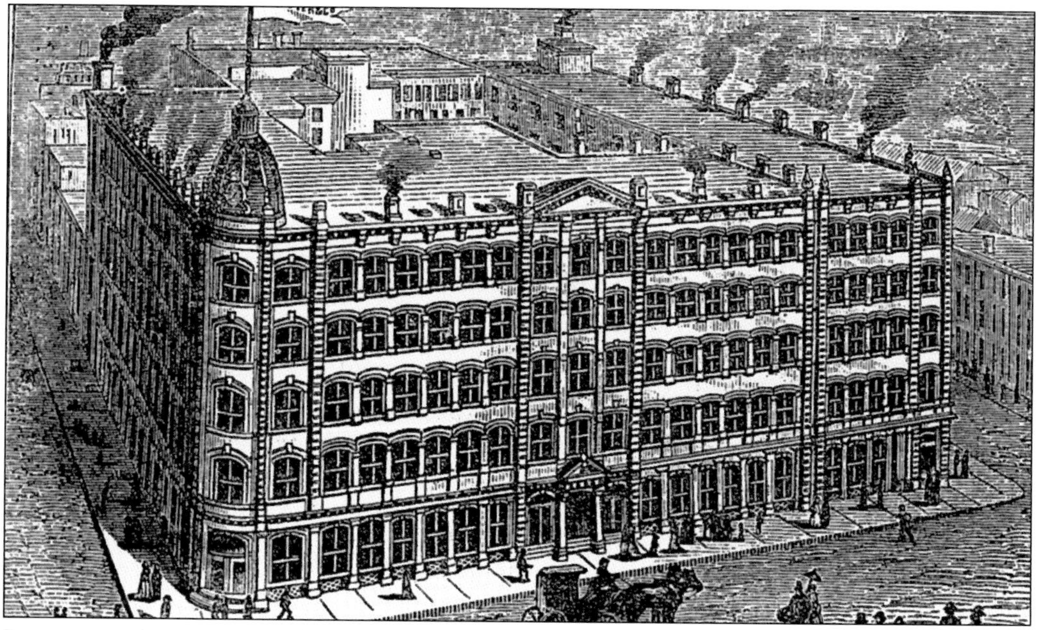

Brewster and Company's 1874 relocation from Broome Street to the west side between 47th and 48th Streets established the carriage industry in a desolate fringe. Its massive, full-block factory was imposing when new according to *Harper's Weekly* on June 9, 1877, and was built in an area called "goatville," on a site that William Brewster, grandson of the founder, recalled as "covered with enormous rocks." When Brewster departed in 1910, its building, looking forlorn and out of place, was slated for demolition, replaced by the Strand Theater in 1914 and in 1990 by the tower at 1585 Broadway.

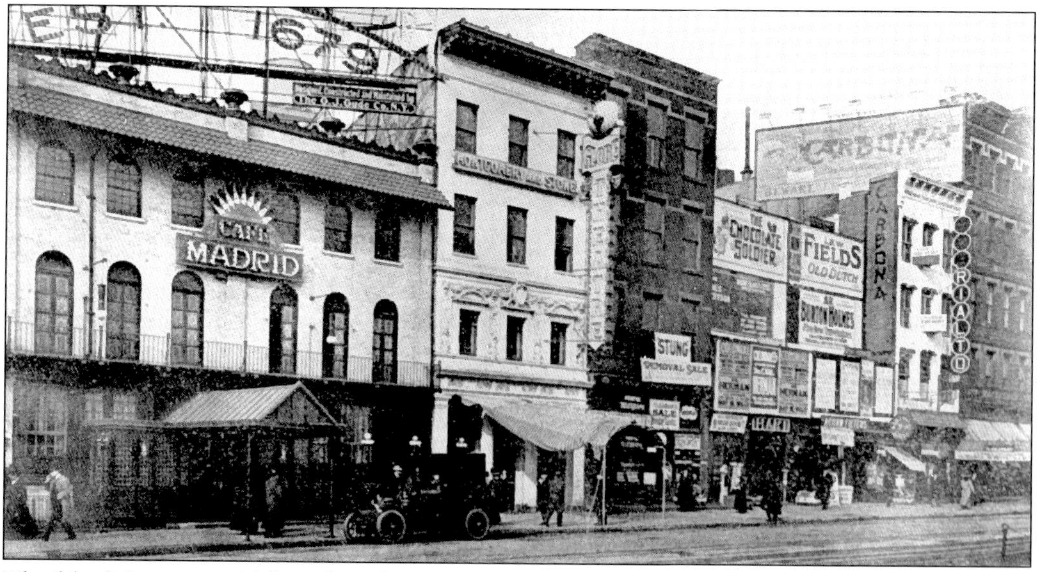

The block between 46th and 47th Streets reflected around 1910 impending change. The narrow Globe entrance opened to an expansive space on 46th Street. It is better known as the Lunt-Fontaine. A new eatery involved big names in Times Square restaurant annals. The Café Madrid, opened in 1905 by George Churchill, was sold to George Rector and Company four years later but was bankrupt in 1912.

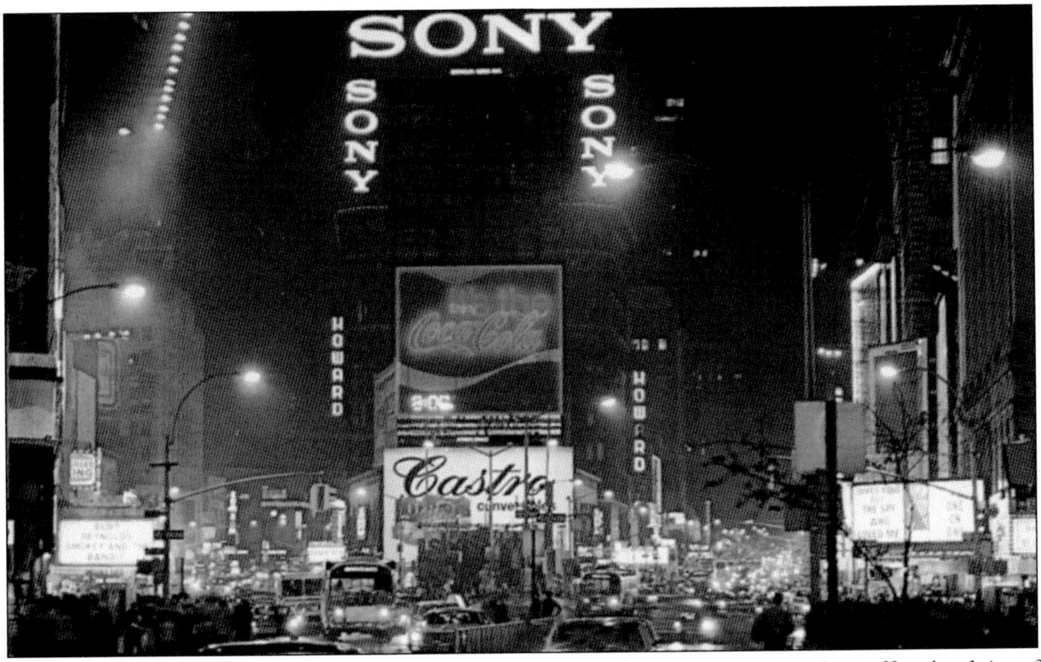

Northern Times Square is actually Duffy Square, named for Francis Patrick Duffy, chaplain of New York's famed 69th Regiment and later pastor of 42nd Street's Church of the Holy Cross. Father Duffy, who was born 1871 in Ontario, Canada, ordained in 1896, and died in 1932, is memorialized by Charles Keck's statue, installed in 1937 and visible in the background.

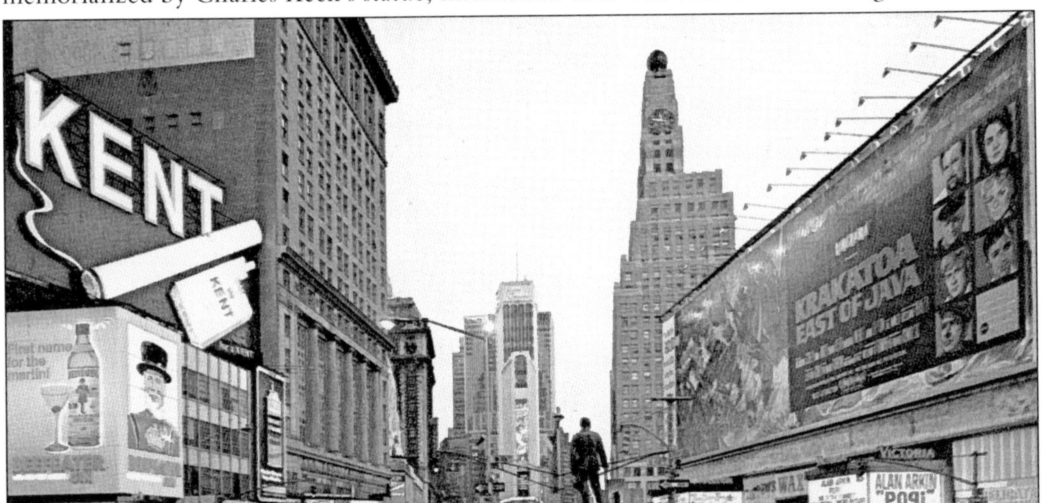

George Lorbor's 1959 statue of George M. Cohan, of *Give My Regards to Broadway* fame, is silhouetted between the Times and Paramount Buildings around 1979. The Loew's State at left on the northeast corner of 45th Street, completed in 1921 to Thomas W. Lamb's design, was demolished in 1987.

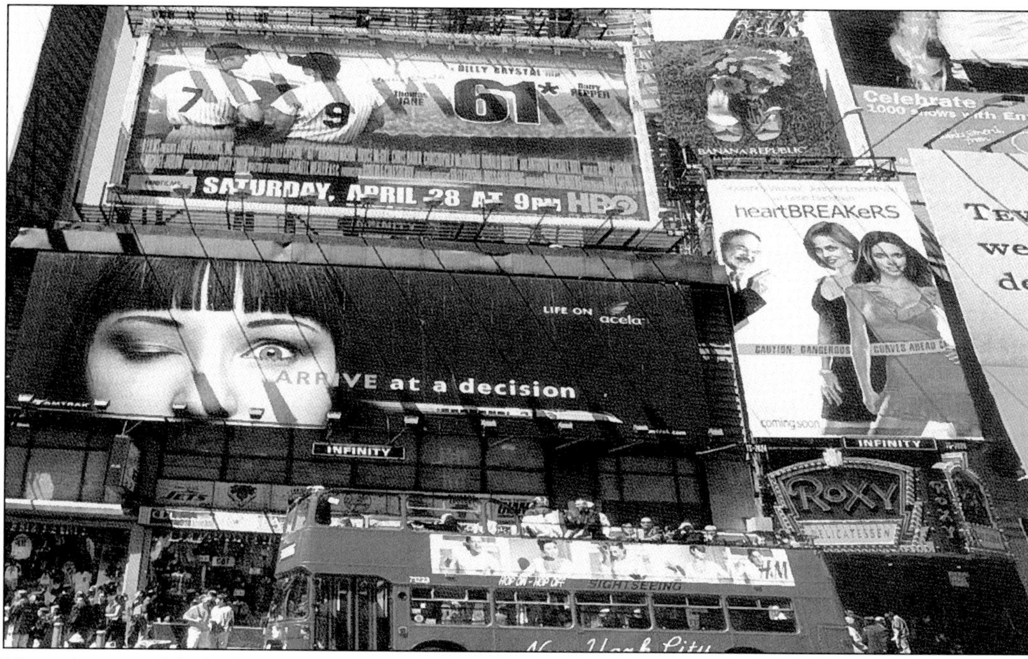

New signs readily hide old structures in Times Square, this on the west side from 46th to 47th Streets. Few diners at the pictured delicatessen remember its namesake, long-gone theater and/or the master movie mogul who built it, S. L. "Roxy" Rothenthal.

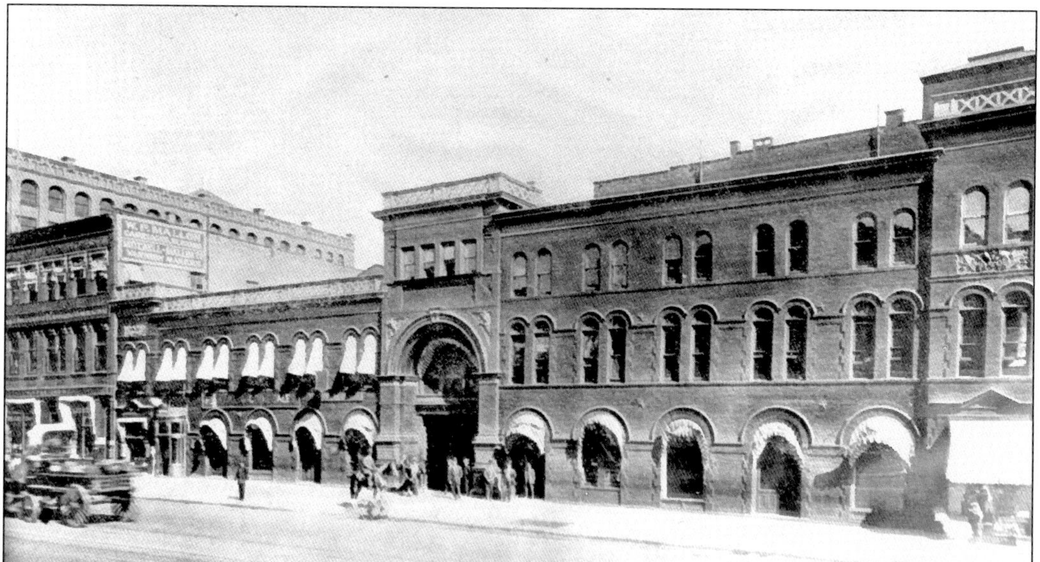

The American Horse Exchange spanned the area's transformation from carriage days to entertainment center. Opened in 1880 for the sale of horses and livestock, the place was destroyed in August 1896 in a calamitous fire that killed dozens of horses. The *c.* 1910 image shows a replacement structure designed by Albert V. Porter. Although activity around 1900 is unclear, the site, secured by Schubert theater interests in 1909, was reported the next year as being torn down, to be replaced by a theater utilizing a portion of the old walls. That theater was the since-rebuilt Winter Garden. One can only speculate what of the horse exchange remains.

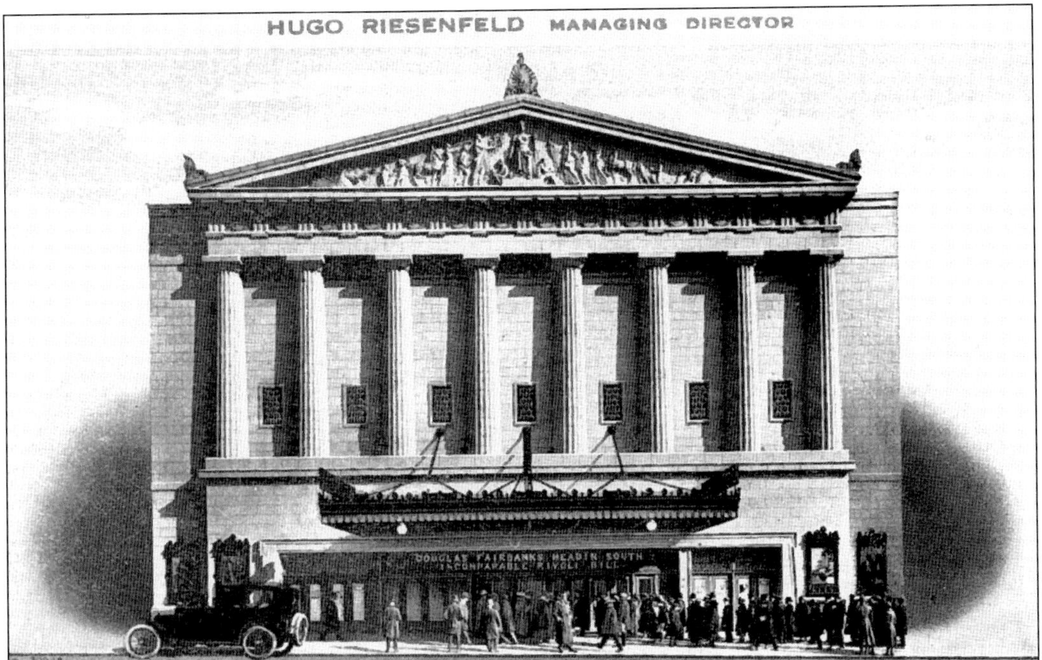

The Thomas W. Lamb–designed Rivoli Theater, which opened on December 28, 1917, marked a new elegance for the "Triumph of the Motion Picture," Rivoli's briefly utilized promotional slogan. Dominating the east side block between 49th and 50th Streets, once a motley collection of structures, the richly decorated edifice prompted metaphoric comparison with the Parthenon. The lush interior, foretelling the palaces built over the next decade, was predominately colored old rose but possessed a dome on which reflected light could appear to change the color pattern of the entire house.

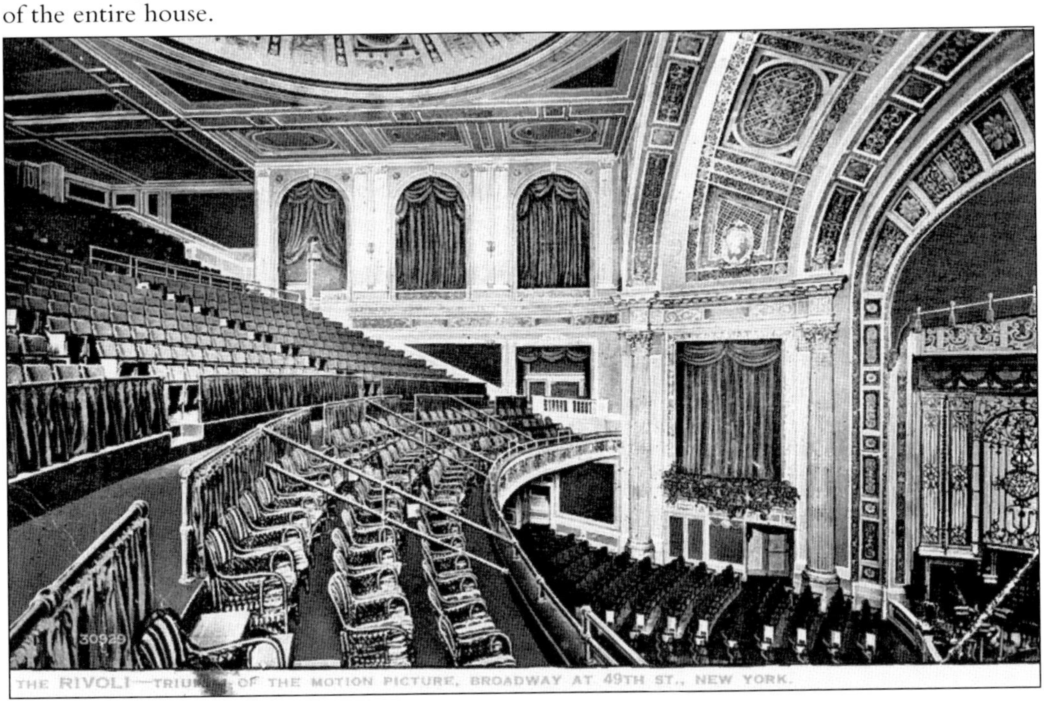

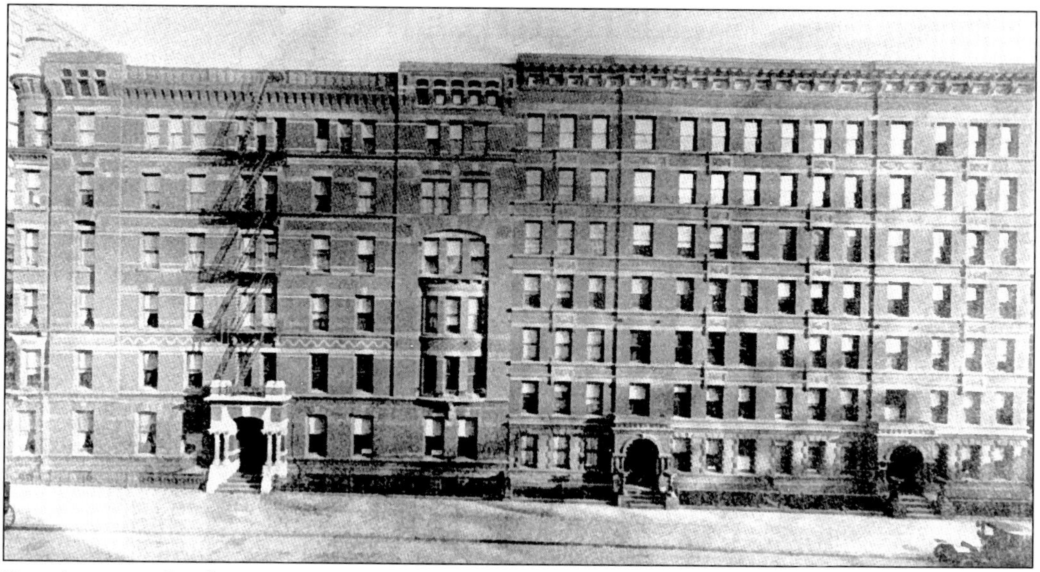

Broadway north of Longacre Square became a premier residential district in the 1870s. Many apartments were built in that and the following decades, including the Pocantico and Windsor. The construction of the subway elevated the apartment district north of Columbus Circle. The older residences endured, typically until replaced by automobile industry structures or hotels. The pictured sites were replaced in 1935 by a taxpayer, in turn replaced in 1969 by 1700 Broadway.

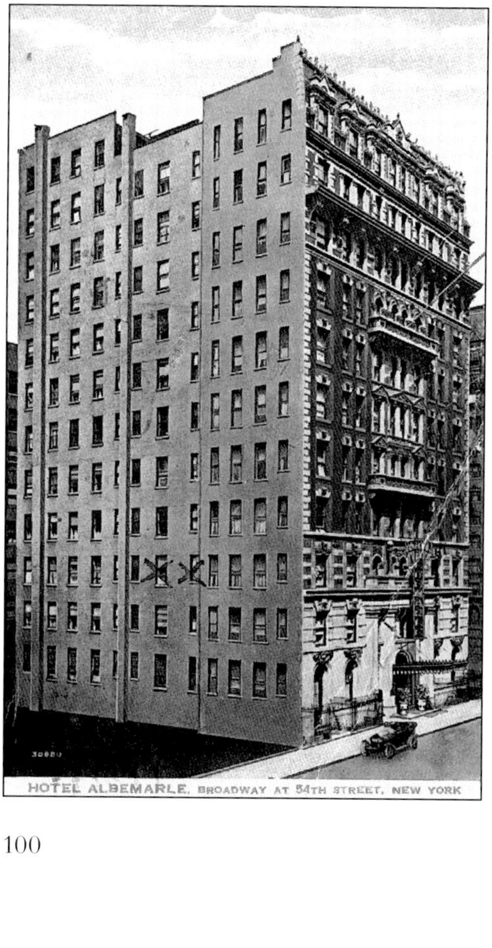

The value of a Broadway address prompted Hotel Albemarle's "inflating" its location to "Broadway at 54th," although "near Broadway" was truthful. Originating in the early 1900s as the Carlton, this Beaux-Arts Albemarle, confused with its 24th Street namesake, had other incarnations, including the Harding after Warren Harding's 1921 inauguration. Known as the Alba when foreclosed by Union Dime Savings in 1935, this failed hotel, remodeled into small apartments, was reported 85 percent rented two years later.

Nathan E. Clark built the Hotel Woodward, designed by George F. Pelham, completed in 1909 on the southeast corner of 55th Street, and named for lessee Robert Graham Woodward. The place is pictured in the 1930s with an edge of the 1917 Ford Motor Company building at right. The well-preserved building (minus its tower) was the Hotel Majestic until around 2005 when reborn after a luxurious interior reconstruction as the Dream Hotel.

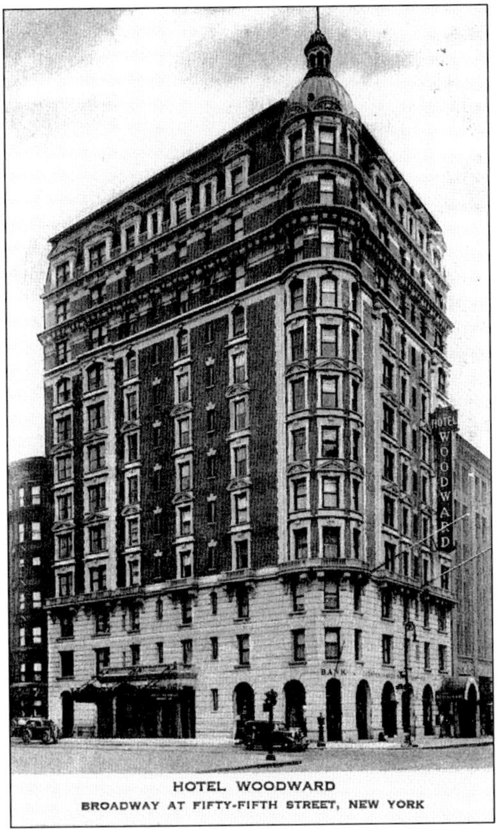

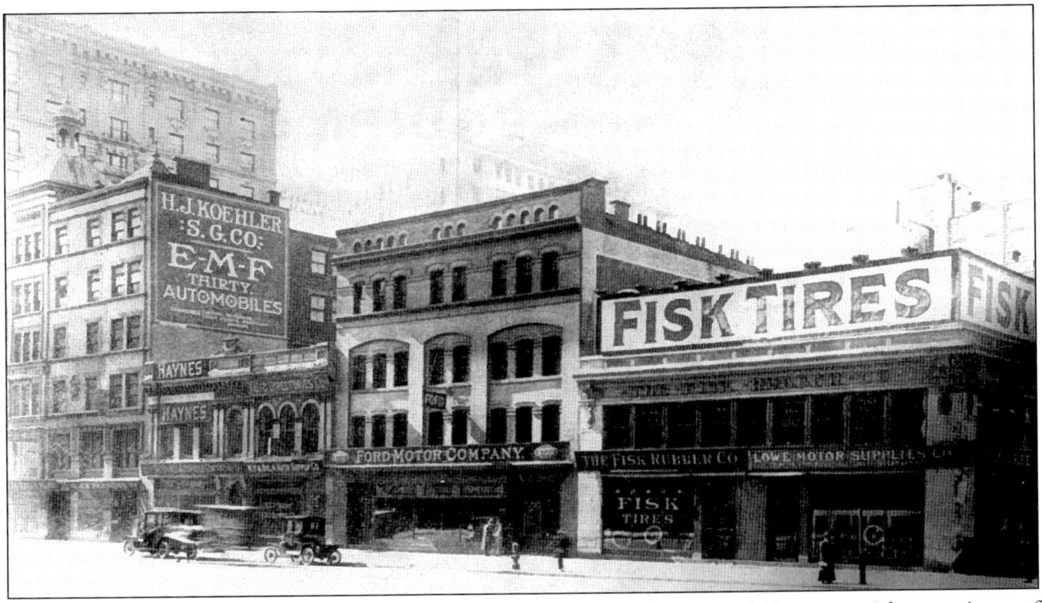

The west side between 54th and 55th Streets was typical automobile row with a variety of low-rise buildings housing eclectic occupants. Ford secured around 1917 an attractive building on the east side. Fisk built the tower on page 107 in 1921. La Premiere, a high-rise from the 1970s at No. 1721, now fills the street.

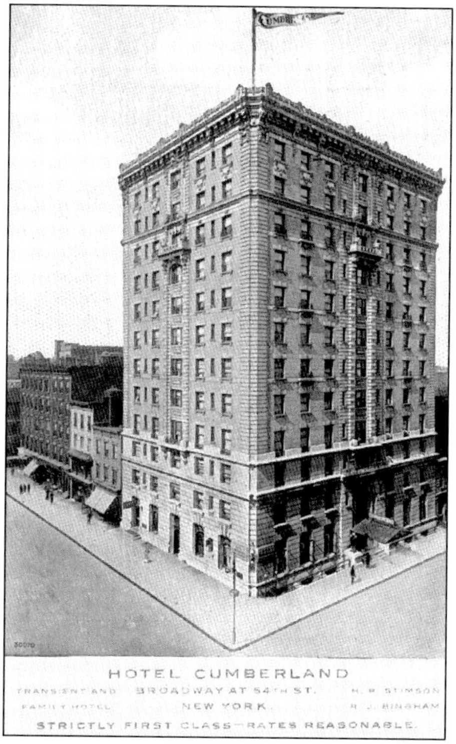

The Hotel Cumberland was completed in 1903 on the southwest corner of 54th Street, formerly filled by the Hotel Bayard. The appealing Renaissance Revival 12-story white-brick structure was designed by Mulliken and Moeller. Looking south, the theater below is now adjacent to Cumberland, while the 53rd Street corner survives absent decoration. The Cumberland has marketed itself to European business clientele since the 1990s.

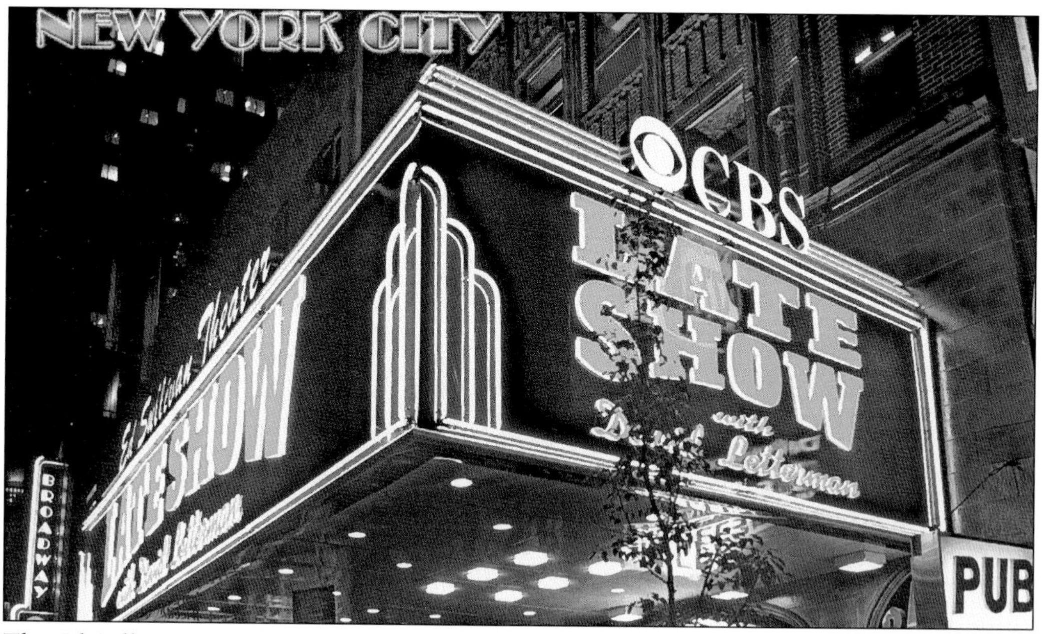

The Ed Sullivan Theater, built in 1927 at No. 1699 by Oscar Hammerstein and named then for his father, was also earlier known as Manhattan and Billy Rose's Music Hall. CBS, its association dating from the 1930s, called it Studio 50 during television's golden age. The now technologically advanced broadcast studio, known for the pictured telecast, was reconfigured in 1993 for a smaller seating capacity within its larger built volume, installed through reversible construction if needs change.

The 11-story Sonoma on 55th Street and the Rockingham filled the east side block. The former was built around 1886 as the Ariston where in 1887 a 10-room apartment rented for $125, not inexpensive, but this was the fashionable apartment residential district. Aging, the area no longer in vogue, the two were demolished in 1936, replaced by a taxpayer. The 1905 Broadway Tabernacle Church, designed by Barney and Chapman, is in the background.

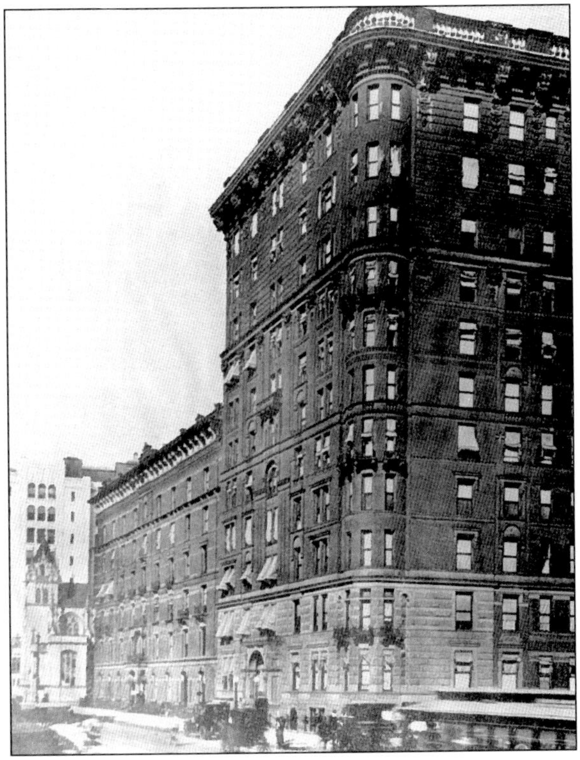

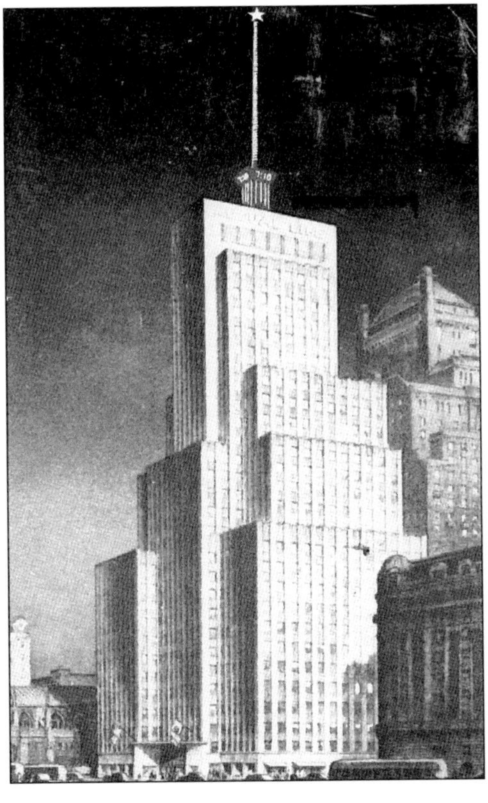

The Mutual Life Insurance Company of New York's 25-story office was the only significant construction on the Times Square–Columbus Circle stretch for two decades following World War II. Erected on the west side block between 55th and 56th Streets, which MONY (Mutual of New York) acquired in a 1936 foreclosure sale and dedicated on April 12, 1950, the design by Shreve, Lamb and Harmon, was a rare postwar application of art moderne. Following the insurer's departure, the building was modernized, dropped its historical name, and looks not unlike this rendering at No. 1740.

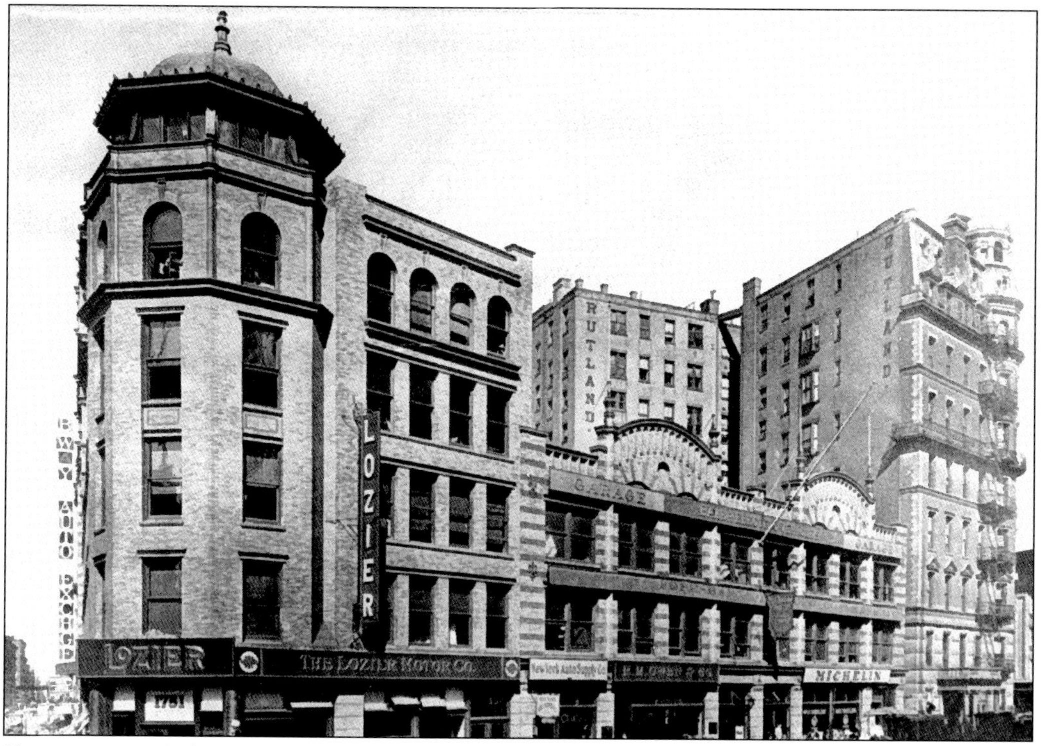

Signage around the 1905 Lozier Building at the northwest corner of 56th Street, designed by Francis H. Kimball, reflects how deeply rooted the automotive trade had become in the 50s blocks by 1910. Lozier filed for bankruptcy in 1914.

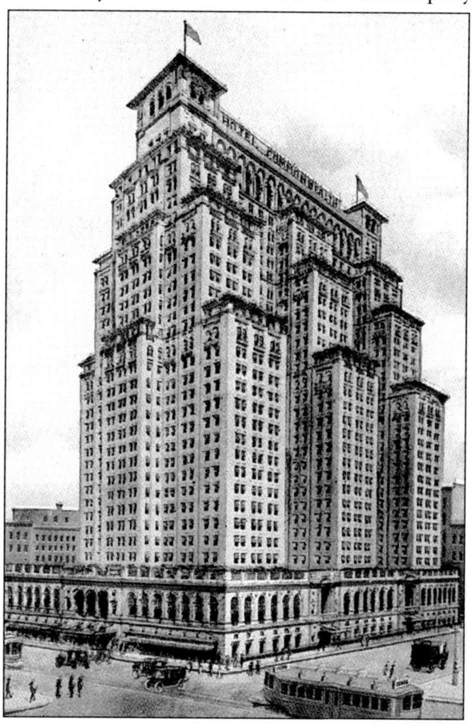

The Hotel Commonwealth is remembered only by dreamers and postcard collectors. Announced in 1916 as a project to erect a 34-story tower, which would be financed on a subscription plan, the Commonwealth Hotel Construction Corporation raised millions, bought in 1918 the full east side block between 55th and 56th Streets, and had Starrett and Van Vleck, and King and Campbell, draw plans. They built nothing. The back of the card proclaimed that a people-financed, profit-sharing plan would raise funds, with $100 shares of stock limited to 10 per person. Financial irregularity and waste doomed the ambitious projections. The dreams ended in court, where the small investors lost the most.

Eight

Columbus Circle and North

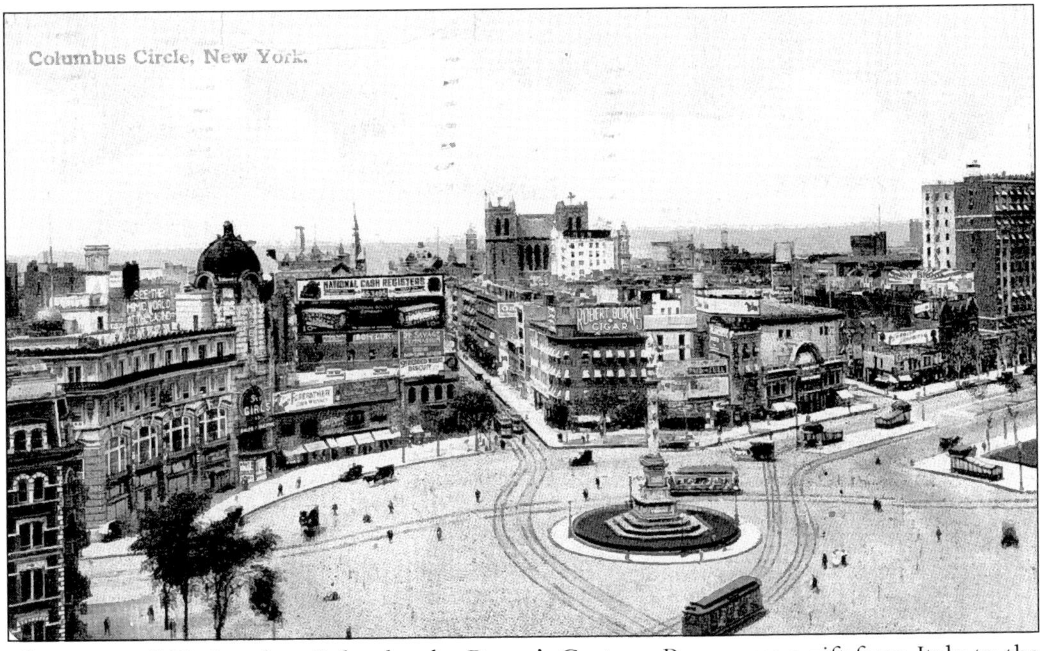

The statue of Christopher Columbus by Rome's Gaetano Russo was a gift from Italy to the United States' people, offered in celebration of the 1892 Columbian Quadricentennial. The figure named the great space, formerly the Great Circle. This *c.* 1910 view depicts 59th Street at center, showing the tower of St. Paul's Roman Catholic Church, and Broadway at right where the 1904 Jermyn Hotel by Mulliken and Moeller stands. Columbus Circle was a thriving entertainment district. Pabst's Grand Circle Hotel is left, adjacent to the Majestic Theater tower. The Little Theater is on the southwest corner of 60th Street, a block later home to the coliseum.

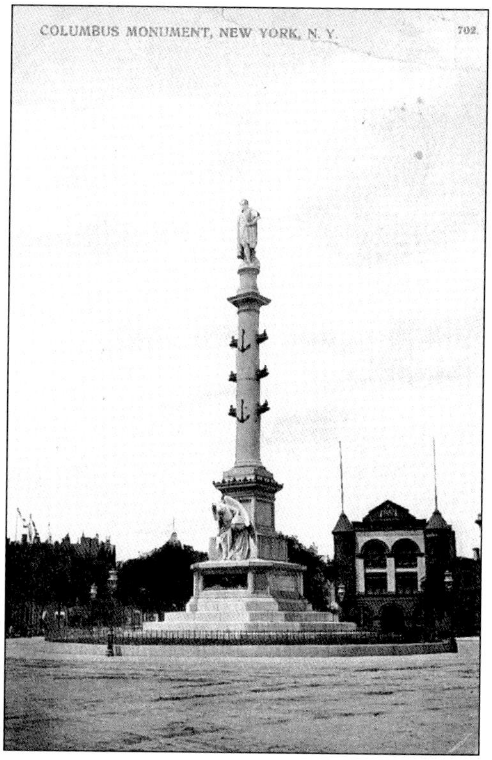

The 14-foot-high figure of Christopher Columbus tops the 77-foot monument. A winged youth examines a globe at the base. Two bronze bas-reliefs depicting Columbus's departure and New World landing are on the north and south sides of the base respectively. The infrequent view north depicts the Durland Riding Academy, completed in 1887 on the short arc between Broadway and Central Park West. The academy reminds one that horse-drawn carriages once changed direction at the circle. The academy relocated several blocks north in 1901. This building, which extended deep along Broadway, was slated for demolition when destroyed by fire on February 15, 1902.

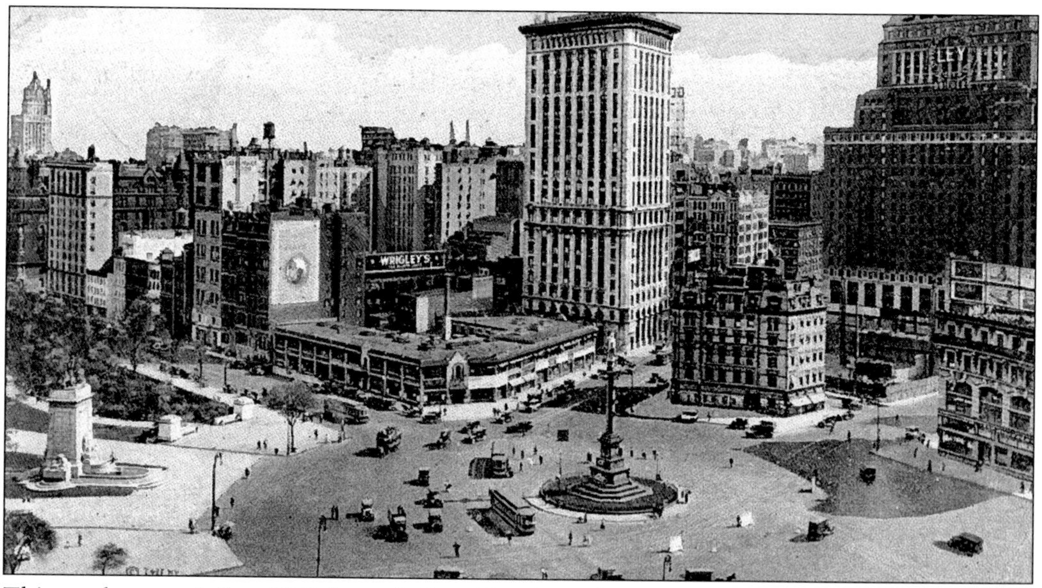

This southeast aerial's *c.* 1922 date is inferred by the Fisk Building at right and the construction site of the Colonnade Building, completed in 1923 north of Fisk. The 20-story, 292-foot United States Rubber Building, on the southeast corner of 58th Street, looms over the squat Ehret Building. Three doors east is the Gainsborough Studio, an apartment for artists with double-height ceilings. The Second Empire Grand Boulevard Hotel on the southern arc had many names prior to demolition for the Huntington Hartford 1964 Gallery of Modern Art, a building reviled in youth, now subject of a preservation campaign.

The 26-story, 318-foot Fisk Tire Building, designed by Carrere and Hastings and Shreve, Lamb and Harmon, was completed in 1921 on the Rutland Hotel site at the southwest corner of 57th Street. Note the temple-styled capital's three-story Ionic pilasters. Automobile row is at the left. The landscaped square was soon filled with the Colonnade Building, the base of the General Motors Building below.

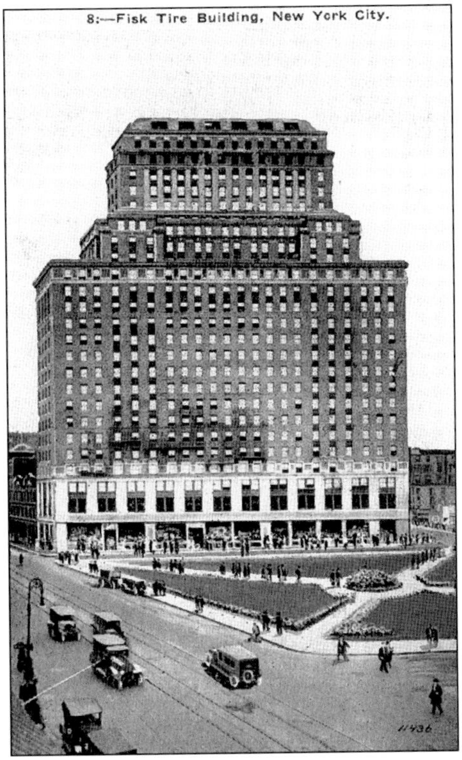

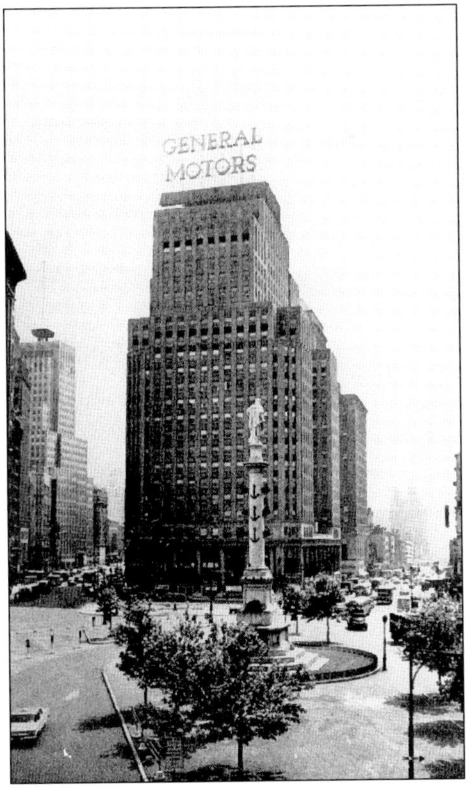

The base of General Motors on the west side from 57th to 58th Streets, or No. 1775, is William Welles Bosworth's three-story Colonnade Building. A 26-story tower designed by Shreve and Lamb was built over it in 1927–1928. The building fills the short block created by Broadway's convergence with Eighth Avenue (right) at Columbus Circle. A glimpse of the Mutual Life Building is left, while the vacant lot at center dates this from the early 1960s, or after the 1960 demolition of the hotel once there and prior to the 1964 Gallery of Modern Art.

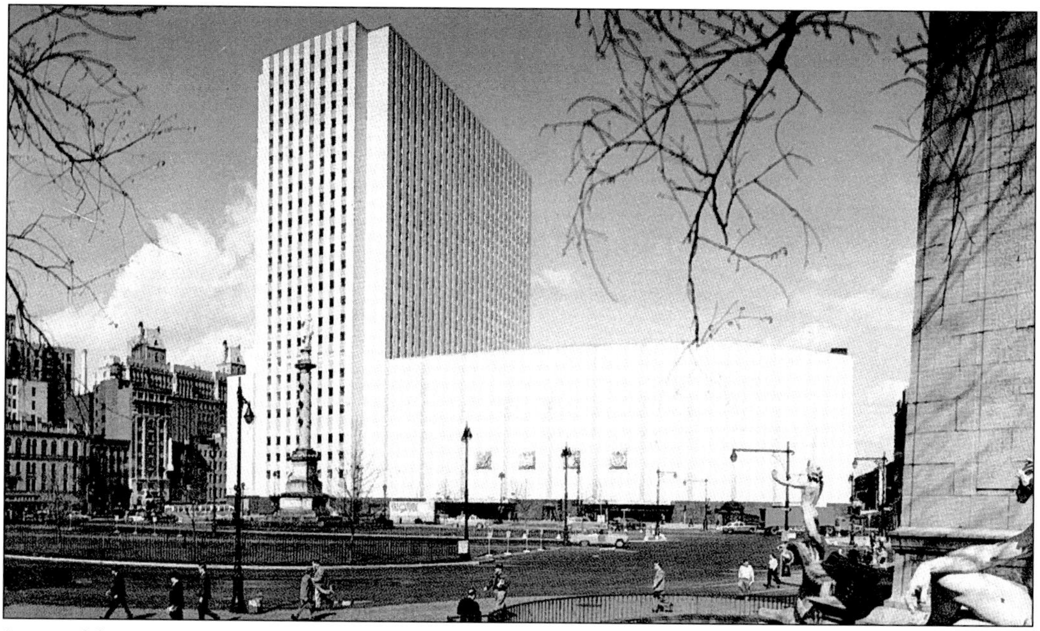

Spurred by 1951's Columbus Circle urban renewal, the 1956 Leon and Lionel Levy–designed coliseum and 10 Columbus Circle, the 26-story tower, had a short, unhappy existence at a prominent location. For three decades it was New York's premier exposition hall. Replacing the 1911 Grand Central Palace, the coliseum touted geographic centrality, air-conditioning of 400,000 square feet, and the ability to handle crowds exceeding 30,000. The coliseum, its exhibition role taken by Javits Center, was demolished in 2000, replaced by AOL Time Warner Center.

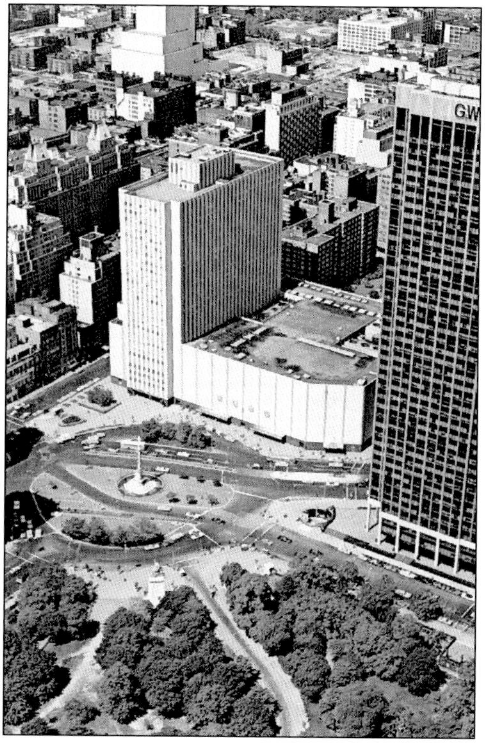

The enormous floor area of the coliseum's exposition space is seen around 1970. Durland's at Broadway was replaced by the two-story American Circle Building, which in turn was replaced 1970 by the Thomas E. Stanley–designed Gulf and Western Building. This office was stripped to its frame in 1996, wrapped in gold glass, and rebuilt as Trump International Hotel and Tower.

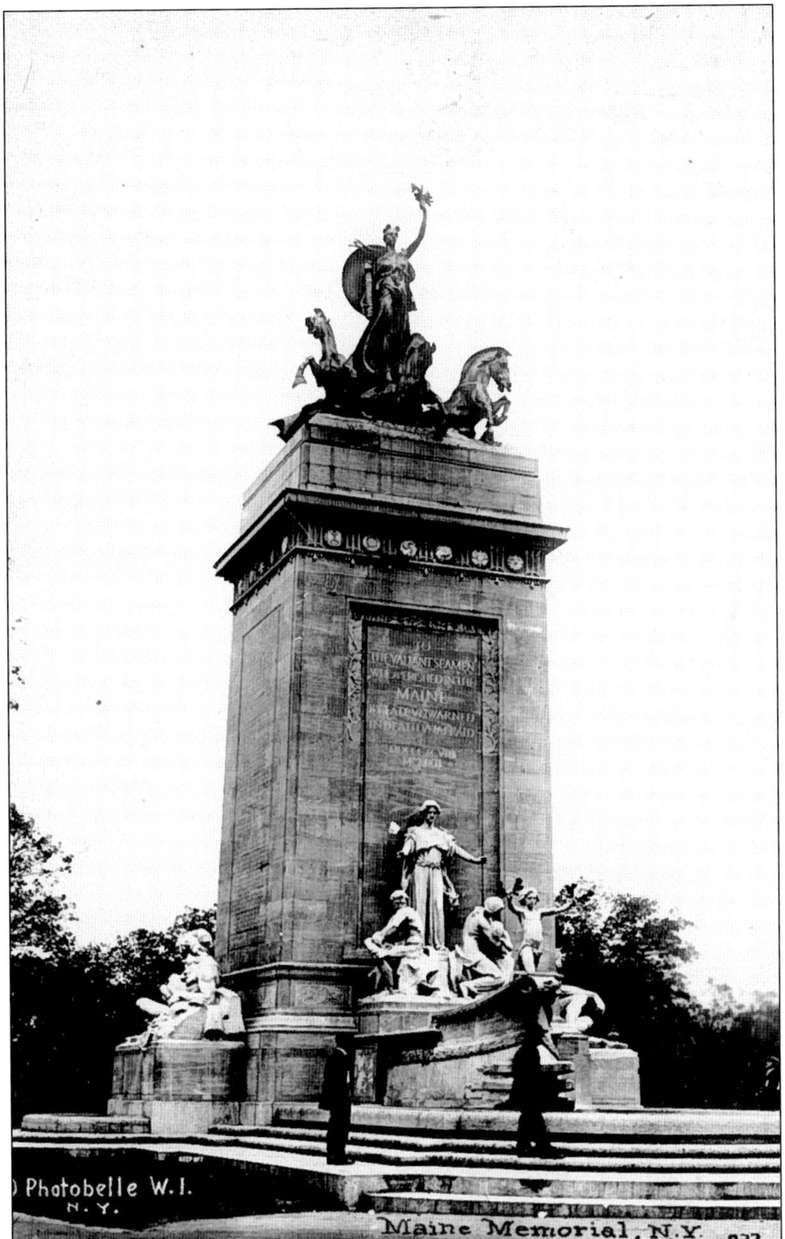

Dedicated to the 258 killed in the February 15, 1898, explosion of the battleship *Maine* in Havana, the National Maine Memorial was completed in 1913, unveiled on Memorial Day, and placed on the circle's park side. Attilio Piccirilli's figure of Columbia Triumphant with a chariot led by sea horses is atop H. Van Buren Magonigle's base, surrounded by 10 marble allegorical figures. Peace reigning over Courage and Fortitude are three under the inscription, facing the circle. In front, a youth holding a laurel wreath and olive branch (since destroyed) stands as on a ship's prow. Two figures personifying the Atlantic and Pacific Oceans are on the sides, the former a youth, the latter an old man. Fund-raising was led by William Randolph Hearst, the yellow-rag journalist who also fanned the flames for the Spanish-American War that stemmed from the explosion.

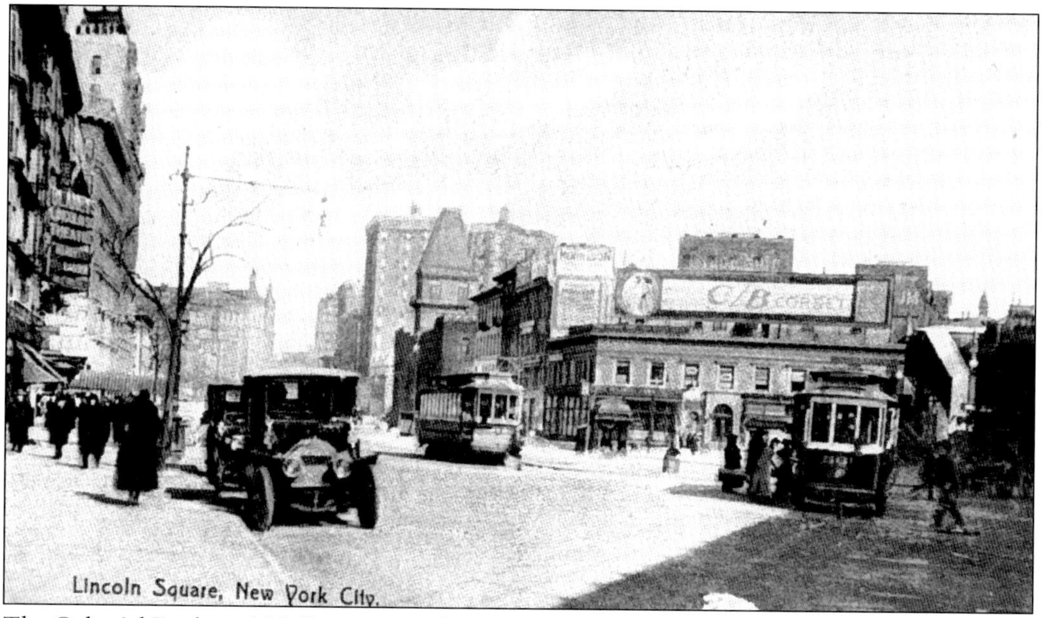

The Colonial Bank on 66th Street around 1912 is behind the streetcars at Lincoln Square looking north. The tower belonged to the 22nd Regiment Armory, a cavernous building filling the 67th–68th Streets block, east to Columbus Avenue. Broadway Arcade at left provided an entrance to Lincoln Square Theater on 65th Street, a building demolished for the Julliard School of Music. Hotel Marie Antoinette is above, while the Ansonia towers are in the background.

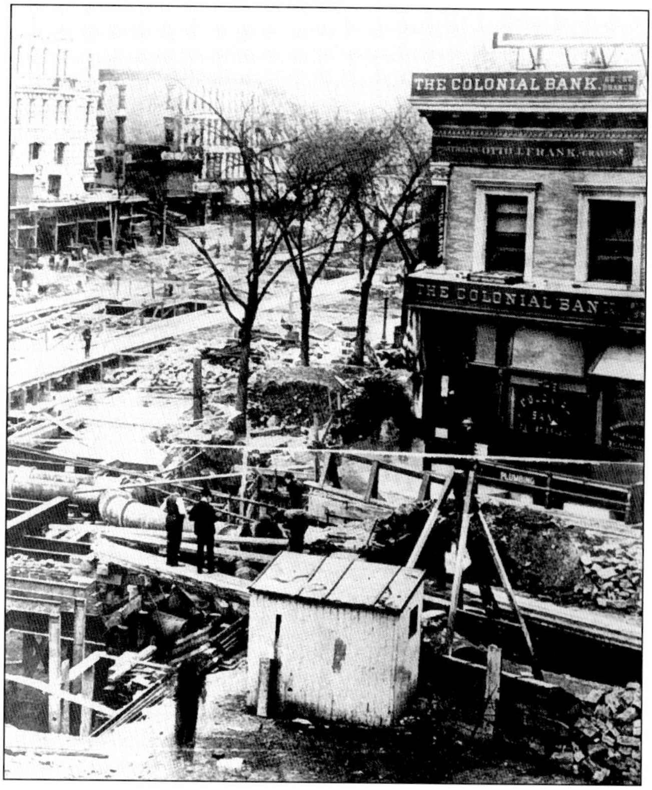

The crossing of Broadway and Columbus Avenue, Empire Square, was renamed in 1906 Lincoln for no documented reason. Change was in the air, or under the ground, Broadway being ripped up earlier for extension of the subway, the Interborough Broadway line to old-timers, or the 1, 2, and 3 trains for newcomers.

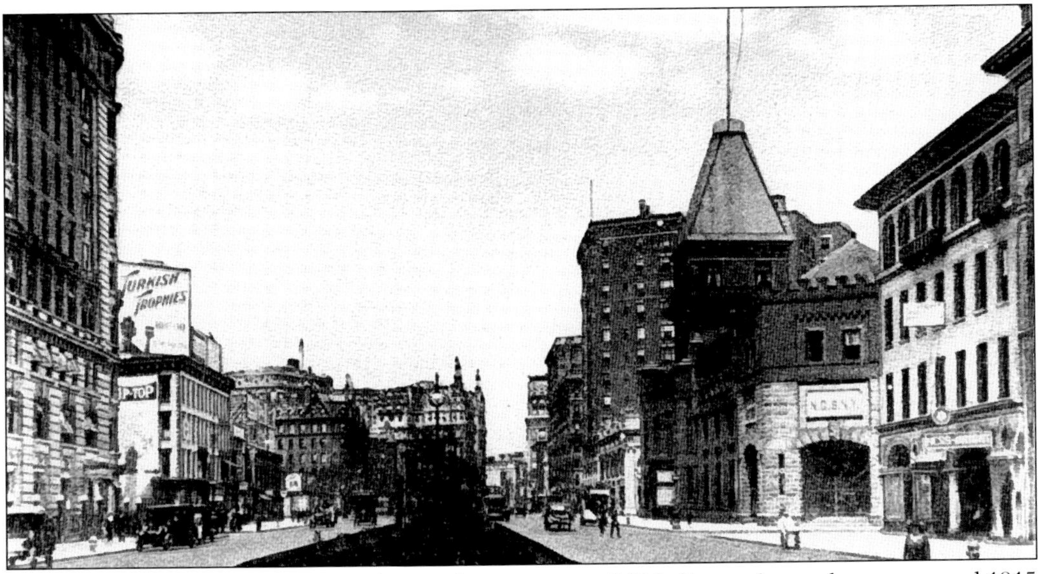

The pyramidal tower at right on the northeast corner of 67th Street draws the eye around 1915 north from Lincoln Square to the armory, completed in 1891 to Capt. John P. Leo's design. Demolished around 1930, a parking lot for a spell, it is now the Ansonia post office. The Hotel Marie Antoinette at left, dating from 1895, was expanded in 1903. The tall structures behind are the Spencer Arms and Ormonde; Ansonia's towers are visible. (Courtesy of Joan Kay.)

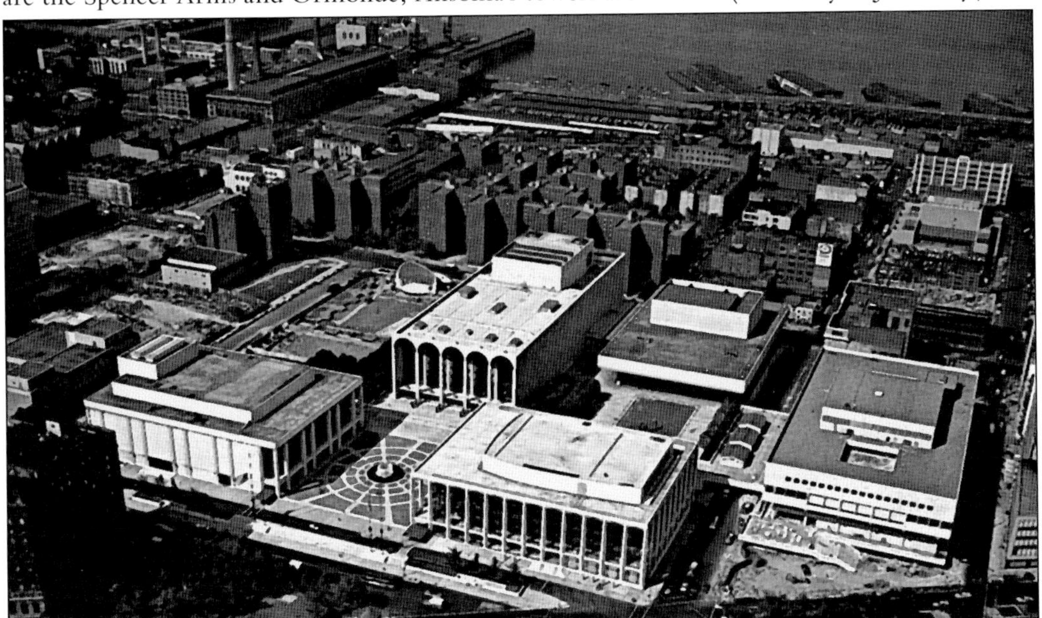

Lincoln Center's original urban renewal project ripped up a neighborhood and brought a performing arts center. Ground was broken in May 1959, while the first component, Philharmonic (now Avery Fisher) Hall, opened in September 1962 where angled Broadway touches the building's corner. Following were the New York State Theater, left, April 1964, and the Vivian Beaumont Theater, above Avery Fisher Hall, October 1965. The Julliard School of Music, the north side of 65th Street and at right, is connected by a bridge. The Amsterdam Houses on Amsterdam Avenue are the brick structures.

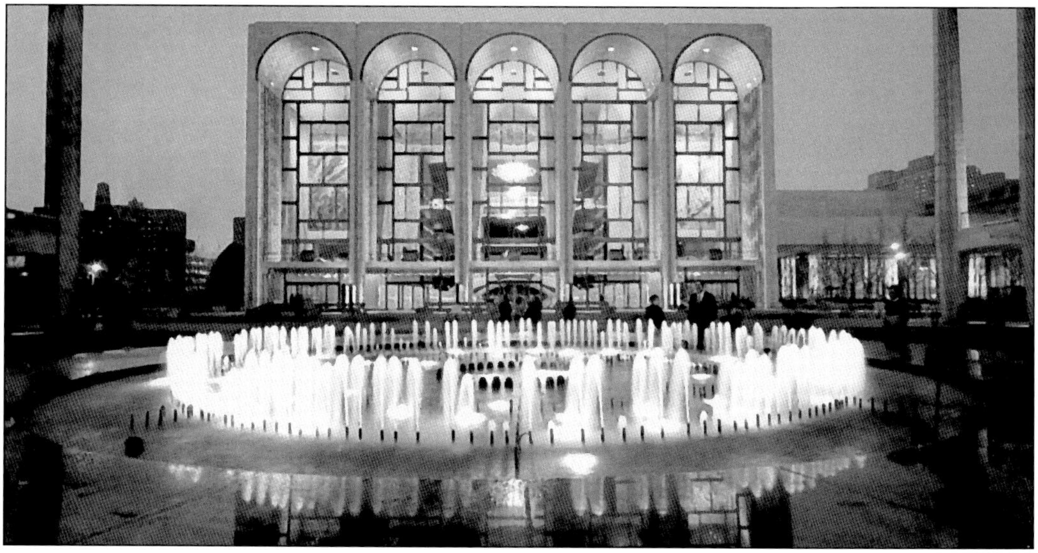

The Metropolitan Opera long ago outgrew its 39th Street home, which counted lack of storage space among its shortcomings. A new house designed by Wallace K. Harrison of Harrison and Abramovitz opened in September 1966 featuring Samuel Barber's *Anthony and Cleopatra* premiere. Marc Chagall's murals, hanging aside the entrances, are visible at dusk. Few may realize that the house, seating 3,900, is as deep behind the stage as in front, where office, rehearsal, storage, and workshop space consume enormous areas.

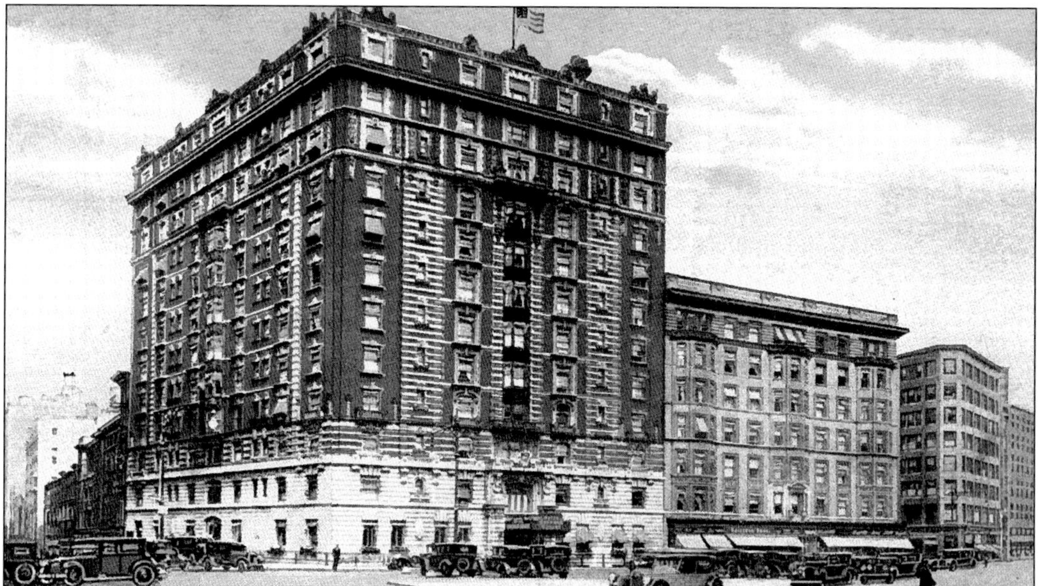

The 12-story building on the northwest corner of 70th Street is the major structure, but the 1893 Sherman Square Hotel originated as the seven-story part with the balustrade on the southwest corner of 71st Street. The taller is the Hotel Regent. The two were joined in 1909 when the former bought the latter. The same-level floors facilitated their physical linkage. The seedy Sherman Square Hotel reflected in the 1960s a neighborhood on the brink. Bought by a developer in 1967, the place, pictured in the 1920s, was demolished in 1969 and replaced two years later by the 41-story residence designated 1 Sherman Square.

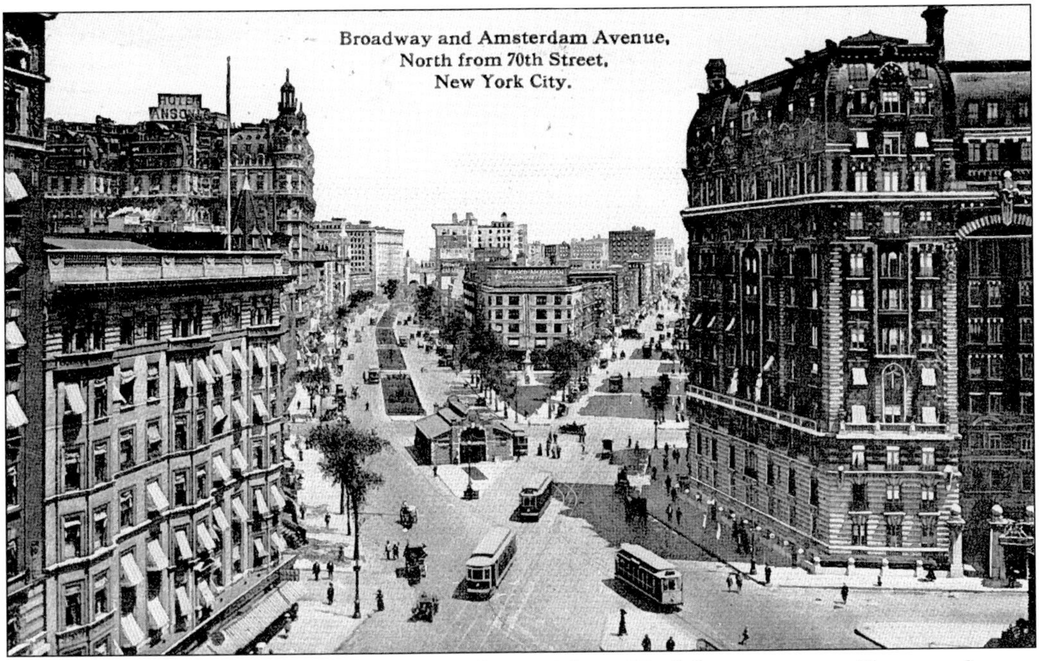

Broadway's bisecting Amsterdam Avenue from 70th to 72nd Streets creates Sherman Square and Verdi Square, south and north, respectively. Note in the center background the 1906 statue of Guiseppe Verdi by Pasquale Civiletti. The Heins and LaFarge subway station is in front in a streetscape dominated by the Dorilton at right and the Ansonia and the original Sherman Square Hotel in left back- and foregrounds. Behind Verdi is the Loring, demolished for the 1928 Central Savings Bank, remodeled in 2000 as condominiums.

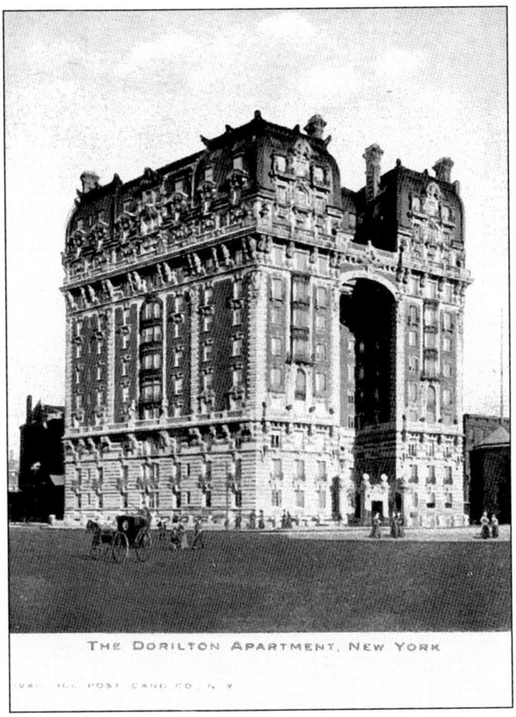

The Dorilton, on the northwest corner of 71st Street, was upper Broadway's first tall apartment following 1904's subway extension. The 12-story building's rich decoration has been the subject of disagreement over its century's existence, but the Dorilton attained landmark stature, even after some finish had crumbled. The Janes and Leo–designed Beaux-Arts extravagance, capped with a three-story mansard, has seen other changes since pictured around 1905, notably stores on Broadway, left.

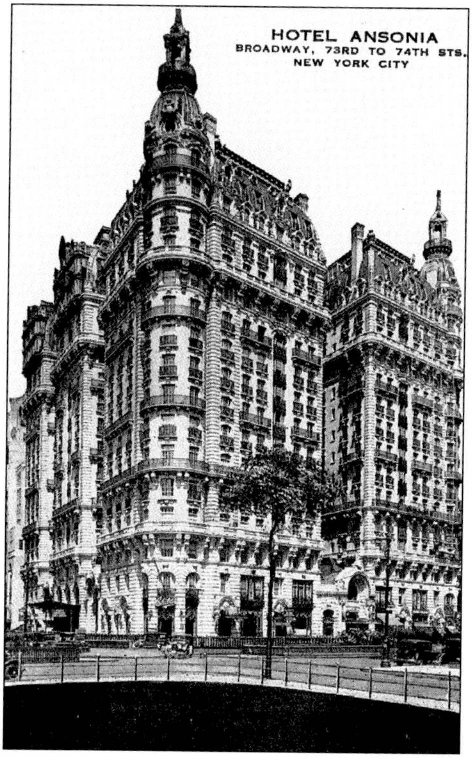

William Earl Dodge Stokes developed the Ansonia apartment-hotel in 1899–1904 on the west side from 73rd to 74th Streets. The 200-foot-tall, 17-story Beaux-Arts palace, designed by Paul E. M. Duboy, was New York's finest of its time and has endured as one of the city's greatest legendary residential landmarks. The Ansonia underwent decline as the West Side changed character, encountering the usual unappealing storefronts and division into smaller units. However, the building rose with the rising tide of a resurgent neighborhood.

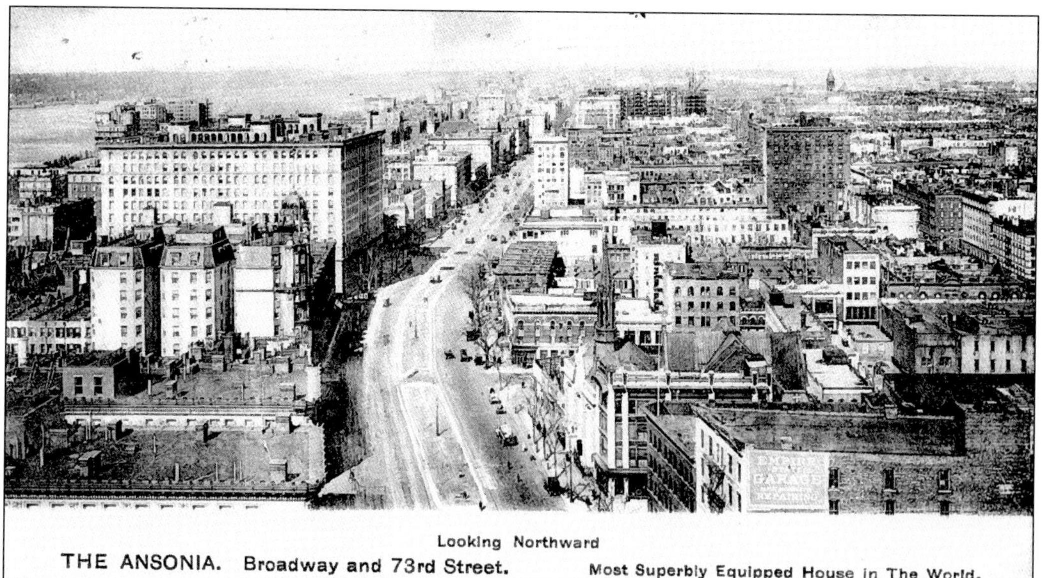

The Ansonia's location on a bend of Broadway dominated the view north and south. Prominent on the west side of Broadway is William Waldorf Astor's 1905 Astor Apartments between 75th and 76th Streets, designed by Clinton and Russell and pictured before the 1914 expansion. The mansard-roofed building is the Avonmore Apartments. This 1909 promotional card fills the back with advertising. The Ansonia's 2,500 rooms, both housekeeping and not, started at $2 ($3 with bath) and ranged higher for suites.

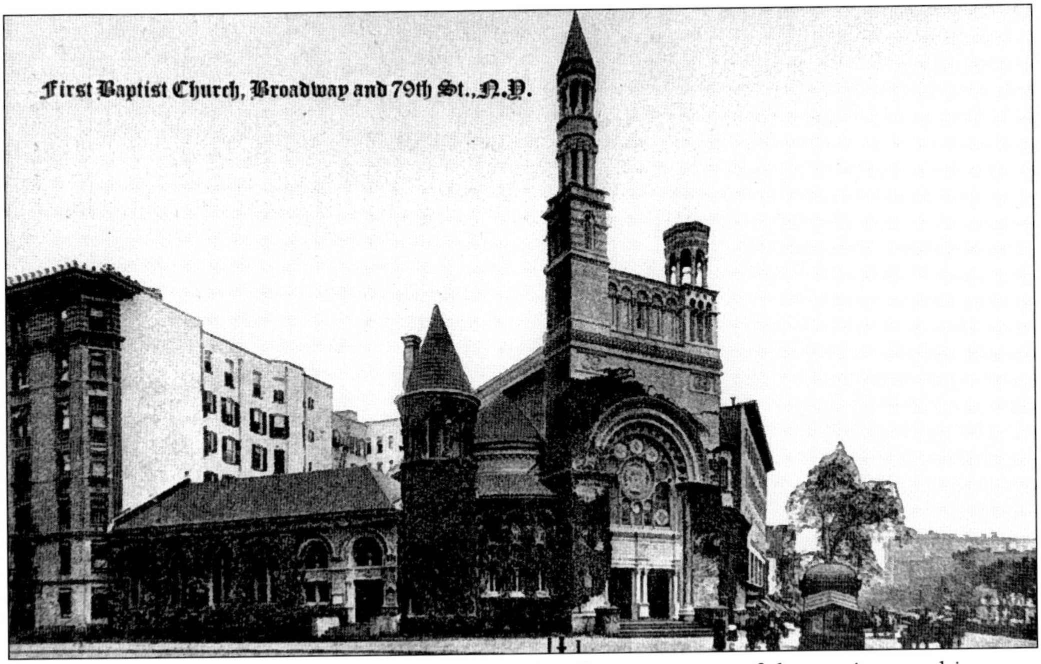

The Romanesque Revival First Baptist Church offers an excess of decoration, making one wonder what is missing and if too much is enough. The edifice at the northwest corner of 79th Street was designed by George Keister. (Courtesy of Joan Kay.)

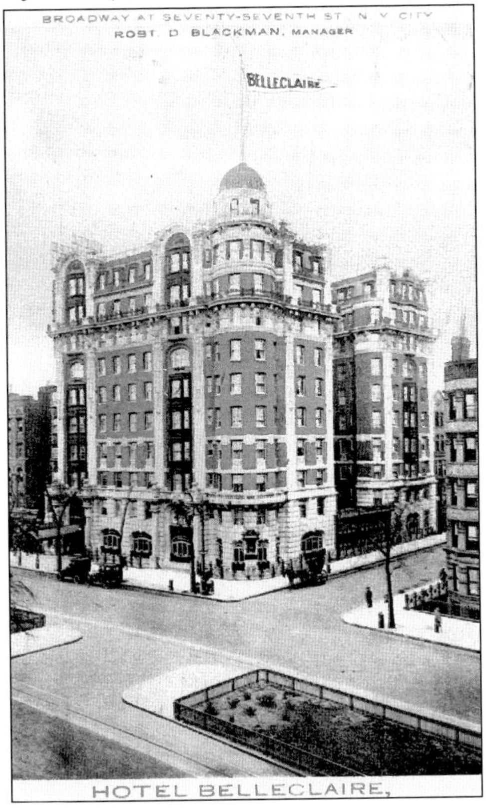

The young Emery Roth designed the Belleclaire, pictured around 1910, when with Stein Cohen and Roth. The 10-story Beaux-Arts hotel on the southwest corner of 77th Street, with elements of art nouveau, was completed in 1903, in the wave of luxury buildings following the subway. One distinction was the dining rooms' varied decor, Moorish, Louis XVI for ladies, or Flemish café. Shabbiness overtook the Belleclaire, which lost its dome and replaced ground-floor public rooms with stores. Recent restoration now mixes tourist-oriented transient rooms with long-term, single-room permanent residences.

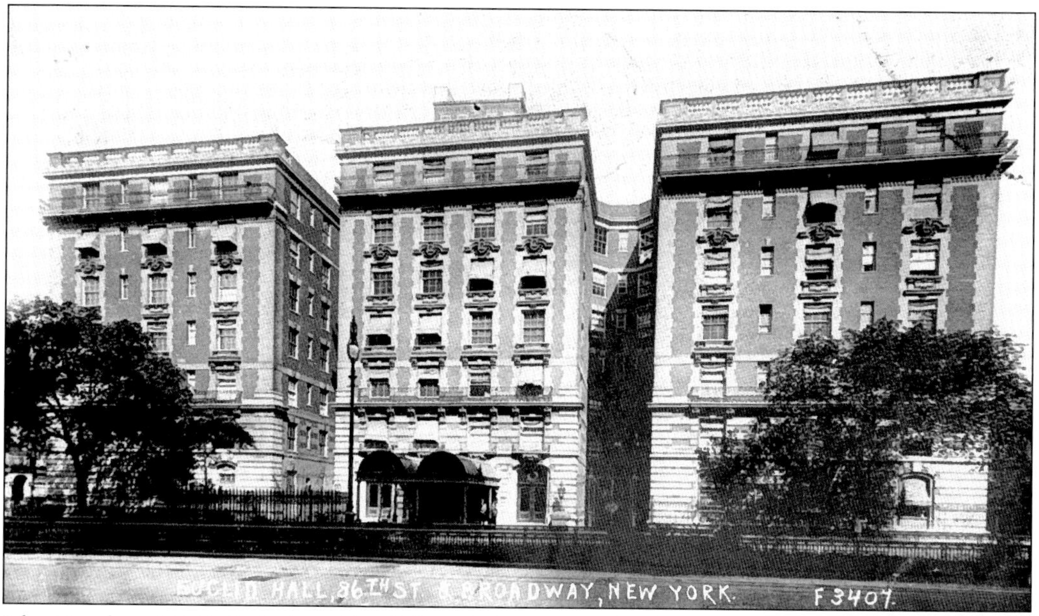

The Hotel Euclid Hall, designed by Hill and Turner, was built in 1903 at No. 2345, the full west side block from 85th to 86th Streets. Briefly fashionable when new, Euclid fell out of favor with changing tastes in living arrangements, slipping to one of the West Side's largest single-room occupancy domiciles. Purchased by the West Side Federation for Senior Housing around 1990, the revitalized building, pictured around 1910, stands, serving an older population, many with social or mental needs. (Courtesy of Joan Kay.)

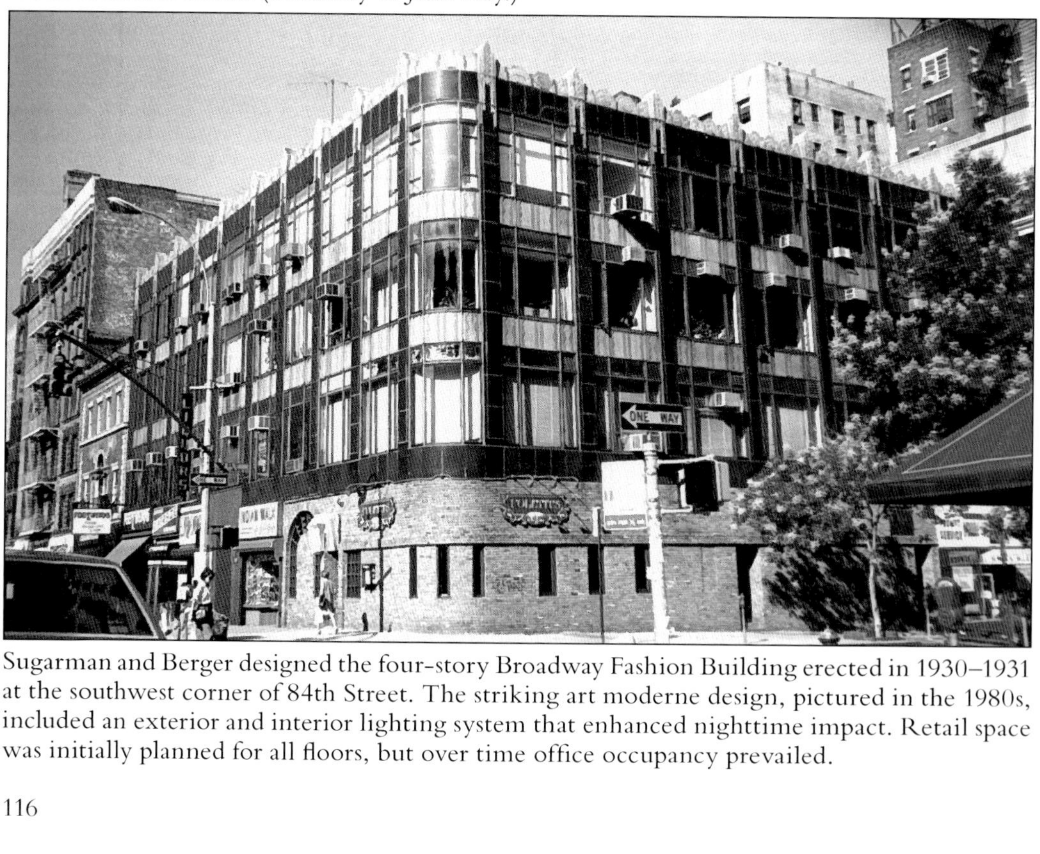

Sugarman and Berger designed the four-story Broadway Fashion Building erected in 1930–1931 at the southwest corner of 84th Street. The striking art moderne design, pictured in the 1980s, included an exterior and interior lighting system that enhanced nighttime impact. Retail space was initially planned for all floors, but over time office occupancy prevailed.

Nine

Above 100th Street

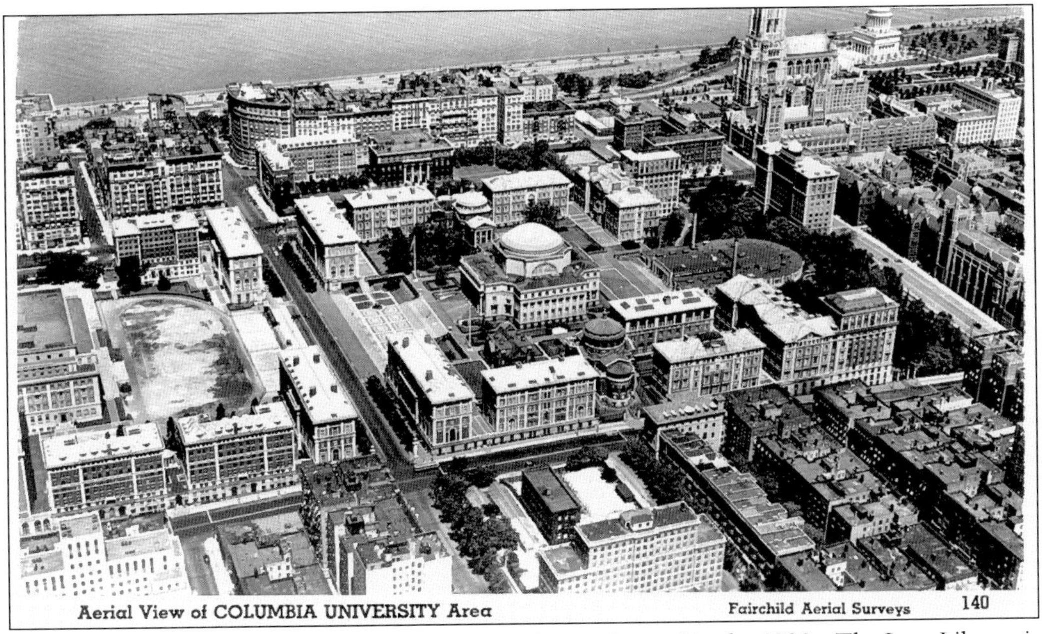

Columbia University campus's core and surrounds are pictured in the 1930s. The Low Library is center, the other domed buildings are Earl Hall, top on Broadway, and St. Paul's Chapel, bottom on Amsterdam Avenue. Claremont Avenue, a short north–south street beginning at 116th Street, is at the top left by the apartment's curved facade. It is the location of Union Theological Seminary, the shorter tower at right. The top right cuts off the peaks of Riverside Church, on Riverside Drive running from 120th Street, and Grant's Tomb at 122nd Street.

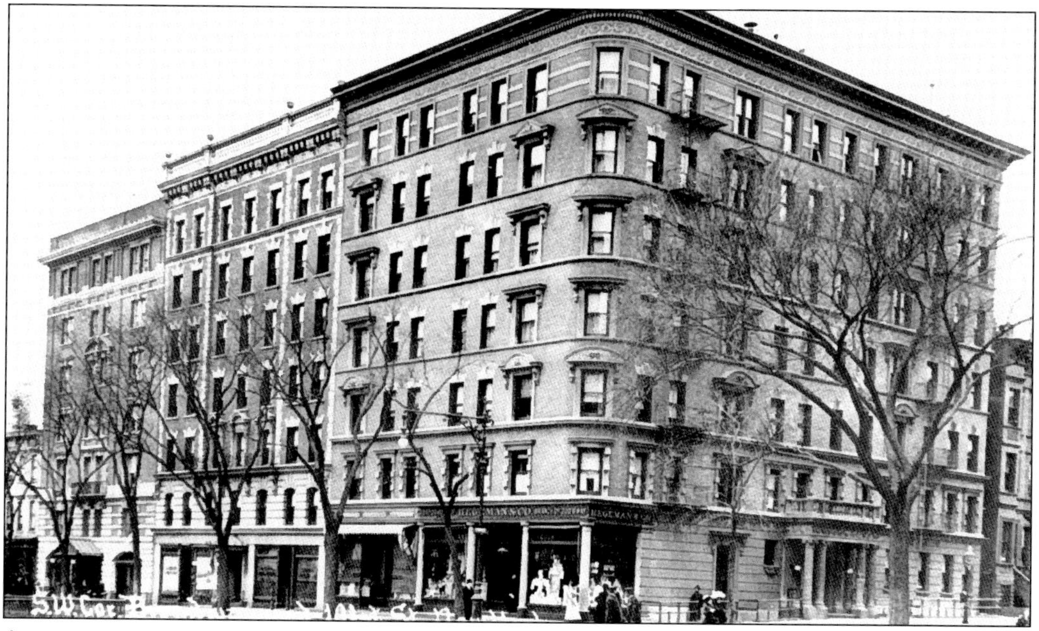

An apartment construction boom followed the Broadway subway's extension. The Broadway is pictured at the southwest corner of 101st Street. Hageman and Company was a large pharmacy chain, having consolidated with Riker in 1910, the time of this card by Thaddeus Wilkerson (1872–1943), a prolific postcard producer from 1909 through 1916. (Courtesy of Joan Kay.)

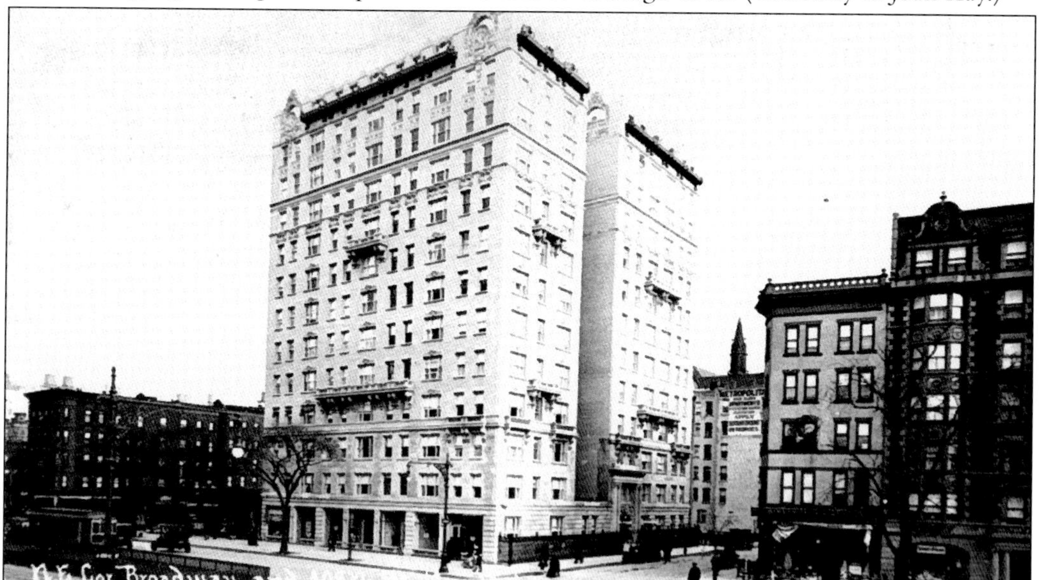

Charles E. McManus bought eight lots at the northeast corner of 108th Street in 1909, hiring Neville and Bagge to design the 12-story Manchester, opening in August 1910. It was limestone-clad with five apartments of six to eight rooms to a floor. The Manchester was planned as a high-quality domicile. The lesser structures at right merit interest, notably the porthole balustrade on the corner and the decorative flourishes on its neighbor. This image is also by Wilkerson, who produced over 400 Manhattan photographic postcards, mostly around 1910 and primarily of Upper West Side subjects. (Courtesy of Joan Kay.)

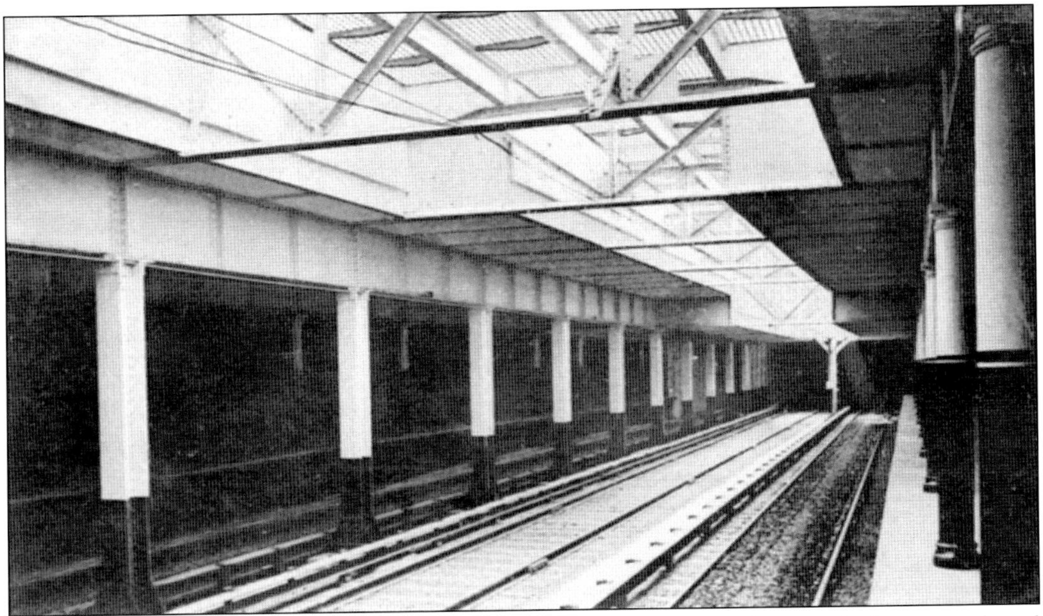

Artistic decor and daylight, when available, brightened subway stations, techniques employed to counter perceived fears of dismal underground environments. Artwork, often mosaics, was tied to the station's area character. On a New Year's Day 1904 official tunnel tour, the *Times* reported, "The 116th Street station was one of the finest on the way, decorated as it is in the Columbia University colors and . . . in addition to the colors, has coats of arms of the college at intervals on the walls."

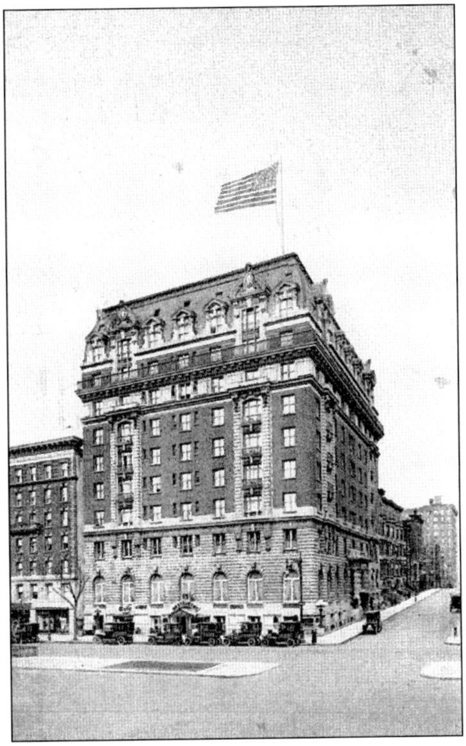

The Hotel Marseille on the southwest corner of 103rd Street, completed in 1905, was described by the architectural press as "joyously exuberant." Henry Allen Jacobs' Beaux-Arts design is enhanced by an appealing capital and richly decorated mansard. The place was known as the Langham, a name confused with the Central Park West apartment between 73rd and 74th Streets. The Clearfield at Riverside Drive is visible around 1915.

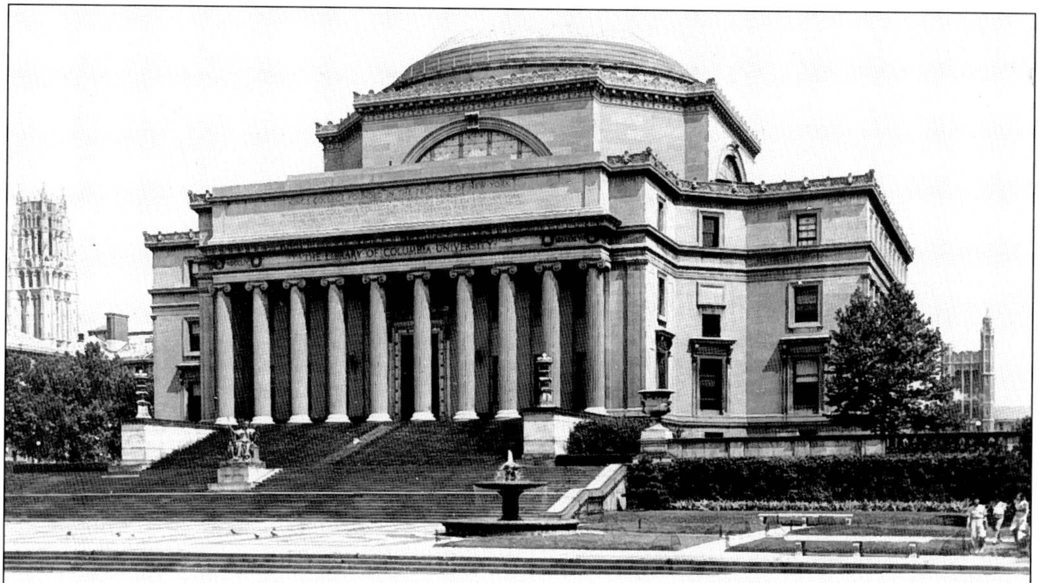

Old Library, Columbia University, New York City 130

The 1907 Low Library was the architectural centerpiece of Columbia's new campus founded a few years earlier. The neoclassical landmark, designed by McKim, Mead and White, was named for Abiel Abbot Low, father of Columbia president Seth Low, leader of the school's move from midtown to Morningside Heights and major financial backer of the library. The card's labeling "old library" reflects 1934's opening of Butler Library. Low, subject of early-21st-century preservation, although used for administration, is still the Low Library in common reference.

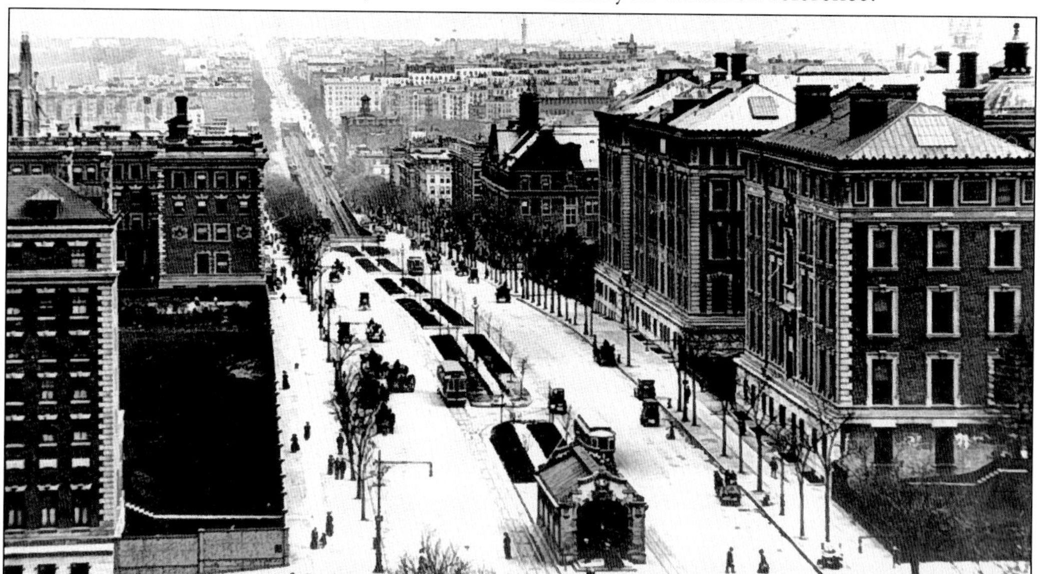

"Three Miles Of Broadway", north from Columbia University, New York. TW

The 1904 Heins and LaFarge 116th Street subway kiosk is in the foreground of this *c.* 1907 Thaddeus Wilkerson card. Above one sees the subway emerge at 122nd Street. Columbia's 1904 School of Mines designed by Alfred W. Brunner is at right, while Barnard is at left. The Broadway Malls, laid out after the Civil War, fill the mid-thoroughfare. The slivers comprise a cumulative 10.5-acre city park. (Courtesy of Joan Kay.)

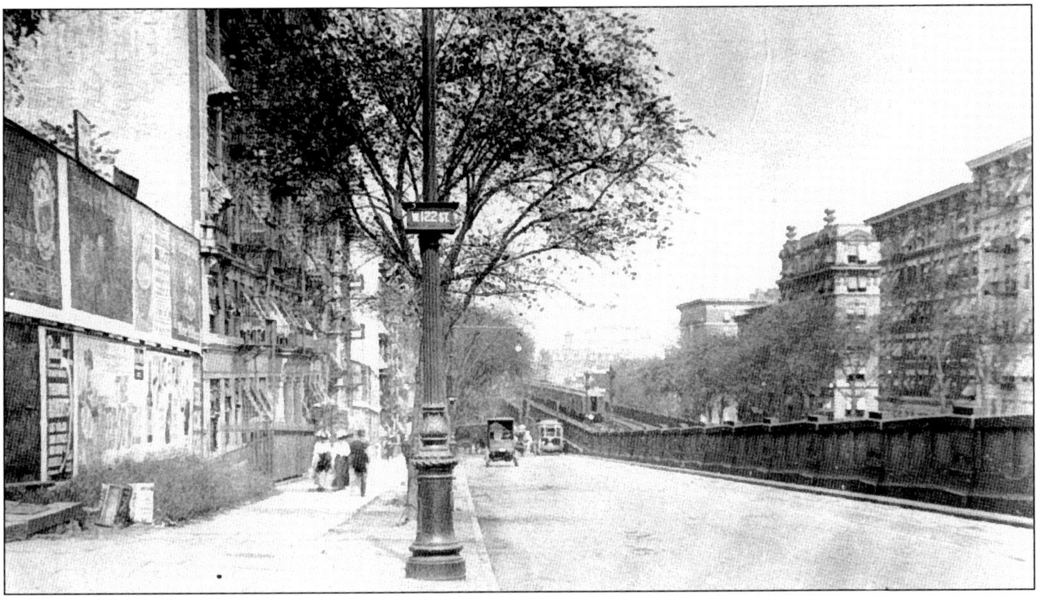

The Broadway subway emerges at 122nd Street to start its elevated run over Manhattan Valley. The *c.* 1910 view north from 122nd Street depicts the start of the line's viaduct, ending at 135th Street. The landscape changed markedly, notably on the east. Northward, current structures include the 1930 Jewish Theological Seminary, the 1957 Morningside Gardens Houses, and the General Ulysses S. Grant Houses. (Courtesy of Joan Kay.)

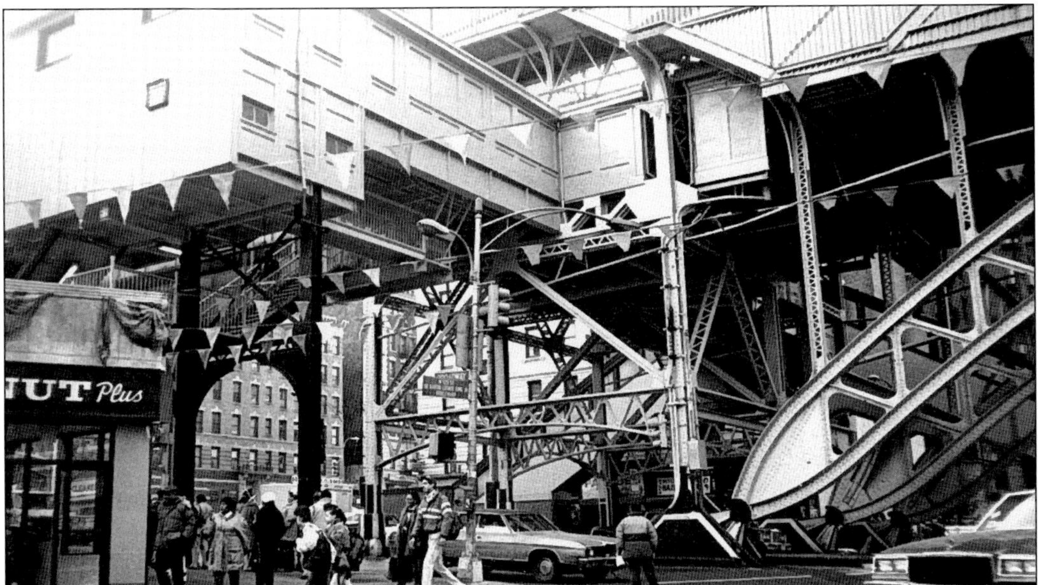

The viaduct, emerging at 122nd Street and running 2,174 feet, has one stop at 125th Street. A massive arched steel frame supports the station. A corner is at the right of this *c.* 1980 John Kowaluk card. The viaduct was designed for aesthetic appeal, unlike the Ninth Avenue Elevated. A 1981 landmark, the 125th Street viaduct's lengthy rehabilitation was completed around 2004.

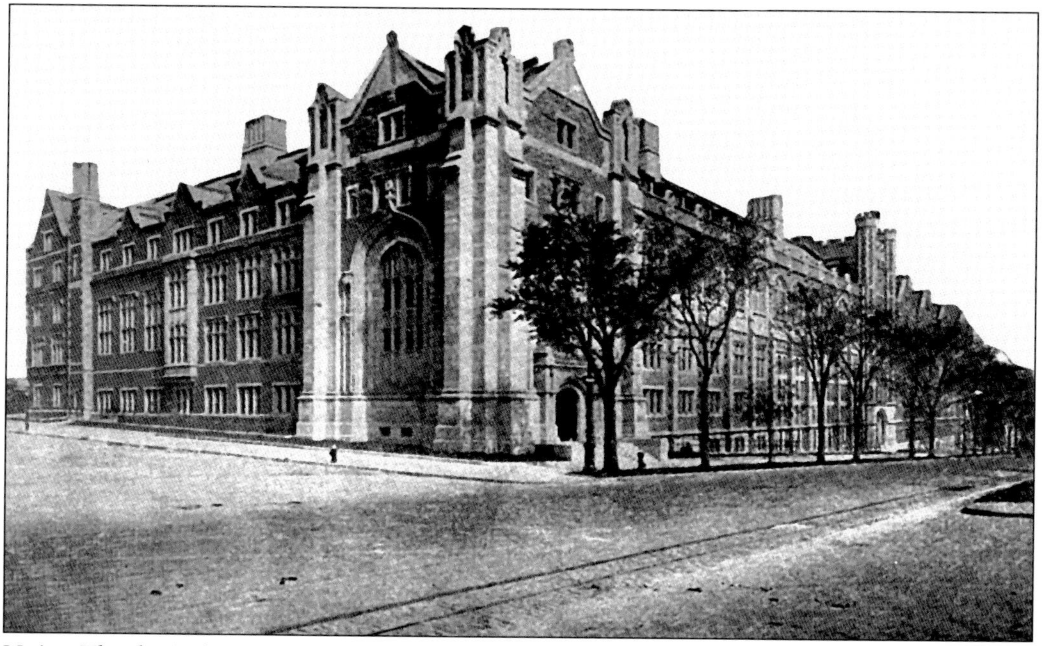

Union Theological Seminary, founded in 1836 on Park Avenue between 69th and 70th Streets, moved around 1910 to Broadway between 120th and 122nd Streets following an architectural competition won by Boston's Allen and Collens. They planned an English Gothic design reminiscent of the collegiate architecture of Cambridge. The entire block to Claremont Avenue at west is lined with buildings creating an interior courtyard.

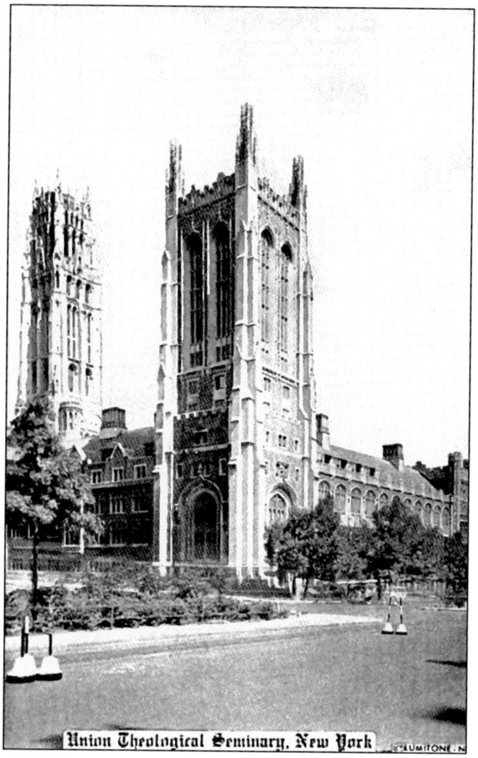

Founded by Presbyterians, Union Theological, nondenominational when uptown, became known for ecumenism and theological inclusiveness. Its tower, completed in 1928, also by Allen and Collens, memorialized John Crosby Brown, who served over 40 years as director. Pictured in the 1930s, it expanded classroom space by 30 percent. The rear tower is Riverside Church.

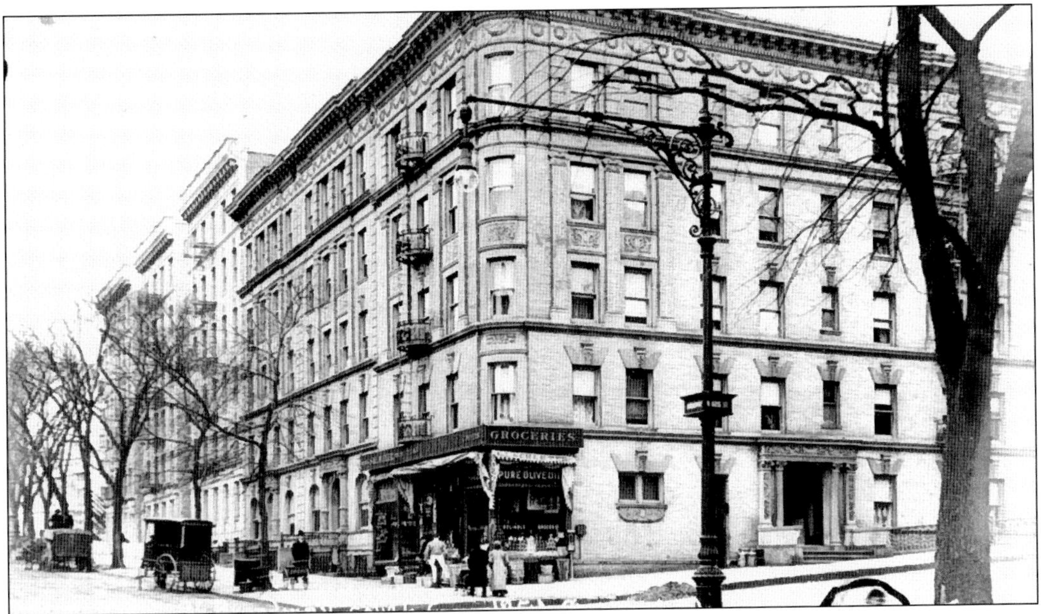

A richly decorated apartment on the southwest corner of 125th Street is pictured by Thaddeus Wilkerson. The row of unusual semicircular fire escapes are the only ones on the street side. The sign is unreadable driving but marks the location. The building is gone. (Courtesy of Joan Kay.)

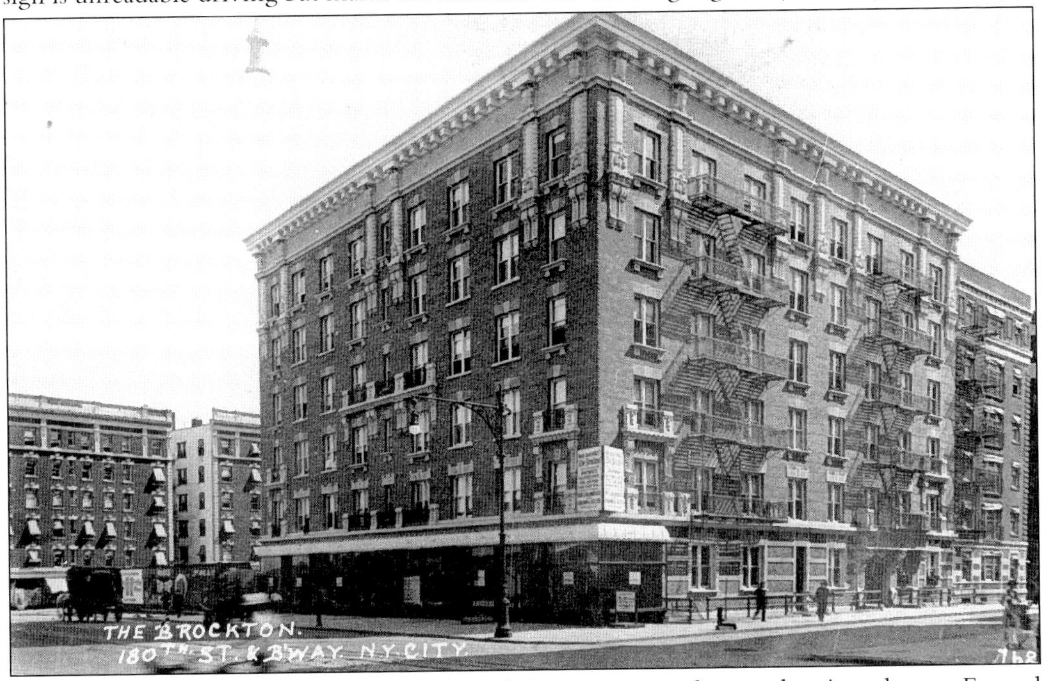

The Brockton, at the northeast corner of 180th Street, appeared new when issued on an Ess and Ess Company card around 1910. The area's land was bought around 1904 by the Fort Washington Syndicate in anticipation of the subway's arrival. It sold only to developers who agreed to erect better elevator apartments. The fire escapes, uncharacteristically on a main street rather than a court, possessed artistic shadows. Beyond the lot is the 1909 Elmsford at 181st Street, George F. Pelham's design. (Courtesy of Joan Kay.)

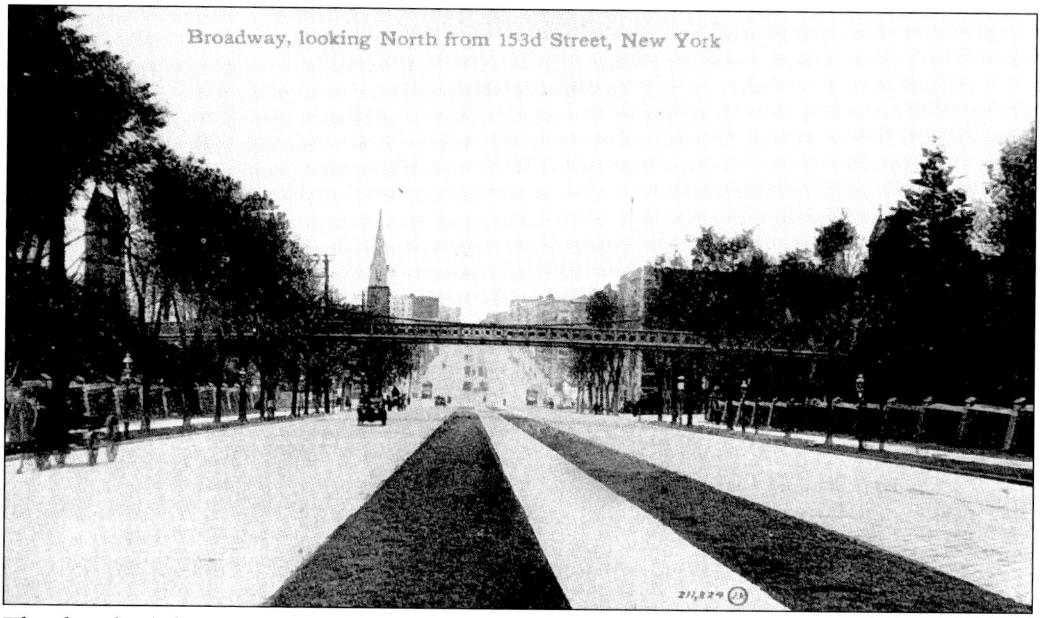

The chapel at left was replaced by Trinity at 155th Street in a corner of its cemetery reserved for a church. The cemetery was laid out in 1846 prior to Bloomingdale Road, a Broadway antecedent, which bisected the graveyard. This view north from 153rd Street shows the bridge connecting the sections. At removal in 1911, the *Times*, on October 15, reported the artistic structure was erected in 1871. (Courtesy of Joan Kay.)

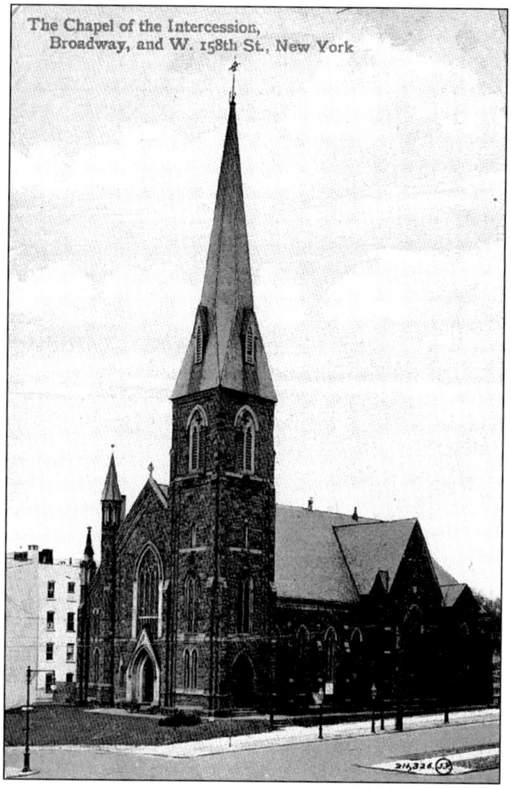

When this handsome Gothic edifice was completed in 1873 by the then-independent parish of the Church of the Intercession, organized in 1847, it was located at 158th Street and Eleventh Avenue. Broadway had not yet reached that far north. Dedicated on September 21, 1873, the 140-by-70-foot structure had a 180-foot tower surmounted by a 10-foot gilt cross. The congregation outgrew this building, was absorbed in 1908 by Trinity, and the church became a chapel.

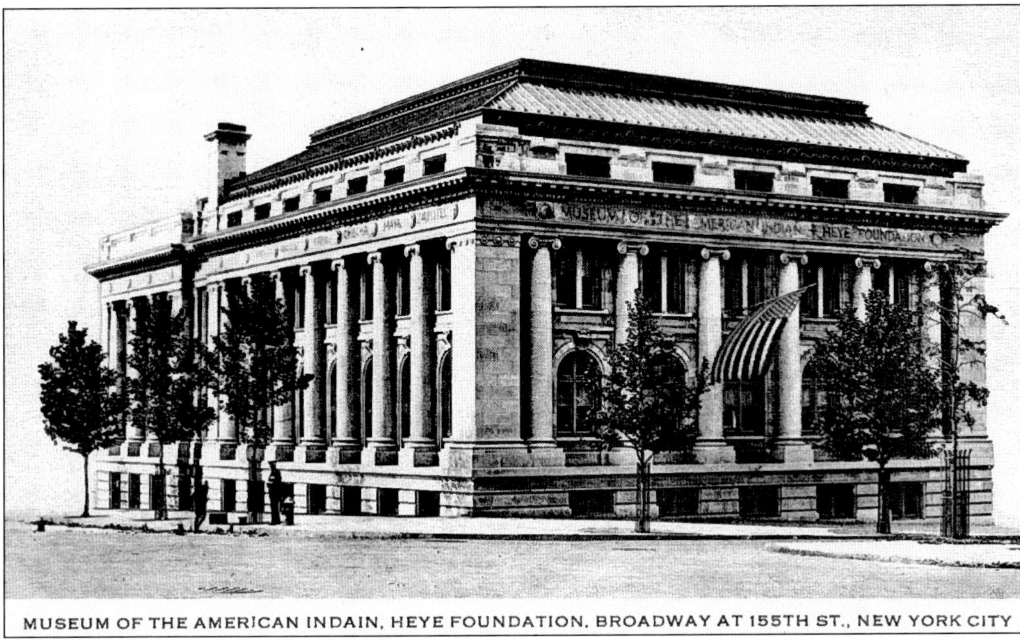

The Museum of the American Indian, begun in 1916 as a replica of American Geographical Society's building, was completed in 1917. Admitting the public for years, it delayed "official" opening until November 15, 1922. George Heye collected prodigious quantities of Native American artifacts, housed and exhibited here until substantial parts were moved to the Smithsonian's National Museum of the American Indian, an adaptive use of the customhouse.

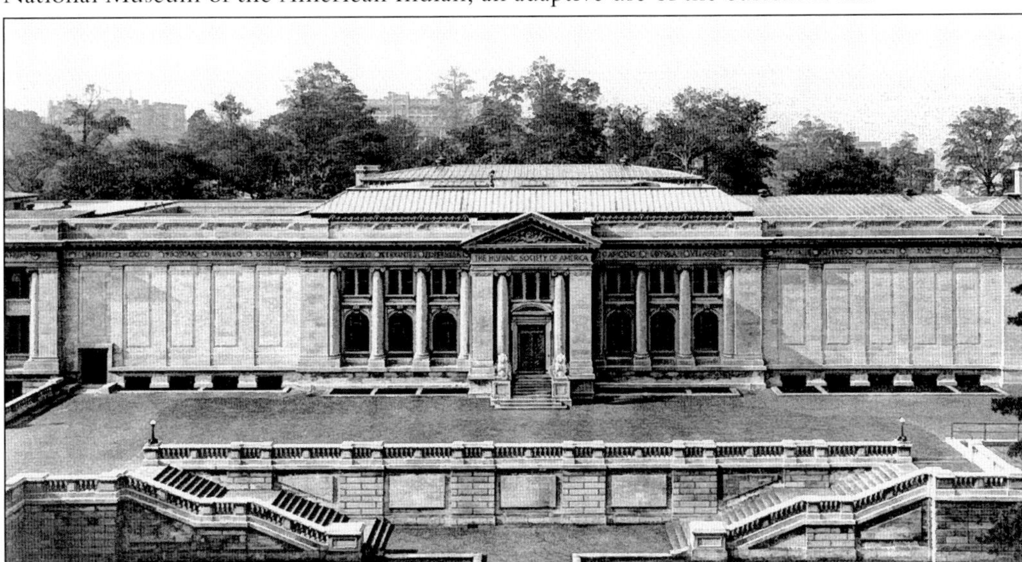

Scholar, art patron, and philanthropist Archer M. Huntington conceived the museum group on the Audubon estate, known as Audubon Park, designed to the master plan of his cousin, architect Charles Pratt Huntington. Statuary was provided by Archer's wife, Anna V. Hyatt Hutchinson, one of the best-known figurative sculptors of her generation. When the Hispanic Society of America, founded in 1904, opened this Spanish Museum by 1910, the building was the seven-bay main block. Stand-alone wings were later connected.

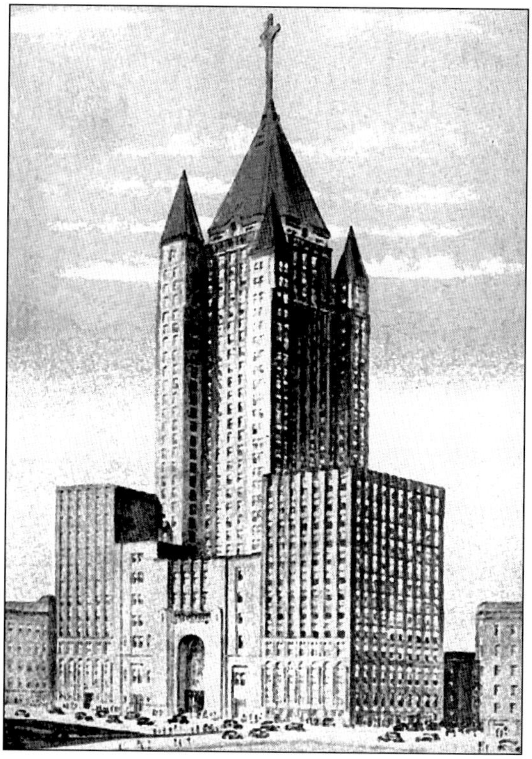

Broadway Temple planned a cathedral-like apartment topped by a cross that would be visible for 100 miles. Although Dr. Christian F. Reisner announced his ambitious plans in 1923, by the 1932 publication of *New York-The Wonder City*, his grand small city itself was unfulfilled and the country was in a depression. Although Donn Barber's rendering for a 41-story skyscraper at 173rd Street was unbuilt, two extant apartment wings were.

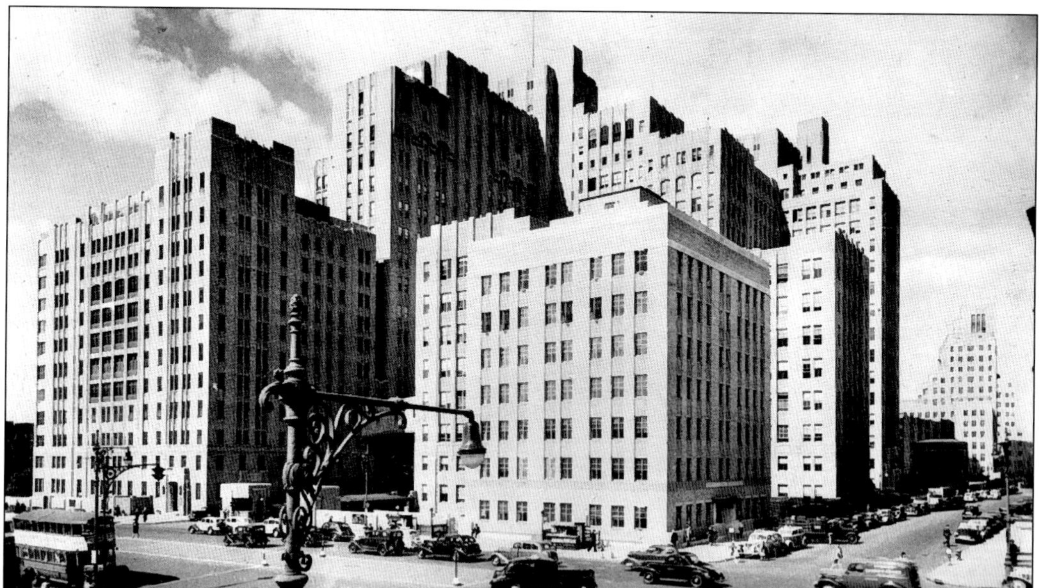

Presbyterian Hospital, on Park Avenue, and Columbia College of Physicians and Surgeons bought baseball's Hilltop Park in 1921, necessitating the Yankees' brief Polo Grounds tenancy before their 1923 stadium in the Bronx. The two organizations planned the world's greatest medical facility and built Columbia-Presbyterian Medical Center, designed by James Gamble Rogers and opened in 1928, pictured in the 1930s. The much-expanded institution occupies three blocks from 165th to 168th Streets, Broadway (east) and Fort Washington Avenue (west).

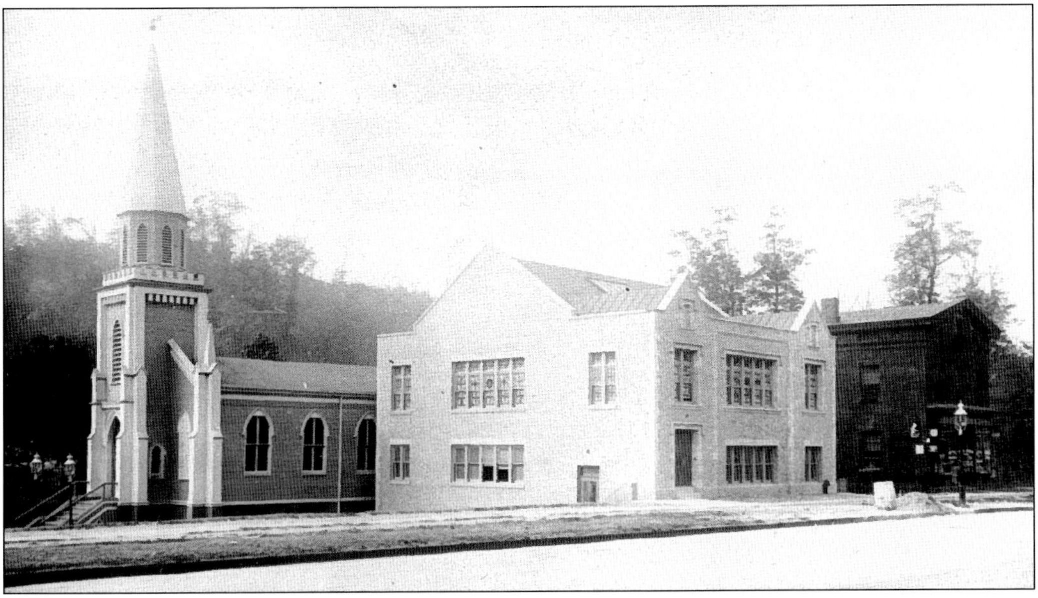

Mount Washington Presbyterian, an outgrowth of Samuel Thompson's 1844 private chapel, built (date unknown) the small edifice at left at Dyckman. The back, around 1910, contains a printed message from architect Eli Benedict, perhaps in conjunction with the foreground's unidentified hall. They were removed following city condemnation for a traffic island. Presbyterians built a new church at 80 Vermilya Terrace. (Courtesy of Joan Kay.)

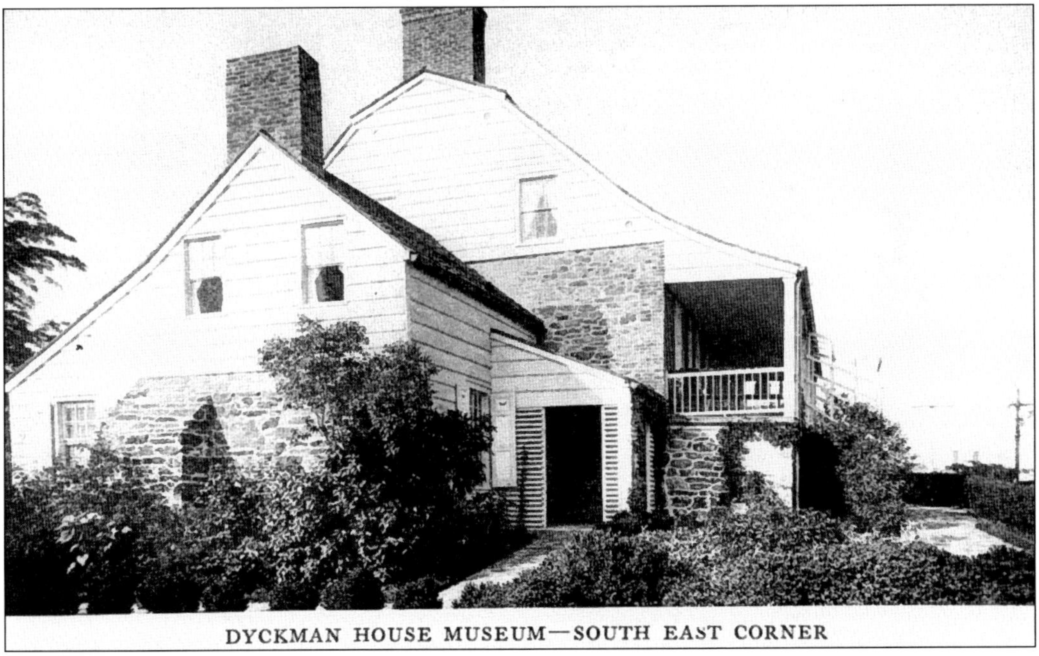

The 18th-century origin of the Dyckman House on the northwest corner with 206th Street, pictured around 1940, the last surviving farmhouse in Manhattan, is the summer kitchen in the foreground. While Jan Dyckman settled the area in 1661, the house was begun by grandson Willem. Expanded greatly, the place was sold outside the family in 1865, bought back in 1915, and given to the city for a restored house museum. (Courtesy of Robert Pellegrini.)